Making Sense
of
Literature

Making Sense
of
Literature

———————

John Reichert

THE UNIVERSITY OF CHICAGO PRESS

Chicago and London

JOHN REICHERT is professor and chairman of the
Department of English at Williams College. He is the
author of a number of journal articles.

THE UNIVERSITY OF CHICAGO PRESS, CHICAGO 60637
THE UNIVERSITY OF CHICAGO PRESS, LTD., LONDON

© 1977 by the University of Chicago
All rights reserved. Published 1977
Printed in the United States of America
81 80 79 78 77   5 4 3 2 1

LIBRARY OF CONGRESS CATALOGING IN PUBLICATION DATA

Reichert, John, 1935–
    Making sense of literature.

    Includes bibliographical references and index.
    1. Criticism.   I. Title.
PN81.R36   801'.95   77-24455
ISBN 0-226-70769-5

*This book is dedicated
to Judy and to
Emily, Danny, and Nancy*

Contents

Preface

This is a book about how we make sense of literary works, both for ourselves and for others. Hence it is about reading and also about criticism regarded broadly as the imparting of one's understanding of a poem or play or novel to another reader. Reading is a private act, and it gives rise to questions like: What does one need to know in order to read literature? What does a reader *do* in order to understand language? And, what happens to a reader in the process of reading? Criticism, on the other hand, is public and pedagogical. As such it raises a slightly different set of questions: How do we convey an understanding of something to someone else? If two interpretations of a work are not consonant with each other, how can we decide which is right? How can we not only persuade a reader that our interpretations and judgments are correct, but demonstrate them to be so?

I would like to think of the pages that follow as contributing to the demystification of criticism. The critics now most in vogue are advocates of particular approaches to literature or theories of literature. The stance of an advocate, like the stance of an ad man pushing a brand name, necessitates making the most of whatever distinguishes your product from another. It means finding a suitably new and esoteric vocabulary to disguise the commonplace, and hence warp it; and it means creating an appearance of controversy, which often enough turns out, upon examination, to be bogus. To the extent that the explanation and justification of a theory become the critic's objective, the literary work becomes a mere occasion for an essay in metaphysics or the psychology of the creative process. What is worse, much of what now passes for critical theory leaves the student of literature with the impression that he won't really be able to think clearly about literature at all until he's first mastered Husserl or Lévi-Strauss, Freud or Nietzsche, Marx or the Kabbala, and decided what ideological cap is most becoming.

What is needed is not another theory of literature (chap. 5 will suggest why) but a view of reading and criticism that cuts through the plethora of competing critical languages to recover and redignify the simple procedures of reading, understanding, and assessing literature that the English language has long been adequate to describe. Hence if there is in this study a reliance on a particular way of asking and answering questions it is on that of the language philosophers and philosophical psychologists loosely associated with Oxford—J. L. Austin, Gilbert Ryle, and their progeny—who offer not a philosophy that accommodates literature in a new way but an invitation first to get straight those familiar concepts, like "meaning" and "purpose," "emotion" and "fiction," "value" and "goodness," that ordinary readers actually use in thinking and talking about what they read.

The book is not without its biases, and they should be announced if not defended here. I believe that we have in this century put ourselves at a disadvantage by our stress on the autonomy of both literature and literary criticism itself. To subvert completely a favorite notion of Northrop Frye's, I would say that the forms of literature are the forms of life. We make sense of a character, a dialogue, a plot, as we make sense of each other and of our lives, and the shapes our experience takes provide the shapes of literature and give them their only value. There are no interpretive procedures peculiar to the interpretation of literature, no evaluative criteria uniquely appropriate to literary works. One botanist of literary studies has done us the considerable service of naming the sixteen different "fallacies" that hang on the tree of literary criticism. Indeed, he says, "all the main kinds of criticism" are "fallacious." And he adds, with insufficient irony, "Adopt *any* one standard as your sole criterion of literary merit and you fall into a fallacy; commit all the fallacies and you near perfection of method."[1] This is nonsense, of course. No "kind of criticism" is inherently fallacious, except perhaps that *kind* in which reason is abused. A critic who argues or interprets or evaluates illogically is violating not local and literary but general principles of argument and inquiry.

As the last paragraph may suggest, the position set forth here is pluralistic, an extension of the view that R. S. Crane urged in his two prefaces to *Critics and Criticism*:

> Most of the doctrinal polemics, with their catalogues of critical "fallacies" and "heresies," that have engaged critics in all times can be reduced to quarrels between opponents who are really talking about different things or talking about them in different ways. And since there is nowhere any authority capable of deciding, among the many distinguishable aspects of poetry, which ones critics ought to fix upon as principles or how these ought to be discussed, it would appear that the only satisfactory approach to the existing diversities of criticism must be one that recognizes a plurality of distinct critical methods—each of them valid or partially valid within its proper sphere—and that insists, consequently, upon ascertaining, in methodological terms, what a given critic is doing, and why, before attempting either to state the meaning or judge the truth or falsity of his conclusions or to compare his doctrines with those of other critics.[2]

As Crane was wont to remind us, however, there is a great difference between pluralism and "a merely amiable tolerance of half-truths, bad reasonings, and preposterous interpretations."[3] And since pluralism is often transmuted into the flabby philosophy of "anything goes if it's interesting," I have taken pains to stress the ways we have of sorting out right readings from wrong ones, better from worse, whatever "approach" to literature they may embody. I have not hesitated to speak freely of how a reader *ought* to respond to a passage in a literary text, however intolerant the idiom may sound. And I try to show in the last chapter that discovering what is *good* about a particular work is not only possible but desirable, however strong the current tendency to confuse evaluation with the exhibition of taste.

My debts are many and of many kinds. That of longest standing is to my teacher William Kennick, who asked the questions I have for many years been trying to answer. I have no doubt drawn with unconscious freedom on the early chapters of Crane's *The Languages of Criticism and the Structure of Poetry*, the opening chapter of M. H. Abrams's *The Mirror and the Lamp*, Barbara Herrnstein Smith's *Poetic Closure*, F. E. Sparshott's *The Concept of Criticism*, and E. D. Hirsch's *Validity in Interpretation*. A debt of another but equally genuine kind I owe to those writers with whose views I have had to wrestle hard in my own thinking and with whom I quarrel in these pages. My former student Scott Shane read the manuscript with properly skeptical and very shrewd attention. Many colleagues have helped me over the years, but I must single out for their benevolent scrutiny beyond the call of friendship Lawrence Graver, Peter Berek, and the late Charles Samuels, all of the Department of English at Williams College, and Charles Karelis, who has never given up trying to get me to tell the truth. Finally, if any pages of this study bespeak a mind well soothed by charming song, I owe them to my wife.

1

Aspect Seeing and the Uses of Criticism

Literary criticism is a social activity. If it is sometimes corrupted by pressures from the marketplace, it is nevertheless fundamentally cooperative, an activity that is both inquisitive and pedagogical. Like Chaucer's clerk, the ideal critic would gladly learn and gladly teach. The persistent liveliness of criticism testifies to our desire to make sense of literature and, when we feel we have done so, to impart our discoveries to others. I am not speaking of published, professional criticism alone. Criticism takes place also on a casual level, in the lobby after the play, among actors and directors arguing about how the parts should be interpreted, between two people who have read the same book, and between the child who weeps when Beth dies in *Little Women* and the parent who reassuringly tries to explain the nature of fiction.

It is natural, perhaps, to think of criticism as a mode of inquiry only, its goal the attainment of true or valid statements about literary works. If you read about criticism, you're likely to discover that criticism is description, analysis, and explanation; that it is argument, dispute, controversy, a mode of inquiry. And you are likely to find that scientific method is the filter through which the spectrum of critical discourse is being viewed. The goal, for example, of E. D. Hirsch's excellent study *Validity in Interpretation* is to demonstrate that criteria can be established to determine which of several competing interpretations of a work is most valid, and since for Hirsch "most valid" means

This chapter is an expanded version of "Model-Making and the Usefulness of Criticism," which appeared in *College English* 34 (1973): 912–26. Copyright © 1973 by The National Council of Teachers of English.

"most probably intended by the author," the argument becomes an application of probability theory to criticism.[1]

Even when the differences between science and criticism are acknowledged—and they usually are—it is still the departures of criticism from some scientific ideal (frequently misconstrued) which are used to define it. Then, depending on the critic's temperament, he either tries to show how criticism can be "improved" (i.e., made more scientific) or, with the joyful resignation of the skeptic, he embraces impressionism.

Such a framework for placing the nature of criticism has its uses, and I do not want to be read as advocating the dismissal of truth and rigor from consideration. Yet I would like to suspend our interest in them temporarily, and try to see the ways we talk about literature in a rather different context. For the scientific paradigm raises at least two disturbing questions.

First, one wants to know what true and valid statements about literary works are good for. One is surely not satisfied, as a teacher, with the imparting of true descriptions and valid interpretations of a work; if one were, one would not take up so much of the student's time with the requirement that he read the work itself. Of course one can imagine several tasks to which true statements about a work would contribute. They can serve, for example, for grounding the broader statements of literary history, as the source from which inferences about the author may be drawn, or, in a testing situation, as evidence that understanding has occurred. But what is the connection between true statements about the text and the *reader* of the text? What use does the inquiry serve?

Second, one wonders whether criticism has received as clear-eyed a treatment as it deserves—a treatment unconstrained by terms and concepts imported from other sorts of inquiry which have their own goals and ways of achieving them. To what extent are terms like "probability," "causal inference," and "hypothesis formation" sufficient for describing the way we talk about a poem, play, or novel?

Let me add, however, that each of the writers from whom I have drawn these terms reveals at some point and in some way that he too is aware of something more to criticism than inquiry and the attainment of truth. Thus, to turn to a practicing critic, Lionel Trilling has written that up to a certain point "criticism in its relation to literary phenomena bears comparison with science in its relation to natural phenomena." "A first undertaking of criticism in dealing with a work of literature is to describe the object of its interest," an activity that includes, first, classification, second, "the observation of the particularities of the work," and third, an "account of the form or structure of the work." "We expect of the critic that he will make every possible effort, in Matthew Arnold's famous words, 'to see the object as in itself it really is' and to describe it accordingly." It is only at a later point, with "the failure of perfect objectivity," that "description becomes interpretation."[2]

Waiving for the time being the question of the failure of objectivity, we should note that even in the midst of this picture of criticism as struggling toward a scientific ideal, Trilling shows himself aware that the critic is not merely trying to "take account of" the structure; he is trying "to make us perceive it." It is not only true beliefs, but perception, which the critic attempts to impart. And that acknowledgment suggests that if criticism can be usefully studied from the viewpoint of the philosophy of science, it ought also to be regarded in terms borrowed from the philosophy of perception or even from that old-fashioned discipline, rhetoric. There is a difference between believing that such and such is true of a given work and actually perceiving it and responding to it in a way consistent with that belief.[3]

Joseph Margolis has written about the pedagogical and inquisitive aspects of criticism in the following way:

> Critics are, fundamentally, teachers. Their comments upon works of art, accordingly, are adjusted to influence, to instruct, to draw attention to, to indicate, to suggest with tact, to remind, to correct, and a thousand other such functions. These uses of language deserve to be carefully catalogued. But it is as a more or less professional discipline, with its own appropriate techniques of inquiry and a distinct sense of making its judgments responsive to challenge, open to correction and confirmation, that criticism chiefly attracts philosophical interest. . . .[4]

The problem here is that if one ignores the techniques by which the critic imparts his perceptions, one can seriously misconstrue his techniques of inquiry. What looks like an argument, an hypothesis, a true or false description when seen from the point of view of the logic of inquiry may look rather different when seen as a strategy for altering perceptions and changing minds. (We will see in chap. 4 how this confusion leads Margolis himself astray.)

There will be time enough for considering the logic of interpretation in subsequent chapters. For the present let us embrace and explore the assumption that one of the important goals of criticism is to induce new perceptions and alter responses—to bring the reader to *see* something in the work that he had not seen, or to see it in a new way, or to see the whole work from a new perspective. One does not teach *King Lear*, I believe, so that students will merely know *about* it. One wants them to *know* it and thereby be able to respond to it more fully and more truly.

It has been argued, chiefly by writers building on Wittgenstein, that all *seeing* is *seeing as*: that vision is an organized and organizing activity.[5] We see vergeben as a German word meaning "forgive," or simply as a German word, or as ink marks on white paper, or as black shapes on a white background, but always *as* something. If we are not in a position to see it as anything at all, we are not in a position to single it out as an object of perception distinct from its surroundings. How we see it will depend on what we know and on what our interests in it are. A native speaker of German who does not speak English will see vergeben differently from an Englishman who is learning German, and both will see it differently from the non-German-speaking expert in type who will see it as an example of ten-point Black Letter. None of these ways of seeing vergeben is wrong. They simply reflect different correct ways of construing or classifying it. But it would be wrong to see it as a German word meaning "pot roast" or as eight-point Goudy Old Style.

The example illustrates the close connection between the visual and the conceptual, and the naturalness of our use of all those terms that do service for both sight and knowledge. We can say "I see what you mean" or "I know what you mean," and "know" is believed to derive from the same root as "ken." The eyes of a person who knows English will behave differently from the eyes of someone who knows only the alphabet when they scan *astitchintime*.

Let us take a hint from this way of talking about seeing. For it is obviously true that in one sense at least all *reading* is *reading*

4

as. We open the newspaper and see something called a letter to the editor, and we read it as that. Then we are puzzled by its contents and try to decide how to take it, whether to read it as an ironic or as a straight-but-stupid letter to the editor. We might read a given novel as an entertaining and moving story, as a piece of socialist propaganda, or as a symptom of what ailed the writer. The use of "as" in these formulations does not imply that the novel is not *really* a piece of propaganda but only *like* one. It merely reminds us that when we read something we focus on an aspect of it.

Can we read something as two different things at once? As an entertaining story *and* as propaganda, say? Certain visual examples seem to suggest that we can't. Try seeing the accompanying diagram simultaneously as a representation of (1) a lampshade seem from above, (2) a tunnel, (3) a square suspended in a frame.

We may know that it can be seen as representing any of the three, but it is not easy to see it as representing all three at once. It doesn't necessarily follow that we can't read something as two things simultaneously. But on the other hand one sort of reading sometimes tends to crowd out another equally appropriate sort of reading. We may be reading a novel as a piece of propaganda (which implies, among other things, being on guard) and get caught up in the story, or vice versa. Or we may be reading *The Faerie Queene* as an allegory and suddenly find that it has "become" an adventure tale and that we've lost track of the theological argument.

Certainly it is hard to read a text as something we believe it not to be. *We* read a particular document as Dr. Johnson's letter to Lord Chesterfield. Chesterfield read it as Johnson's letter to him. There is a world of difference between the two ways of reading, and though I may pretend to read it as Johnson's letter to me, I can't really do it. How we read a piece of writing depends on such matters as our situation, our conception of the author's intention, our relationship to the text and its author, and the sort of text we believe it to be. These considerations exclude certain ways of reading in a given case, but they do not determine which of the admissible ways of reading we shall follow. That is a choice we make according to our interest and purpose. We are also constrained, however, by the number of ways of reading that we have at our disposal. You can't read John Crowe Ransom's "Piazza Piece" ("I am a gentleman in a dustcoat trying / To make you hear.... I am a lady young in beauty waiting / Until my truelove comes....")[6] as a dramatic dialogue unless you possess that "genre" as one of your ways of reading or making sense of something. It is a characteristic shortcoming of untutored readers that they can read poems only as rhymed advice. It is a characteristic shortcoming of highly tutored readers that they can't read any poem as rhymed advice.

Not all criticism presents itself as aspect training, but most of it can be so regarded, and many critics are quite aware that that is just what they are doing. One may, for example, regard the major developments in the history of Shakespeare criticism as discoveries and instructions in new ways of reading or watching, responding to or making sense of the plays. To do justice to any single new perspective or way of reading would involve a lengthy exploration of the formulation, clarification, and application of it, but the method can be indicated briefly with a few examples, such as this passage from G. Wilson Knight's essay "On the Principles of Shakespeare Interpretation," the preparatory chapter of *The Wheel of Fire*:

> To receive the whole Shakespearian vision into the intellectual consciousness demands a certain and very definite act of mind. One must be prepared to see the whole play in space as well as in time. It is natural in analysis to pursue the steps of the tale in sequence, noticing the logic that connects them, regarding those essentials that Aristotle noted: the beginning, middle and end. But by giving supreme attention to this temporal nature of drama we omit what, in Shakespeare, is at least of equivalent importance. A Shakespearian tragedy is set spatially as well as temporally in the mind. By this I mean that there are throughout the play a set of correspondences which relate to each

6

> other independently of the time-sequence which is the
> story.... Now if we are prepared to see the whole
> play laid out, so to speak, as an area, being simul-
> taneously aware of these thickly-scattered correspon-
> dences in a single view of the whole, we possess the
> unique quality of the play in a new sense. 'Faults' begin
> to vanish into thin air. Immediately we begin to realize
> necessity where before we saw irrelevance and beauty
> dethroning ugliness.... We should regard each play as
> a visionary whole, close-knit in personification, at-
> mospheric suggestion, and direct poetic-symbolism.[7]

Whether Knight discovered a valuable way of seeing, and
whether he succeeded in finding what he calls "the true focus
demanded by the poet's work," is not at issue here and could be
resolved only by investigating his attempts to see the individual
plays in these terms. All that we need note is that he explicitly
sets out to readjust our focus, our way of thinking about
Shakespeare's plays generally. The rest of his critical writings on
Shakespeare are attempts to see the individual plays and groups
of plays from the new perspective, not to banish the temporal
understanding of them but to add a complementary one "of
equivalent importance." In the process metaphor plays a central
role: see the whole play laid out as an area, see the whole play in
space. And the justification is a claim about what the new focus
will achieve: "We begin to realize necessity where before we saw
irrelevance."

Another fine example is C. L. Barber's *Shakespeare's Festive
Comedy*, the opening chapters of which are a prolonged education in a way of seeing, reading, or understanding. Barber
introduces his reader to the notion of "forms of experience which
can be termed Saturnalian," "the experience of moving to
humorous understanding through saturnalian release." Again:
"the saturnalian pattern appears in many variations, all of which
involve inversion, statement and counter-statement, and a basic
movement which can be summarized in the formula, through
release to clarification."[8] He goes on to offer examples of
Elizabethan holiday customs and pre-Shakespearian entertain-
ments which embody this pattern in a fairly simple way. By the
time the reader is led into Shakespeare's comedies themselves,
Barber has shown him, among many other things, what the
terms of the formula mean and how they operate in describing

7

certain kinds of human experience. If the reader has never himself experienced the clarification that holiday misrule can produce (which seems unlikely), he has at least been led to see it as a plausible or possible outcome of such release. We have been given both a general description or narrative of a kind of experience and a variety of instances of it.

Anyone who has read Barber's book knows how difficult it would be to do justice to the subtlety with which he then applies his formula to the individual comedies. He succeeds always in sustaining the distinction between holiday or ritual on the one hand and the drama on the other, and the abstractness of the formula fades away when the specific experiences of the characters in the plays are described. His argument has two thrusts to it which need to be distinguished. The first is historical: the book offers some causal hypotheses about how the comedies came to be what they are. The second, with which we are concerned, is heuristic: we are instructed, through analogies, in a way of seeing and hence of responding to certain experiences. I want to quote and italicize one of Barber's justifications for approaching the comedies through these analogies, for it relates his procedure clearly to the general critical function I have been describing. It is that "so much of the action in this comedy is random when *looked at as* intrigue, so many of the persons are neutral when *regarded as* character, so much of the wit is inapplicable when *assessed as* satire" (p. 4, my italics).

There would seem to be at least two standard methods of showing someone how to read something in a certain way. The first is by classifying it—naming it or saying what *sort* of work it is. The second is by comparing it with something else. The two boil down to about the same thing, the offering of a model or paradigm simpler, more familiar, more easily grasped than the work itself, to help the reader organize it. The classification is useful only for someone who is familiar with the class, who can make some comparisons of his own, and who already knows what it is to read something as, say, a parable, a reflection of enlightenment thought, a spoof, a tract, an unconscious working out of anxieties, a piece of propaganda, a revenge tragedy, or a psychomachia. If you can't get your point across by saying "read it as a parable" or by defining "parable," you resort to examples—stories or behavior analogous to the work in question in respect to the aspect of it you are trying to make known.

The problem with general categories, as everyone knows, is that they are general, and if the critic is to sharpen our focus, he must make finer discriminations, frequently with the help of metaphor and analogy, comparison and contrast. Any generic conception, and any analogy, is in danger of distorting or oversimplifying the work. But there is no way to do without them. The mere enumeration of the facts of a work will teach nothing and lead to chaos. An ordered and hence instructive laying out of the facts has already been subjected to generic treatment and reflects the classificatory or analogical principle of its ordering.

Not only criticism but reading itself involves a great deal of comparison making. To read something as a poem, for example, is to read it in the light of our past experiences of poems. This does not mean that we necessarily make conscious comparisons with other particular poems, but simply that in some vague way we assume a likeness between the words at hand and poems. We construe what we read by regarding it as a member of a class of similar writings. This is particularly the case when we come to something that's hard to piece together: we search for analogies that may give us a clue. We can get some notion of how fundamental this analogical mode of thinking is, both for readers and for critics, by identifying some of the major kinds of critical models. What follows should be read as suggestive, however, and not as a systematic or exhaustive treatment of the subject.

WORDS AND SENTENCES

First there is the act of discovering and saying what a given word in a passage means. By far the most common procedure for explaining the meaning of a word is that of offering a synonym for it. We can postpone the notorious intricacies of semantic theory by noting that usually when one asks "what does 'x' mean?" the answer comes back in the form " 'x' means 'y' " where 'y' is a word or phrase that is like 'x,' or analogous to it, with respect to meaning. "Means" means, roughly, "is equivalent to." Synonymous terms are terms that can be interchanged in a sentence without altering seriously what the sentence says or does.

The Soul selects her own Society—
Then—shuts the Door—
To her divine Majority—
Present no more—
Unmoved—she notes the Chariots—pausing
At her low Gate—
Unmoved—an Emperor be kneeling
Upon her Mat—
I've known her—from an ample nation—
Choose One—
Then—close the Valves of her attention—
Like Stone—[9]

Reader A thinks he understands Emily Dickinson's poem. Nothing in it troubles him; everything makes sense. Reader B is troubled, however, and his troubles begin in the first stanza when he tries to figure out the third and fourth lines. He realizes that "present" could be either the adjective "présent" or the imperative "presént." But he can't make "majority" go very well with either. Reader A points out to him that in this passage "majority" may well have its relatively uncommon meaning, "the status of legal age when full civil rights and personal rights may be exercised legally." And since that phrase is a bit cumbersome to substitute for the single word, a few other perhaps less accurate but more helpful synonyms (verbal analogies) are offered, like "will" or "capacity to make choices." At this point (hopefully) something will click for B, who will say "Ah! Now I understand the stanza. So 'present' must be an imperative verb."

An anecdote may bolster this analysis. I once overheard a heated discussion about whether "valves" in the penultimate line of Dickinson's poem suggests hearts or mollusks when one participant, armed with a dictionary, announced that one (archaic) meaning for "valve" was "either half of a folding door." There followed an audible sigh suggesting that we all "saw" at last, though the sigh of course did not preclude further debate about secondary meanings, connotation, intentional ambiguity and the like.

The point of this rather labored treatment of a fairly simple idea is that when we want to explain (or discover) the meaning of a term we offer (or try out) alternative synonyms. Several aspects of this procedure have a bearing on what is to follow:

10

1. A full account of the meaning of a word in a passage may well include some descriptions of its uses: it is a transitive verb used here in the plural, its object is such and such, and so on. But no *descriptions* of use will suffice to explain the term to someone who doesn't know what the term means. For that purpose the meaning must be *rendered*; an analogous term must be provided. It will be little help to most readers who come upon the question "Can one be ephectic otherwise than unawares?" in Beckett's *The Unnamable* to learn that "ephectic" is a rare word, Greek in origin, used here as a predicate adjective.

2. The usefulness of an analogy ceases once it has achieved its purpose. Once the reader knows what "majority" means in Dickinson's line, he no longer needs to substitute "capacity to make choices" for it.

3. Accuracy or exactness is by no means the only criterion for determining an effective critical analogy. We surround a meaning but, since analogies are not identities, probably never hit it on the head. We might help a reader understand "majority" with other (nonsynonymous) analogous expressions like "minority" and "seniority." The ultimate test of an analogy lies in what it allows the reader to see and understand.

4. Of course arguments can arise about what a word actually means in a passage—about which synonym is the "right" one. And one will have then to determine what criteria one wishes to employ. Is the "fit" with the context all that counts? Or does one yield to the pressure of the author's other writings, his customary uses of the term? Is it legitimate to ask which meaning makes the poem better? (Do you like the dramatic shift inward from doors and gates to the valves of the heart? Or the metaphorical consistency of folding doors?) But though such arguments are important in their own sphere, they take us away from the reading experience itself and the ways in which practical criticism can aid and influence it.

It is but a short step from synonym to that most necessary and useful of critical procedures, the paraphrase, which, as its etymology suggests, is also a species of analogy. Paraphrase can get at a good deal more than the meanings of the individual words and can bear a useful likeness to the passage, speech, or poem in a number of respects. A paraphrase is designed to show forth some particular aspect of the original, and hence one can imagine a number of quite different but equally helpful paraphrases of the same passage. It may embody, for example, a grammatical or logical structure similar to that of the original, or it may render those features of the passage that suggest tone, attitude, rhetorical purpose, and the like. (A full account of the process of clarifying stanza 1 of Dickinson's poem would no doubt include a paraphrase showing how "present" and "majority" might work together grammatically in the sentence.) A hint of irony in the original can be magnified, made obvious, in the paraphrase. A metaphor can be expanded or it can be translated into literal terms, depending on the purpose for which the paraphrase is designed. In short, a paraphrase can imitate not only the meanings of the individual words in the original, but all those features of it that make it an utterance, symptomatic of a speaker doing something, as well as saying something, in a specific situation. The critic who paraphrases is saying in effect, "try reading this sentence as you read this other sentence; try seeing it as having this sort of meaning, spirit, tone."

Critics get nervous about paraphrase precisely when they misconstrue its function as that of rendering everything in a poem with exactness. But the critic who paraphrases is trying to show us something, not everything. Cleanth Brooks worried that paraphrases "lead away from the center of the poem—not toward it."[10] For the reader who is already located at the center of the poem, that is no doubt true. But the act of criticism— presumptuous as it may sound—surely assumes that the critic can bring the reader closer to the center than he was, and from that point of view paraphrase—as Brooks's own practice excellently demonstrates—is indispensable.

ACTIONS

All literary works either dramatize or relate events, from the briefest alteration of feeling or mood in a lyric to the crowded, complicated plots of a novel by Flaubert or Dickens. And a great deal of critical energy is spent in attempting to understand the ways in which the events in a given work hang together. Hence the frequency of statements like the following:

> The essential story of *Macbeth* is that of a man, not naturally depraved, who has fallen under the compulsive power of an imagined better state for himself which he can attain only by acting contrary to his

normal habits and feelings; who attains this state and then finds that he must continue to act thus, and even worse, in order to hold on to what he has got; who persists and becomes progressively hardened morally in the process; and who then, ultimately, when the once alluring good is about to be taken away from him, faces the loss in terms of what is left of his original character.[11]

Pickwick at first yields himself to a life made up of unrelated adventures separated from one another by a vacancy of sleep and forgetting. These experiences have very little connection with one another. Each adventure has a real duration, with a beginning, middle, and end linked together in a rhythmic continuity. The stages of this rhythm are the sudden discovery, when the window is thrown open, of a new experience into which Pickwick throws himself with youthful effervescence, the evaporation of this bubbling excitement, a return to exhausted calm, and, finally, the blotting out, through sleep, of all that has happened.[12]

Emma [Bovary's] life is a pool in which, occasionally, stones are thrown. Or, more exactly, it is a series of pools, each one a little bigger than the preceding one, first the father's farm, then Tostes, then Yonville, finally Yonville plus Rouen. In the stillness of each of these pools, at a particular time, a stone is thrown. This throwing of the stone is invariably the appearance of a new lover. From the moment he comes out, there start waves of emotion, which for a time broaden Emma's life; up to the moment when, the lover having gone, the emotion being spent, Emma is brought back by a retrogressive process to her starting point.[13]

What sorts of statements are these, and what functions do they have? One would probably characterize them as descriptions of plots, and usually in a critical essay they would be preceded or followed by an enumeration of supportive or exemplary instances. None of them, of course, is or could be a complete description of all the events that occur in a given work. In fact, the most usual purposes that descriptions serve are hardly relevant to these accounts of plot. They are certainly not designed, as most descriptions are, as aids to recognition, since critical conversation ordinarily takes place between people who are already familiar with the work, and who know perfectly well what happens in it. Nor would it do justice to these statements to treat them as mere plot summaries, designed for jogging the memory or other subcritical purposes.

Surely the key to the function of the statements quoted lies neither in their accuracy nor in their completeness, but in their simplicity, their internal coherence, their abstractness. Insofar as accounts of plot are aimed at producing understanding, they function much the way synonyms and paraphrases function. Each, you will notice, is a brief narrative in its own right, simpler, more compact, more readily grasped than the work it "describes," but analogous to it. The experiences that the characters undergo in the critic's narrative make sense, and the reader is invited to make the same *kind* of sense out of the more complex experiences of the characters in the work.

The story that Crane tells is not *the* story of *Macbeth* but a version of it (and there have been many other versions). He narrates events, offers psychological explanations, asserts cause-effect relationships, and makes moral judgments, all in a condensed form the coherence of which is readily perceived. The coherence is obtained at the cost of detail and complexity; the gain is a means for subsequently bringing the detail and complexity of the work into focus.

Of course if a description of a plot contained actual inaccuracies it would be discounted. If Emma Bovary took no new lovers, if Pickwick never behaved with youthful effervescence, one would be entitled to suspicions. But such inaccuracies are usually easily spotted. The differences between the narrative models critics offer of the same work are less often differences of accuracy than of omission and inclusion.

Note that it is not only Poulet's metaphor of stones tossed in a pool that leads one to construe his plot summary as a model of or analogue to *Madame Bovary*. That figure is in fact a metaphor within a metaphor, introduced to suggest a correspondence between the plot of the novel and Flaubert's use of expanding circles in several descriptive passages. The basis for calling Poulet's paragraph a model is simply that the micro-story he tells includes only a very few of the many characters and events of the novel itself and arranges them in a narrative that highlights certain patterns and repetitions. Even the use of the generic term "lovers" plays down for the moment the differences between Charles, Leon, and Rodolphe. The model could easily be stripped of the pool metaphor and achieve much the same effect.

IDEAS

Narrative models, since they narrate a series of events, are useful chiefly in rendering temporal structures for a work—the relationship between beginning and end, cause and effect, conflict and resolution, and the like. Conceptual models are used when temporal relationships are ignored for the sake of understanding other kinds of relationships among characters or ideas in a work—relationships usually of a qualitative or ideological sort.

In an essay on Shakespeare's *Henry IV* plays, for example, William B. Hunter, Jr., invites the reader to see the ethical relationships among Hotspur, Hal, and Falstaff in Part I in terms borrowed from the *Nicomachean Ethics*, according to which any particular virtue is defined as a mean between an excess and a deficiency of a quality. Thus Hal exhibits the proper concern for honor, Hotspur and Falstaff the excess and deficiency of that concern; Falstaff exhibits cowardice, Hal courage, Hotspur foolhardiness, and so on.[14] Or again, drawing on a related but different ethical theory, Samuel Holt Monk urges readers of the fourth book of *Gulliver's Travels* to understand the relationships between the Houyhnhnms, the Yahoos, and Gulliver himself in terms of the theory of the Chain of Being and its traditional ethical implications. The Houyhnhnms, like creatures higher than man on the Chain of Being, are, according to Monk, "purely rational," "pure intelligence"; the Yahoos, like creatures below man, are "purely sensual"; Gulliver himself is "the symbol of humanity," the "middle link," which partakes of the qualities of creatures both "above" and "below" him.[15]

Once a conceptual model such as these has been described and "attached to" the work, inferences are drawn from it, frequently by incorporating the conceptual model into an account of the narrative or plot. Thus Prince Hal "rejects both extremes" when he kills Hotspur and disowns Falstaff, and the plays show him "choosing and practicing the ideal mean." And Gulliver's horror of the Yahoos and adulation of the Houyhnhnms becomes for Monk an act of "denying his place in and responsibility to humanity, by aspiring above the middle link, which is man, to the next higher link, that of the purely rational."

It will be seen that one great strength that conceptual models such as these possess is that, insofar as they work well for the reader, they provide a compelling argument for saying that certain characters and actions ought to be judged in a particular way. It makes a good deal of difference for our response to Gulliver whether we see Houyhnhnm society as a utopia or as a higher link on the Chain of Being, since we know from reading Pope that the emulation of the angels is an act of sinful pride.

The two conceptual models I have cited are unusually explicit ones. It is not necessary, however, that a conceptual model be drawn from a clearly defined and well-established body of ideas. (Nor, one supposes, need they always be tripartite.) A model is operative whenever certain features of a work are selected for comparison and contrast—operative indeed in the very act of selection, in the choice of terms used to describe the features selected, and in the necessarily partial gathering of evidence used to support the selection. In this sense Barber's concept of "release" is a conceptual model, much like the concepts of excess or pure intelligence. When we divide characters or groups of characters by such terms as protagonist and antagonist, naturally exuberant and unnaturally repressive, innocent and experienced, or as representative of eros or agape, or of art or nature, we are employing conceptual models. As these examples suggest, the model may be an obvious literary one, close to the surface of the work and to the author's intent, or it may not be. These terms embody the simplifying, sense-making ways we have of organizing our perceptions of the qualitative relations among people. They may occasionally be oversimplifying (analogies can hobble), but we cannot do without them. We may find more of the details of book 4 falling into place when we regard the Yahoos as actual, the Houyhnhnms as ideal, or we may not wish to place Hal "between" Falstaff and Hotspur. But we can hardly see such characters at all as undifferentiated agents in a neutral world. We rely for sight on the critic's or our own classificatory schemes and metaphors.

16

MINDS

Many of the statements we make about characters in a play or novel, or about the speaker or narrator of a poem, are like the statements we make about real people. We attribute to them motives and intentions, feelings and attitudes; we grant them existence in a time and place. We say, for example, that the narrator of Browning's "Soliloquy in a Spanish Cloister" is located in a place where, unseen, he can observe Brother Lawrence puttering about the garden, and we say, too, that he is petty, jealous, hypocritical, and lustful. This elementary act of interpretation, on which the reading of all imaginative literature depends, involves imagining a personality behind the words spoken and the deed performed. We read the words and think of the deeds *as if* there were a Hamlet who speaks and acts, a Pip who recounts his past to us. The description of these fictional characters presupposes a nonfictional model—an implicit reference to the sorts of people who would speak or behave in a certain way.

To talk about Hamlet or Pip or the speaker of a poem at all is to commit ourselves to that assumed analogy between fiction and life that makes the understanding of fiction possible. How far the analogy may be carried is determined by the nature of the work, by how full or complete a character has to be assumed or imagined to make his words and deeds make sense. There is no pat answer to the question of the extent to which we are justified in speaking of Hamlet's or any other character's childhood or of his experience prior to the opening of the play. We grant him a childhood, of course, and a sufficiently detailed past to account for what he says and does. Furthermore, we are more generous in our interpretations of words and deeds in literature than we are in life. We recognize that the best model for understanding what a fictional character says or does may be one that we would not accept as plausible for understanding a real person. The personality theory that best explains a Greek tragic hero or a character in a comedy of humors need not be one that would satisfy our present psychological knowledge. (Similarly, we might recognize the wheel of fortune or the laws of Marxist economic theory as governing the actions in a particular work of literature whether we subscribe to such forces in life or not.)

17

We use such "person" models both in reading and in criticism. Take, for example, Pound's famous pair of lines entitled "In a Station of the Metro":

> The apparition of these faces in the crowd;
> Petals on a wet, black bough.[16]

Part of our understanding of this poem has to do with seeing how the two lines are related to each other. And one way to get at the relationship is to ask in what sort of actual situation two such phrases might be spoken in conjunction with each other. What kind of utterance is it? A response to the question "what do you most enjoy looking at"? The beginning of a list of particulars about which a generalization is going to be made? Most people would answer that it is like the verbal mental process one indulges in in a certain mood when the sight of one thing brings something else to mind. And the answer usually occurs intuitively or spontaneously. One does not ordinarily have to stop and search for the appropriate models, any more than one has to stop in midsentence to get the grammar straightened out. One knows almost immediately what sort of utterance to read it as.

It is only when difficulties or ambiguities arise, or when the natural psychology of the utterances is burdened with other distracting elements, that the analogy-finding process becomes necessary and exposed to view. *Lycidas*, for example, is a long poem with many themes, difficult sentence structures, some interpolated speeches, rich diction and imagery, metrical and phonological complexities, and so on. It is not always easy to see the resemblances between the poem and the natural meditation of a person expressing grief and seeking consolation. So one of the critic's activities may be to show within these distractions what sort of actual utterance it is like, what sorts of emotional and logical development it has. The passage on fame and "the homely slighted shepherd's trade," for example, has not always made spontaneous sense to readers, or so at least the history of *Lycidas* criticism suggests. How can we understand the shift from grief over Lycidas' fate to a long passage on the speaker's own life and career? So the critic (in this case M. H. Abrams) steps in, spelling out his version of what any reader tries to do for himself.

Consideration of this particular death raises in his mind a general question about the pointless contingencies of life, with its constant threat that fate may slit the thin-spun thread of any dedicated mortal prior to fulfillment and so render profitless his self-denial. . . . This turn away from Lycidas to the circumstance of those who have survived him is not insincere, nor does it constitute a digression or an indecorously personal intrusion. It is entirely natural and appropriate; just as . . . it is altogether fitting and proper for Lincoln, in the course of the *Gettysburg Address*, to turn from "these honored dead" to concern for "us the living."[17]

Analogy functions in two ways here. There is the explicit comparison with Lincoln's speech, illustrating the naturalness of this *kind* of transition. But there is also the analogy with ordinary thought processes on which the interpretation is based, or which, in a sense, *is* the interpretation: *See* this as an instance of the consideration of a problem giving rise to a question. *Imagine* a person thinking that way and the passage will make sense.

An even more recalcitrant passage is the sudden shift from the despairing thought of Lycidas' bones washed by the seas to "the bottom of the monstrous world" to the exalted confidence of the vision of the "blest Kingdoms meek of joy and love." It is harder to "fill in" between the second and third lines of the following transitional passage than between Pound's two phrases:

> Look homeward Angel now, and melt with ruth,
> And, O ye *Dolphins*, waft the hapless youth.
>   Weep no more, woeful Shepherds, weep no more,
> For Lycidas your sorrow is not dead. . . .[18]
>
> [Lines 163–66]

Here are two attempts to relate the transition to a natural thought process, the first by Abrams, the second by Wayne Shumaker:

[The speaker] has tried to interpose a little ease by strewing imaginary flowers on Lycidas' imagined hearse. *But this evasion only brings home the horror* of the actual condition of the lost and weltering corpse. By extraordinary dramatic management, it is at this point of profoundest depression that *the thought of Lycidas' body sinking to "the bottom of the monstrous world" releases the full implication of St. Peter's speech,* and we make the leap from nature to revelation, in the great lyric peripety: "Weep no more...."[19] [My italics.]

The Irish Sea has become a resistless, unsympathetic force which deals with the body of poet-priest-shepherd exactly as the Hebrus has dealt with the severed head of Orpheus, tossing it about with the indifference with which it would toss a plank broken from the hull of the wrecked ship. The effect is overwhelming.... Relief, however, is at hand, for *the depressing thought of a tossed and ruined body generates immediately, by contrast, that of a redeemed and joyous soul.*[20] [My italics.]

Whether or not these remarks will make the poem hang together for a reader depends partly on how familiar and hence persuasive the analogies are. Can one imagine a person contemplating a particular death circling back to thoughts of his own death and of the purposes of life? Can one imagine evasion bringing home horror, or one thought "releasing the full implication" of an earlier thought, or the thought of a ruined body, "generating immediately, by contrast," the thought of a redeemed soul?

This sort of analogy making is not limited to the ways we connect sentences and paragraphs. Consider, for example, the so-called pastoral conventions in *Lycidas*: the procession of mourners (Neptune's herald, Cam, St. Peter), the pathetic fallacy through which the woods, caves, and vines also "mourn" for Lycidas, the strewing of flowers, and so on. One way that the critic "explains" such elements in the poem is to point out that other elegists include similar devices in their poems. It's the sort of thing one does in writing a pastoral elegy. But one can also, again, point to their analogues in nonliterary experience— to the need for talking about the death with other people, to the wish that one's own feelings were shared not only by other people but also by the "world" itself, to the need to engage (in order to "interpose a little ease") in absorbing ritual activities.

We are never asking, with poetry or drama, whether the

speaker is *really* undergoing such and such a thought process. *Lycidas* is a good example of this fact, because it is clearly *not* the natural meditation of a person expressing grief and seeking consolation, if by "natural" we mean ordinary, commonplace, just what you or I would say in a similar situation. It is, in Dryden's phrase, "nature wrought up to a higher pitch." But, insofar as criticism succeeds in explaining the development of the poem in the ways I've described, it is the *sort* of thing you or I might say—similar in many ways, but also very different. It may be *seen as* a natural expression, though that "lens" leaves certain other aspects of the poem temporarily out of focus.

Form and Structure

Let us regard the form or structure of something as the principle according to which its parts may be seen to be related to each other. That the explication of the structure of an utterance is performed by classification and analogy can be illustrated by noting how we talk about the syntactic structure of a sentence. Consider, for example, the sentence "I persuaded Noam to leave." Here, first, is a traditional "schoolmarm" parsing:

a) *I* is the subject of the sentence, *persuaded Noam to leave* the predicate. *Persuaded* is the main verb. *Noam* is both the object of *persuaded* and the subject of the infinitive *to leave*.

Here is another parsing, indebted to Chomsky,[21] who would say that the underlying deep structure of the sentence is:

b) Noun Phrase — Verb — Noun Phrase — Sentence
(I — persuaded — Noam — Noam will leave)

And here is yet another:

c) The syntactic structure of "I persuaded Noam to leave" is what it has in common with "Pete urged Jack to run" but not with "Noam heard my argument and decided to leave."

Method *a* proceeds entirely by classification and would make sense only to someone who knew the grammatical taxonomy. Method *c* proceeds entirely by analogy and contrast. Method *b* combines the two. Chomsky classifies and also offers a two-sentence paraphrase ("I — persuaded — Noam" and "Noam will leave") that makes explicit the double function of "Noam" but weakens the causal relationship between my persuasion and Noam's decision to leave. All three methods render the structure

21

by telling us what to see it as, either as an instance of a class of structures, or as the structure of something else.

In these terms each of the critical procedures we have been considering is a way of exhibiting or naming the form of a work or passage. For example, a paraphrase may exhibit the same grammatical or semantic structure as the passage in question; Hunter's interpretation of Hotspur, Hal, and Falstaff asserts the conceptual relation among them (the principle is that of exemplifying excessive, proper, and deficient possession of various qualities); and our account of Pound's poem relates the two lines to each other according to a psychological principle of association. We have glanced at a few of what one might call the psychological substructures of *Lycidas*—problematic transitions in the total psychological structure that moves through several emotions toward a state of peace. But that is not the only way of talking about the poem. Jon Lawry has argued for "considering the poem as in part a dialectical process, in the Hegelian sense: the initial dogmatic proposition (thesis) is opposed by a skeptical second (antithesis); from their encounter there arises a third statement, one of mystic certainty (synthesis)."[22] Northrop Frye has argued that "the Adonis myth in *Lycidas* is the structure of *Lycidas*."[23] (Frye likes to collapse his critical analogies into methaphoric statements of identity. But clearly, unless one is talking about how the structure got there, one could also say that the Lycidas myth in the Adonis story is the structure of the Adonis story. For interpretive purposes the point is that the two stories are analogous, and the Adonis analogy will work only to the extent that it is for the reader simpler and better understood than the poem.)

But this discussion already suggests that there is something peculiar about talking about *the* form or *the* structure of a literary work without designating the sort of structure one has in mind. Abrams is talking after all about the psychological structure of the poem, Frye about the conceptual structure of its images and events, Lawry about its logical structure. To talk about the structure of a work is necessarily to talk about an aspect of it, and any work will have several structures according to what aspect of it is being considered. In other words, there will be more than one principle according to which its parts are related. Thus in considering Marvell's "To His Coy Mistress," one

22

might want to call attention to its verse structure (tetrameter couplets), its psychological structure (the increasing urgency and intensity of the speaker's feelings, the accelerating pace), and the syntactic, quasi-logical structure of its verse paragraphs (Had we but ... But at my back ... Now therefore....). One might also wish to consider various conceptual structures, such as the pairing off of spatial and temporal images which remain apart in the beginning ("World enough, and Time," "walk, and pass," "Vaster than Empires and more slow") but gradually merge ("Desarts of vast Eternity") until time has become through metaphor an object to devour or be devoured by, and finally a "Sun" whose inexorable motion can be opposed only by making "him run."[24]

Of course we also read the poem as an attempt to persuade a coy mistress, thus organizing its parts according to a rhetorical principle, the purpose of persuasion. We can speak not only of the various ways in which the parts of the poem are related, but also of the relationship of those several arrangements, subsuming, say, the syntactic structure under the rhetorical structure, or explaining the psychological development (increasing urgency) as the effect on the speaker of the paradox emerging from his own argument. Finally, we may subsume this entire network of structures under some governing poetic purpose, seeing the poem as Marvell's attempt to dramatize, say, certain emotional consequences and concomitants of desire. In every case we are bringing to the poem our storehouse of knowledge about how discourse can be arranged, seeing the poem through the lenses provided by these models and altering the models when the fit is inexact.

CONCLUSION

Surely by now the reader—even the reader who has been persuaded that criticism makes more use of analogy than he realized—is asking whether there aren't nevertheless better and worse critical analogies and models. Aren't these procedures subject to certain tests for accuracy or validity?

The answer is certainly in the affirmative. It makes better sense to read "In a Station of the Metro" as representing a process of association than as a shopping list. And sometimes two critical analogies are genuinely incompatible. Monk, as we saw, invites us to read book 4 of *Gulliver's Travels* as a story about a man who aspires above his place. R. S. Crane invites us to read it as a story about a man who sees perfection and is naturally thrown off balance by having to leave it.[25] Monk's critical metaphor is the Chain of Being as it was interpreted by writers like Pope. Crane's is Plato's story about the cave of shadows and the prisoner who leaves it and is shown the sun. Upon his return he is "blinded by the darkness" and makes something of a fool of himself. The two ways of reading book 4 are as incompatible as Pope's and Plato's attitudes toward the pursuit of the ideal. They lead to contrary evaluations of the Houyhnhnms, of Gulliver's behavior, and of the point of the satire. If you believe that one of the critics is right, you can't read it in the other's fashion.

We will turn in chapter 4 to the question of how to tell whether an interpretation represents a true understanding or a misunderstanding of the work. I prefer at this point to dwell on the fact that criticism is in part a rhetorical and heuristic enterprise and to stress the misconceptions that can arise from prematurely construing it within a logical rather than an analogical framework. If the two ways of regarding the critic—as truth teller and as perception inducer—turn out to be more harmonious than this introduction has suggested, so much the better.

To regard criticism as aiming not just at true statements about, but at new perceptions of a literary work, is to admit among the others a purely pragmatic test for its success—with all the tangles that purely pragmatic tests ordinarily entail. That is, one test of an interpretation is whether it actually provides the reader with the new way of perceiving that it is intended to provide him with. That means, of course, that in this sense an interpretation may work for some readers but not for others. Its success will depend in part on such logically extraneous factors as the reader's familiarity with and attitude toward the area from which the model has been drawn. (A person versed in and committed to psychoanalytic theory will react differently from the layman to a psychoanalytic model.) Furthermore, since the critic is trying to lead the reader into the work, not to provide an exact equivalent for it, certain inaccuracies—chiefly in the direction of oversimplification and exaggeration—are not only allowable but necessary and desirable.

The problem with this pragmatic test, of course, is that a critic can lead a reader to see something in a text that *isn't there*. I may be so persuaded by the cogency of the critic's model and the evidence he adduces that I become blind to the contrary evidence or to other, better ways of understanding the work. Nevertheless, the pragmatic test does provide an important and powerful negative criterion. If reader after reader is simply unable to *feel* the plot of *As You Like It* as a movement through release to clarification, or to understand the development of *Lycidas* as a natural psychological one, that would constitute very good evidence that the critical models were ill-suited to the works in question.

One is right, then, to counter the purely pragmatic criterion with the claim that the function of criticism is not merely to let us see the work in some new way, but to let us see it *as it really is*. But questions about what something really is—especially when we are asking for more than a label or an enumeration of parts—tend to turn into questions about what the something is like, or what *sort* of thing it is. And these are questions which obviously allow a variety of answers. Different models can be used to interpret the same work. As we saw, for example, Poulet invites us to see Madame Bovary as the story of a woman responding emotionally to a succession of lovers. But Mary McCarthy, in another admirable essay on the novel, offers a very different formula. She says that "the diffusion of ideas in the innocent countryside is the plot of *Madame Bovary*."[26] She has in mind the many characters in the novel (not just Emma herself) whose behavior is determined by what they have read or heard—by poems, romances, newspapers, religious education, and so on.

These two ways of understanding the novel are not isomorphic. That is, McCarthy is not merely saying what Poulet is saying in a different way. Poulet brings Emma clearly into the foreground, letting the other characters fall into place around her, while McCarthy plays down Emma's centrality and treats her career as an important one among other parallel careers. Even if one of these two critical perspectives could be shown to embrace more of the text than the other, there would be no reason to reject the weaker one. For each is offering *a* means, not the only means, of understanding the events in the novel. And a single event may be understood, in literature as in life, as having more than one aspect.

Furthermore, if we glance back now at Arnold's maxim about "seeing the object as in itself it really is," something curious about the phrasing emerges. Not only do questions about what something is turn into questions about what it is like. Arnold's own visual metaphor points in two directions, toward objectivity and toward aspect seeing. It should remind us that "the object" is never just one thing. The object at the corner of my house is not only a Norway maple. It is a beautiful shade tree, a determining influence on what can be planted in the soil around it, and a threat to both the foundation and the roof of the house. It *really is* each of these things and to "see it as in itself it really is," and to know what to do with it, one must see it as all of these things.

When two interpretations of a work are actually in conflict with each other, either the work is fundamentally ambiguous or at least one interpretation is wrong. But there is a strong tendency, when criticism is regarded as a truth-telling activity, to mistake differences of point of view with conflict or logical incompatibility. (And phrases like "the essential story" or even "*the* plot" nourish the mistake.) The analogic of criticism, and its relationship to perception and response, suggests that the question "what is the best interpretation of a work?" is only tangentially and occasionally like a scientific question. It is more tellingly like the question "what is the best seat in the house for hearing *Der Rosenkavalier*, or for watching a Balanchine ballet?" One can observe the performance only if one is in the theater to start with, and one can see or hear much from several seats, but there is no seat from which one can see or hear it all.

It is widely claimed that one of the tests of a scientific hypothesis is its predictive capacity. To the extent that it predicts well other events beyond the event it was designed to explain, its validity is established. This aspect of hypothesis testing points up nicely one of the fundamental features of criticism as we have been considering it. Our critic in the role of interpreter or teacher is not concerned with the discovery of general laws that will apply beyond the work. His target is an understanding of the individual literary event in its uniqueness. In this respect his task is somewhat like the historian's as it was conceived by philosophers like R. G. Collingwood and Michael Oakeshott, both of whom stressed the uniqueness of historical events and the need to "get inside" them.[27]

We have assumed all along that one of the prime values of a literary work resides in the experience it affords. And if we value the *otherness* of the literary work—its integrity as the product of the artist's imagination—then we seek to experience the work as fully as possible for what it is. At this point the measures of accuracy and validity merge with the pragmatic measure. Interpretation points beyond itself and into the heart of the work where it can never quite reach. To know (truly) that *Lycidas* is a certain sort of poem is something. But to know *Lycidas* as the poem it is is much, much more.

2

Meanings, Speech Acts, and the
Turns of Language

If we are to supplement the pragmatic test of an interpretation with other, less subjective ones, we must explore the nature of reading, and of understanding language, in greater detail. In chapter 1 we emphasized the kinds of information which readers bring to a text and which, therefore, one reader can call upon in his effort to educate another. But a literary work has a power of its own, like any speech, essay, or sentence, and is not receptive to every shape we attempt to impose on it. To understand that power—to understand, that is, how a writer can use language in such a way that it will place constraints on the kinds of sense we can make of it—it is necessary to consider language itself, its uses, and its capacity to be understood.

In such a study the problem of meaning is central. Knowing the meaning of the words and sentences of a poem may not be tantamount to a full understanding of the poem, but it is a necessary beginning, not only for literary works but for any written or spoken discourse whatsoever. And it is on the fact that we cannot arbitrarily or whimsically attach whatever meanings we wish to past utterances that the stability and power of the written word rests.

This chapter begins, then, with an attempt to sort out some of the various kinds of meanings, a topic on which I believe there has been significant, clarifying progress in the last twenty years.[1] We will try to see what is involved in understanding the meaning of words and sentences. And using this as a foundation, we will consider what is involved in understanding metaphorical, ironic, and fictional discourse. For these three ways of using language, if they are by no means exclusively literary, are nevertheless of obvious interest to anyone who wants to understand how we make sense of literature.

Let us begin with what philosophers of language call *natural* meaning, which is involved in expressions like: "The recession means trouble for the poor." "Those clouds mean rain." "That look on his face means he's angry." "The fact that he asked for a drink means that he must be feeling better." "Means" means "implies" in these cases, and the sentences all propose an inference that can be drawn from some fact or other. They are distinct from expressions involving nonnatural meaning by virtue of their predicating meaning of objects, events, appearances, and the like, rather than of people or words. Compare the very different propositions "That look on his face means that he's angry" and "He meant that look as an expression of anger." The first asserts an inference about the man's feelings, and says nothing about his intentions. The second interprets the man's intentions, and makes no commitment as to his feelings. The first involves natural meaning, the second nonnatural meaning.

If we restrict ourselves to the sort of meaning we attribute to people and language, a variety of senses of "means" remains. Sometimes it means "refers to," as in "When he asked for his shoes, which ones did he mean?" Sometimes it means "intends," pure and simple, as in "I meant to finish it, but I didn't have time." At other times it has to do with how a remark or gesture or facial expression is intended to be taken. "I didn't mean that. I only meant it as a joke." Or, "I meant it sarcastically." Closely related to this sense is the "means" in a sentence like "What he means by 'aggravated' is 'annoyed,' not 'worsened,' " where we seem to be talking of what a speaker means (intends) a word to mean, or what meaning or sense he intends it to have in a sentence. Then there is the somewhat vaguer "means" in "Bill's a fool!" "What do you mean, he's a fool? He's chairman of the board." The request for meaning here is a request for a justification of the remark, not for the meaning of the sentence.[2]

Meaning in the examples given in the last paragraph was predicated of people. Now let us consider the following two sets of sentences in all of which it is words or expressions that are said to mean something:

1. What is the meaning of "ineffable"? "Ineffable" means "unspeakable." The two words mean the same thing. They have the same meaning.

   "Birdie" has two meanings: "little bird" and "a score of one less than par."

   What does the expression "ontogeny recapitulates phylogeny" mean?

2. What does "fall" mean in Hopkins's lines, "O the mind, mind has mountains; cliffs of fall / Frightful, sheer, no-man-fathomed."

   What does the sentence "Here! creep, / Wretch, under a comfort serves in a whirlwind" mean in Hopkins's sonnet?

The difference between these two groups is that the first exemplifies questions and answers about the meaning that expressions have apart from some actual use of them, the sort of meaning (for words) that one looks up in a dictionary, while the second exemplifies questions about what a word means in some actual uttered or written sentence. We might call the first "type meaning," the second "actual meaning," or, following Grice, "timeless meaning" and "occasional meaning." You have to know what "ineffable" means generally in order to use it correctly or understand it on some particular occasion.

The very fact that questions like "What does 'ineffable' mean?" can be asked and answered points to the stable aspect of language and reminds us of the sense in which a word means exactly the same thing every time it is used. (Or, in the case of a word like "birdie" that has more than one sense, it will have one meaning or the other.) It is important to dwell for a moment on this stable aspect of language, for one sometimes hears it said that "no word ever has exactly the same meaning twice."[3] But this Heraclitean notion makes havoc of any attempt to explain our ability to understand each other. "Birdie" means "a score of one less than par" every time it is used in reference to a golfer's score, whether it's a par three or par four hole. And "I have a headache" means the same thing whether you say it or I say it, whether the headache is mild or severe, and no matter what caused it. We don't have to learn a new meaning (even a *slightly* new meaning) for every word every time we hear or read it. The meaning of a sentence ought not to be confused with the sum total of information communicated when a person utters it. The fact that a man says "I have a headache" in a particular social situation might mean that he's bored and wishes to go home, or that he is tired, or drank too much. But these are cases of natural meaning involving inferences drawn from a set of facts; they are not interpretations of the meaning of the sentence itself. (Of course, to the extent that husband and wife, say, speak a private language, in which "I have a headache" sometimes means "Let's go home," one might speak of these two expressions as having the same meaning in that domestic idiolect.)

What does the *means* mean in a sentence like " 'ineffable' means 'unspeakable' "? I would suggest that it means something like "is equivalent to." It functions like the "is" in "a basket is a wicker vessel" or the "equals" in "the whole equals the sum of the parts." It asserts synonymy between the two words. If we ask what "perhaps" means, the answer would be that it *means* "possibly" or "it may be that." And that italicized "means" means "is equivalent to ———— with respect to meaning." Spelled out further, it means "can be substituted for ———— in sentences without changing the meaning of the sentence."

Of course requests for the meaning of a word are not always fulfilled by a synonymous expression. If asked for the meaning of "horse," we might point to several horses and say "those are horses." If asked for the meaning of "good," we might reply that it is the most general adjective of commendation. Blue is the color of the sky on a clear day, and so on. We are likely to give such responses (1) if there are examples of the thing at hand, (2) if the synonyms are likely to be less familiar than the word in question, (3) if we wish to explain the differences between two synonyms, as when we point out that fleece is untreated wool, or (4) if there is no synonym handy. The English language does not provide ready synonyms, for example, for basic words like "and" and "I." Whatever synonyms we might conjure up, like "the speaker who is addressing you at this moment," are ungainly, to say the least.

In fact, however, when we respond to a request for meaning in these secondary ways, we do not (and cannot) preface our answer with "the meaning of 'x' is. . . ." These methods of definition may more properly be thought of as explanations of meaning or descriptions of the way a word is used. They do not tell us, though they may lead us to understand, what the meaning of the word in question is.

Writers don't always use quotation marks on the right side of a meaning equation. One can find examples of sentences like " 'shay' means chaise," or "the meaning of 'mazarine' is deep blue." But there is reason to think that such transcriptions are slips of the pen—harmless enough, to be sure, for all purposes save that of exploring the meaning and grammar of "means" and "meaning." "The meaning of 'mazarine' is deep blue," for example, might lead us to ask what a deep blue meaning is. And we would be similarly puzzled to learn that one meaning of "comical" is funny, or that the meaning of "ineffable" is unspeakable.

These examples illustrate the fact that the complements of sentences beginning "the meaning of 'x' is . . ." are not words used in the ordinary way. In " 'mazarine' means 'deep blue,' " "blue" is clearly not being used as an adjective. Few people have laughed at the meaning of "comical" and a person who knows the meaning of "ineffable" is able to speak it. It is preferable to say that "rapidly" means "quickly" rather than that it means quickly, because we would want to avoid the implication that some words mean things more quickly than others.

What sort of complements are these expressions? They seem to be nominal expressions, referring to words. We can say either that "rapidly" means "quickly" or that the word "rapidly" means the word "quickly." The latter formulation sounds odd because it is an unnecessary, though legitimate, clarification. It is unnecessary because in the context of "the word 'x' means . . ." we don't expect anything *but* another word or synonym. For the same reason it sounds odd to say "I like the food steak," but the oddity doesn't suggest that steak is not a food. "I like the color saffron" does not sound as odd because the category word is needed to make it clear that it is the color rather than the flower or the seasoning that I like.

Dennis Stampe, in a highly illuminating article called "Toward a Grammar of Meaning," argues against the view that the meaning of a word is another word. He tries in his examples to avoid quotation marks or italics on the right side of the equation and writes *"feu* means fire" rather than *"feu* means *fire."* He considers expressions like "the word 'rapidly' means the word 'quickly' " not only odd but incorrect or "deviant":

> It is often permissible to incorporate into a sentence information concerning the kind of thing being referred to, by the device of placing the referring term in apposition to some categorizing expression. Thus, we may say 'The *word feu* means fire,' placing the referring expression *feu* in apposition to an expression saying what sort of thing *feu* refers to. But by contrast we cannot say 'The word *feu* means the word fire,' without automatically altering either the sense of *mean* or contradicting the original assertion: for the only constructions which can properly be put on this latter sentence are the (unlikely) one according to which *means* means 'refers to,' and one according to which the sentence says, what is false, that *feu* means 'the word fire'—that being instead what the phrase *le mot 'feu'* means.[4]

But Stampe is wrong to say that these are the only two constructions one can put on "the word *feu* means the word *fire*." One can also say that the sentence says, what is true, that *feu* means *fire*.

Stampe instructively points out that "mean" is a so-called middle verb. Such verbs require a complement, do not permit the passive transformation, and do not admit qualification by adverbs of manner. They are also intransitive. "Middle verbs include *resemble, have, cost, lack, weigh* ('He weighed 200 pounds')" (p. 270). We should note that *mean* has one thing in common with *resemble*, but not with the other middle verbs, that reinforces the view that both sides of a meaning equation are nominal expressions referring to words. If "x" resembles "y" in a certain respect, then "y" must resemble "x" in that respect. Similarly, if "feu" means "fire," "fire" must mean "feu." Synonymity, like resemblance, is a symmetrical relation. This similarity is what we would expect on the assumption that "mean" expresses a relationship of equivalence, identity, or resemblance. The word "chaste" resembles the word "chased" in one respect; it resembles the word "pure" in another respect. "Chaste" sounds like "chased"; "chaste" means "pure."

Stampe goes on to argue that expressions like " 'Ineffable'

means unspeakable" (deferentially omitting the second pair of single quotes) are derived, through a series of transformations from a base "string" like "By *ineffable* Agent means *unspeakable.*" That is, according to Stampe, expressions telling us what a word means are elliptical expressions substituted for expressions telling us what people mean by the word. Though I have no reason to think that either expression is derived from the other, it is certainly true that if "ineffable" means "unspeakable," then it is also true that by "ineffable" people generally mean "unspeakable," and vice versa. It is the constancy of what people use a word to mean that accounts for the stability of meanings.

I suggested earlier that to say that "x" means "y" is to say that "x" can be substituted for "y" in a sentence without changing the meaning of the sentence. That definition would of course be circular if there were no distinction between the meaning of a word and the meaning of a sentence. But there is such a distinction, even though the two are closely related. As P. F. Strawson points out:

> We must acknowledge, as two complementary truths, first, that the meaning of a sentence in general depends, in some systematic way, on the meanings of the words that make it up and, second, that for a word to have a particular meaning is a matter of its making a particular systematic contribution to the meanings of the sentences in which it occurs.[5]

Now we do not ask for the meaning of a whole sentence as often as we ask for the meaning of a word. This is so because we usually grasp at least some part of a sentence's meaning. But if we do ask, say, for the meaning of "ontogeny recapitulates phylogeny," the answer would be another (long-winded) sentence—perhaps, though not necessarily, a sentence substituting a synonymous expression for each term in the original. We render the meaning of a word with a synonym, the meaning of a sentence with a paraphrase.

To understand what it means for two sentences to mean the same thing, let us introduce into the discussion J. L. Austin's seminal insight into the nature of speech acts. Austin pointed out that when we speak meaningfully to someone we are doing something—something that is distinct from merely uttering an audible string of words, and distinct as well from producing certain effects on our listener. When I say to someone, in a given context, "I have fifty dollars in my pocket," I am making an assertion—namely, the assertion that I have fifty dollars in my pocket. And I have made that assertion whether or not (a) it is true, (b) I believe it to be true, (c) I convince the person I am speaking to of its truth. If I then say "I promise to give them to you," I have, in so saying, made a promise, whether I intend to keep the promise or the money, and whether or not I do in fact keep the promise. Doing such things (asserting, promising, asking, commanding, apologizing, and so on) is, in the vernacular, what language is *for*. It is because they can be used to perform such acts that sentences and words have meanings. And it is because there are more ways than one to make a particular promise or ask a particular question that we can say what the meaning of a word or sentence is. Furthermore, it is by means of such acts that we can accomplish other things with language—like expressing feelings and attitudes, or enraging, assuaging, cajoling, and informing people.

Austin dubbed these acts "illocutionary acts," and he distinguished them from the "locutionary" act of vocally uttering the sentence and the "perlocutionary" act of affecting the listener in some way. One can think of these not as separate acts but as three different ways of describing a single act, much as one and the same movement can be described as sticking one's hand out the car window, or as signalling for a left turn, or as annoying the driver of the car behind.

The difference between illocutionary and perlocutionary acts is illustrated best by examples. Thus Alston lists, as illocutionary acts, reporting, predicting, admitting, asking, suggesting, congratulating, promising, and thanking, while perlocutionary acts include persuading, deceiving, encouraging, irritating, frightening, boring, and bringing someone to believe something or do something. Generally speaking, the illocutionary force of a sentence can be made explicit. Thus if "I will be there" is spoken as a promise, that fact could be made explicit by restating the sentence in the form "I promise that I will be there." And "It's raining" can be restated as "I assert that it's raining." There is a certain formality in the explicit forms, and ordinarily the illocutionary intent is indicated by such devices as word order, stress, syntax, and intonation. (See Searle, p. 30.) It is also useful to note that one performs a perlocutionary act by performing an illocutionary act, and not vice versa. You reassure someone

·(perlocutionary) by telling him something (illocutionary). You convince someone of some fact by making certain assertions, and not the other way round.

Searle claimed that more than one illocutionary act can be performed simultaneously:

> There may be several different non-synonymous illocutionary verbs that correctly characterize [an] utterance. For example suppose at a party a wife says "It's really quite late." That utterance may be at one level a statement of fact; to her interlocutor, who has just remarked on how early it was, it may be (and be intended as) an objection; to her husband it may be (and be intended as) a suggestion or even a request ("Let's go home") as well as a warning ("You'll feel rotten in the morning if we don't"). [Pp. 70–71]

It is possible to object to this account, however, for if there are levels here, there are only two of them: there is a difference between the sense in which the woman's remark is a statement and the sense in which it is an objection, a request, and a warning. For the woman has objected, suggested, and warned *by stating something* and she has *not* stated something by objecting to something, or by suggesting an idea, or by warning someone. Put differently, not all the kinds of information that a sentence may intentionally or unintentionally convey are pertinent to a description of its illocutionary aspect. What Searle's example illustrates is that a particular illocutionary act may have, and be intended to have, different perlocutionary effects on different hearers.

At this point we may begin to enumerate some of the things that are involved in understanding actual speech and writing. One brings to them, of course, prior knowledge of word meanings, of syntax, of how illocutionary acts are performed, and the like. But understanding a particular utterance also entails figuring out what the speaker or writer meant by his words, what syntactic structure he intended, what illocutionary act he was performing. These are decisions we always make, though the fact that we make them is driven home only when they prove difficult—when it is uncertain which sense of a word (like Dickinson's "majority" or "valves") was intended, or when the syntax or the specific illocutionary force of a sentence is ambiguous. Thus to understand "Here! creep, / Wretch, under a comfort serves in a whirlwind" it is necessary to recognize that two illocutionary acts are being dovetailed—first a command, then a statement—the last two words of the first ("a comfort") being also the first two words of the second. Or, on a less esoteric level, knowing the meaning of a simple remark like "You will leave tomorrow," when it is used on some particular occasion, involves knowing whether the sentence is meant as a statement (in answer to a question, say), as a command, or, with a rising inflection, as a question.

Beyond these decisions about "non-natural" meaning, however, there remain other questions which one would try to answer in seeking a fuller understanding: questions about the intended perlocutionary effect of the utterance, and other questions about its "natural" meaning—the inferences that may be drawn about the speaker and the situation from the fact of his having said what he said. It so happens that all of these questions are sometimes formulated in terms of "meaning" in one or another of its several senses, a fact which helps to account for the vagueness of questions about meaning in literature. Suppose someone asks, "What is the meaning of Hopkins's sonnet 'No Worst, There is None'?" It seems to be the case that one can know what every word and sentence in a poem, play, or novel means and yet still ask what the work *as a whole* means. It may be a question about what social or biographical inferences can be drawn from the fact of the author's having written it, or it may be a question about the author's perlocutionary intentions: What effects was he trying to achieve? Was he being satirical? What "moral" was he exemplifying through the story? Why did he write it? These are often answerable questions, but they need to be put in a more precise way. "What does it mean?" won't do, except as an encouragement to say *something* interesting.

Two sentences have the same meaning, then, if they can be used to perform the same illocutionary act. And two words or expressions are synonymous if they can be interchanged in a sentence without changing the illocutionary act the sentence is used to perform. To the extent that one is making the same assertion when one says "What I did was courageous" that one is making when one says "The action I performed was coura-geous," the two sentences have the same meaning. And if one

37

meaning of "brave" is "courageous," then one must be able to make the same assertion by substituting "brave" for "courageous" in either sentence.

Many pairs of words, of course, are only roughly synonymous. One can distinguish between a request for a "draught of vintage"—to use an example from Keats via William Alston—and a request for a "drink of wine." They constitute slightly different speech acts, though they mean roughly the same thing. Applying Alston's test for synonymy, we might note that if you seriously requested a draught of vintage you would not be satisfied by a bottle of plonk, and if handed one you might legitimately claim to have been misunderstood, whereas if you had merely requested a drink of wine you would have no cause for complaint.[6]

DENOTATION, CONNOTATION, AND SELECTION RESTRICTION

A view of meaning that antedates the theory of speech acts is the view that if two words have the same meaning, they will also have the same denotation and connotation. It will be useful to see how this traditional view may be developed in such a way as to be brought into harmony with the theory of meaning implicit in the theory of speech acts.

Logicians define a word's denotation as the class of all the things to which the word is correctly or regularly used to refer. And its connotation is the set of qualities that defines membership in that class. The denotation of "mongrel," for example, is the class of mongrels—all those dogs we might use the word to refer to. Its connotations are the qualities that something must possess in order properly to be called a mongrel. "Dog" denotes a larger class than "mongrel," and hence its denotation includes the denotation of "mongrel." The connotation of "mongrel," then, contains an additional quality—mixed-breed-ness—which distinguishes the smaller from the larger class. If one of the regular uses of "vintage" is to refer to old, high-quality wine made from the grapes of a single harvest, then the word's denotation is all wine of that sort. And the word connotes age, high quality, made-from-the-grapes-of-a-single-harvest-ness, and so on.

It seems that we would be issuing roughly the same command whether we told our neighbor to get his mongrel or his dog of mixed breed off our lawn, though the latter request might strike the neighbor as playfully euphemistic. So it is apparently the case that if two expressions have the same meaning they have the same denotation. This is not to say that the meaning of a word *is* its denotation; the meaning of "mongrel" isn't a class of animals. But, in the case of nominative expressions, there is a clear relationship between meaning and denotation. Two expressions that are equivalent in meaning have the same denotation.

The term "regularly" (or its sometime substitute "correctly") reminds us from another vantage point that meaning is dependent on use. Communication can take place only because people use words in the same ways over and over again. Those ways or regularities can be described, and a description of a word's denotation and connotation explicates one of its uses— namely, its use in referring. The community of users may of course be very large, or it may be as small as two speakers or a single person talking to himself, provided the members use words in rule-abiding ways.

If it is true that referring can be done only with noun phrases, then the logicians' definitions of denotation and connotation apply only to expressions that can function that way. But the rules describing the normal use of other parts of speech would constitute something analogous to connotation. Though "courageous," because it is an adjective, may not be used for referring to anything, we may specify what sorts of people or behavior it is used to characterize. Perhaps, stretching the meaning of "connotation" slightly, we could say that the connotation of "courageous" is the set of qualities that defines a person or act as courageous. Similarly, with a verb we may say what sort of action it predicates of its subject, with a conjunction what sort of relationship between things it may be used to express, and so on. In each case, whether the word whose regular uses we are describing is a noun, adjective, verb, or preposition, the regularity of use is a precondition for the word's having a fixed meaning or meanings.

We say that one meaning of "on" is "over and in contact with." The speech-act theory points out that the two expressions are frequently interchangeable. The notion of connotation shifts our perspective only slightly and suggests that the two expressions connote, in our broader sense of that term, the same spatial relation.

In talking about denotation and connotation we are talking

about individual words or expressions and classes of things, actions, relationships, and so on, to which they are linked through the regularities of speech. There is another set of rules or regularities, derivative from these, which describes the way words and expressions are combined in sentences. These the linguists call "selection restrictions."[7] The connotation of a word will place certain constraints on the words to which it may be grammatically related in a sentence. We know that a sentence beginning "I saw a big red . . ." will ordinarily be completed by a count noun designating a concrete object, not by an abstract noun (like "democracy") or a mass noun (like "electricity" or "bread"), for "red" connotes a quality that only objects can possess, and "a" connotes singularity. As a rule, in a sentence of the form "I persuaded —— to consider the matter seriously," the blank will be filled in by a noun phrase designating a person or persons, because of the connotations of "persuade" and "consider."

Speakers of English will recognize sentences like "He water-proofed that idea" or "prepositions smell loud" as irregular because they violate selection restrictions. Waterproofing is something one does to concrete objects, and hence "waterproof" takes a concrete object as its object. "Smell" in its transitive sense takes an animate subject, and a physical subject in its intransitive sense. The connotations in these sentences fail to match up properly, and the result is what is sometimes called "sort crossing," sometimes a "category mistake."[8]

METAPHOR

Now it so happens that we sometimes speak irregularly on purpose. That is, we sometimes violate language rules, intend that our listeners know we are violating them, and nevertheless manage to be understood. And among the occasions when this would seem to be the case are those when we wittingly or wittily violate selection restrictions and hence speak metaphorically.

Alston defines metaphor as "using a word intelligibly without using it in any of its senses." As an example he quotes Cummings's lines "the sweet small clumsy feet of april came into the ragged meadow of my soul." "By any recognized method of distinguishing senses of terms, there is no sense of the word 'feet' in which we can speak of the feet of a month; nor is there any sense of 'meadow' in which a soul can have a meadow."[9]

40

This analysis won't quite do. Surely we can tell that "feet" is being used in its anatomical rather than its prosodic sense, "sweet" primarily in its general approbative sense (= "pleasing") with only a hint of its purely gustatory and olfactory sense, and "meadow" in its only sense. Every word in the sentence is being used in one of its standard senses, and we have no difficulty telling which.

Let us say rather that in metaphor the rules governing the combination of expressions are being broken—not by mistake of course, but by design. The connotation of "feet" would lead us to expect an animate noun after "of," and souls do not contain physical things or places. The effect is that of treating April *as if* it were animate, the soul *as if* it were spacious.

When Frost wrote, of an old man living alone on a winter night, that "all out-of-doors looked darkly in at him," he used a verb that would normally take an animate subject with a subject of a very different sort. When Emily Dickinson called prayer "the little implement / Through which Men reach / Where Presence—is denied them," she was identifying an activity with a physical object. It is, of course, so commonplace to use object language to describe mental activity that simply calling prayer an implement would scarcely seem metaphoric. But the word "little" drives us in the direction of metaphor, and with the subsequent lines—"They fling their Speech / By means of it"— we are there.

The metaphors we are considering here are explicit metaphors in the sense that both of the terms whose connotations are at odds with each other—the vehicle and the tenor—appear in the sentence. That is, a dictionary containing an exhaustive list of the selection restrictions for each word would tip us off to the presence of sort crossing. There are also implicit metaphors, where the sort crossing can only be known from the context of the utterance. These include name calling and sentences where the act or thing referred to is not literally specified. In such cases either the referent must be already understood by the listener or the metaphor is dying, commonplace, and hence obvious. Thus, unless we are at a county fair, or in the hands of an arsonist, there is implicit metaphor in "What a pig!" and "Let's try to light a fire under the chairman."

The line between literal and metaphoric uses of language is not altogether clear and distinct, and that for several reasons. First, since the meanings of words sometimes change through time and may vary slightly from community to community, it is not always clear whether selection restrictions are being violated; a decision by *fiat* would often be untrue to the fluidity of the situation. One man's idiom may be another's mystification, and many an idiom consists of terms that were once metaphorical but are no longer so—for people who know the idiom. Second, and more perplexing, not every violation of selection restrictions results in metaphor.

There would seem to be a spectrum running from literal (that is, regular, normal) speech at one extreme, through metaphor, to nonsense at the other. A decision about whether a given expression is literal or metaphoric depends on our sense of whether or how far it departs from regular usage. A decision about whether it is metaphoric or nonsensical depends on our ability to discover a point to the irregularity:

> Flowers bloom in the spring.
> Spring is coming.
> She is bringing her bouquets with her.
> Spring has a light touch.
> Spring is a perhaps hand.
> Spring thinks perhaps rocks.

There is a certain delight in trying to recuperate meaning out of nonsense, and nothing provokes the attempt more forcefully than the claim that a certain expression is indeed nonsensical. (Let me test that assertion by claiming that the first of my examples is literal, the second a dead metaphor and hence now literal, the next three clearly metaphorical, the last nonsense.) Chomsky provided just such a challenge with his allegedly nonsensical "Colorless green ideas sleep furiously,"[10] most of the readings of which have been utterly banal, but one of which, a poem by John Hollander, deserves quotation:

COILED ALIZARINE
for Noam Chomsky
Curiously deep, the slumber of crimson thoughts:
    While breathless, in stodgy viridian,
Colorless green ideas sleep furiously.[11]

While it is a truism that no metaphorical expression is precisely equivalent to a literal paraphrase of it, it is also true

42

that making and understanding metaphor depends on our ability to conceive of a rough literal equivalent. If we are asked what a metaphorical expression means and we can't even approach a paraphrase, we can hardly be said to understand the metaphor at all. We learn to speak before we learn to speak metaphorically. Intentional deviation from rules depends on a knowledge of the rules.

When we speak metaphorically, after all, we *mean something* by what we say, even though we do not mean what we say literally. So the actual meaning of a metaphorical assertion can be rendered by another expression that makes roughly the same assertion, and that expression itself may be either literal or metaphoric. The meaning of "She had a heart of stone" could be rendered as "she was unemotional and incapable of love," or as "She was cold-hearted," or perhaps even as "she had no heart." The point is not that there are no differences whatsoever among these expressions, but simply that they do mean roughly the same thing. Furthermore, if any one of the assertions is true, the others are true also. If it is metaphorically true that she had a heart of stone, then it is literally true that she was unemotional.

I said earlier that not every violation of a selection restriction results in metaphor. It may, after all, result in an actual mistake, confusion, or falsehood. Suppose you ask someone what a prayer is and he replies that it is a little implement used for flinging things. He then claims to own one and fetches a small sling from the bottom drawer. He has clearly not spoken metaphorically and his answer to your question comprised a real category mistake based on a misunderstanding of the meaning of "prayer." The example is preposterous, but category mistakes are commonplace, and they may result not only from lexicographical mistakes but also from mistaken notions of what the world is really like. Determinations about whether someone has spoken metaphorically, or about whether an assertion ought to be taken literally, are related to our beliefs, and to our conceptions of what those we listen to believe. Colin Turbayne has argued that "there are no metaphors *per se*,"[12] and, drawing on some of his examples and others like them, we can imagine or recollect substantive quarrels over whether propositions like the following are literally or metaphorically true or false:

The world (or man) is a machine.

Sound is vibration.

Bodies attract each other.

The reason instructs the will, which in turn seeks to control the appetites.

The objects we perceive as being "out there" are actually in the mind of the perceiver.

The ego strives to bring the id into subjection.

Genes contain and convey coded information.

A poem is an experience similar to the experience the poet had on rereading his poem.

The genre of a poem determines its form.

We may, then, imagine cases where a speaker says something and means it literally, while his listener regards it as gibberish taken literally, but is willing to grant it a degree of metaphoric truth. We would say that something was *said metaphorically* only if we believed that the speaker was sort crossing, or violating selection restrictions, for a reason, and that if challenged on the literalness of his remark, he would acknowledge that he meant it figuratively. As for the remark itself—taken out of context and regarded as a type sentence—it would appear to be a mistake to try to determine whether it is *"per se"* metaphorical or not. We might say that it can be taken as a metaphorical statement or that we can imagine believing it or saying it meaphorically, or we might agree that it is absolutely absurd taken literally and that it can make sense and does make good sense taken metaphorically. Such conclusions are based on the discovery of a point to the remark when regarded as metaphor— that is, a reason why it might have been metaphorically meant or intended. We come back, in our thinking, to some speaker, in this case imagined rather than real.

IRONY

Irony has this at least in common with metaphor: both concepts can be used to qualify the way a particular actual utterance is *meant*. Or to put it slightly differently, they qualify the way a speaker intends what he says to be taken or understood. "I didn't mean it literally; I meant it metaphorically." "I didn't really mean it; I meant it ironically." In both cases we are dealing with a sense of the verb "mean" that takes people rather than words as its subject. It means "intend," and it is close to the "mean" in

"I mean to go downtown," closer still to "I meant the gift as a token of my affection" or "I only meant it as a friendly nudge." It is quite distinct from the "means" in " 'ineffable' means 'unspeakable.' "

Irony is also like metaphor insofar as it must be regarded as a swerving away from regular speech, an intended breaking of rules. Just as one must learn to speak literally before learning to speak metaphorically, so must one learn to speak "straight" before acquiring the ability to speak ironically. But to understand irony we must return to our investigation of illocutionary acts, for the rules that irony plays off against are not rules describing the proper combinations of words with each other, but rules describing the conditions under which illocutionary acts are performed. No dictionary or list of selection restrictions could help us discover that a sentence might be meant ironically. "You look elegant, my dear," contains no category mistakes, and whether it is a sincere compliment, or affectionate or bitterly impatient sarcasm will depend on the context in which it is said.

Let us note that there is a difference between uttering (or writing) a sentence and performing an illocutionary act. The novice who types "The quick brown fox jumps over the lazy dog" is hardly making a genuine assertion about some fox, and the would-be Hamlet gesturing dramatically as he pronounces a soliloquy before his mirror is not really claiming that the question is "To be, or not to be." There are many situations in which one can utter, say, a promissory, assertive, or imperative sentence without actually making a promise, an assertion, or a command. If, for instance, one utters a sentence in order to discuss its meaning, or to practice one's pronunciation, or to tell a joke, or to report what someone else has said, one is not in fact performing the illocutionary act for which the sentence might be used. Certain conditions must obtain for an utterance to be "good," or in Austin's terms, for it to "secure uptake." These conditions, which vary according to the kind of illocutionary act involved, have been analyzed in some detail, and with certain differences in approach, by both Alston and Searle.[13] We may be content with adumbrating the concept by means of a few examples:

a) A promise would not "secure uptake" if the speaker were not speaking audibly to the person to whom the promise is made, or if it were a promise to do something in the past, or if it were obvious to both parties that the speaker would perform the promised action in the normal course of events anyway. (If both parties know that the speaker is going to do whatever he promises to do with or without promising, the promise would have no point.)

b) One has not made an actual assertion if it is obvious to both the speaker and the listener that the speaker does not believe the assertion to be true, or that the listener already knows that the speaker believes it to be true.

c) One has not really made a request if it is obvious to both parties that the listener is in no position to comply with the request, or that the request has already been complied with, or that the speaker does not wish it to be complied with.

We would say that a person has performed a real illocutionary act only if he intended his utterance to be taken as such, that is, as counting as a genuine assertion, request, or whatever. For example, a promise to your friend that you will repay a loan counts as an expression of your intention to repay the loan. Now you may not actually intend to repay it, but if you promise to repay it, you imply that you do so intend. (In fact, you intend to make your friend believe that you intend to repay it.) An insincere promise, then, is a promise nonetheless, provided you *purport* to intend to do the thing you promise to do. And as a promise counts—promises being what they are—as an expression of intent to do something, so an assertion that something is the case counts as an expression of belief that it *is* the case, and a request that something be done counts as an expression of a desire that it *be* done. We would call an assertion a lie only if (*a*) the speaker believes the assertion to be false, but (*b*) wishes his hearer to *think* that he believes it to be true. If it is obvious to both parties that the speaker neither believes what he is saying nor wishes the listener to think he believes it, no real assertion has been made at all.

We can distinguish, then, among three kinds of utterances: real, sincere illocutionary acts, where the speaker intends, believes, or wishes whatever he purports to intend, believe, or wish; real but insincere illocutionary acts, where the speaker purports to intend, and so on, without actually so intending; and mock illocutionary acts, where the speaker purports nothing at all by the sentence he utters or writes.

A sentence like "Mary, will you marry me?" may be uttered in a variety of situations in which it would not be used to make an actual request, and hence would be a mock request. Jack may be rehearsing his proposal en route to Mary's house, or he may be using it as a sample sentence in a linguistics class. Or he may be joking, or more generally, asking the question ironically. In all these cases at least some of the conditions described by Searle fail to apply, and at least Jack knows it. The request is not to be taken seriously. And if Jack is joking with Mary or speaking ironically, as distinct from speaking insincerely, then Jack must intend that Mary or some third person also recognize that some of the conditions are in abeyance. Something in the situation, such as a mutual understanding, a preceding remark, an unusual inflection, or the fact that Jack and Mary are already married to each other, must be recognized as indicating not only that the request is not to be taken seriously, but also how it is to be taken (for example, as a sarcastic rejoinder to Mary's latest insult, or as a spontaneous and hyperbolic expression of affection).

Of course irony is open to misinterpretation. John may send signals that Mary to her sorrow fails to receive. Or he may (since one may be ironic at someone else's expense) aim the signals not at Mary but at the others seated at the dinner table. Questions about whether an utterance is ironic are questions about how the speaker or writer intended his remark to be taken. One may try to save a stupid remark or a sentimental poem by treating it as if it were intended ironically, as when we say, with irony of our own, "He *couldn't* have meant that *seriously!*" But a claim that a piece of discourse is ironic is a claim about intentions.[14]

Ironic utterances, then, would seem to fall into the category of mock illocutionary acts, occasions in which the conditions rendering an illocutionary act "good" are absent or held, by mutual understanding, in abeyance. But the category of such mock speech acts is very large indeed, and our present task is to distinguish irony from other such utterances. Consider, for example, the following speakers and writers:

1. A person quoting something said or written by someone else.
2. A professional writing advertising copy, composing greeting card verse, or writing a speech for his employer.
3. A translator turning the sentences of one language into sentences of another.

4. A linguist uttering or writing on the blackboard a sentence whose features he wishes to consider or describe.
5. A politician rehearsing a speech prior to delivering it.
6. An actor speaking his lines in the performance of a play.

One almost distinguishing feature of irony is that the ironist *pretends* to perform an illocutionary act. When Jack asks his wife Mary to marry him, he is pretending to ask for her hand—pretending, of course, without any intention of deceiving her. This feature rules out cases 1–4, but not 5 and 6. The actor is pretending to perform all those illocutionary acts performed by the character whose part he is playing. He is also pretending to be the character. And if the character speaks ironically, then the actor is pretending to pretend to perform an illocutionary act. Similarly, the person rehearsing his speech is pretending to perform those illocutionary acts which he will actually perform in time—even if he is rehearsing alone, his own audience, before a mirror.

We can, I think, cut irony out from this smaller herd by remembering that in the case of a mock assertion the speaker does not purport to believe the assertion to be true. Nevertheless, in most of our examples, he *may* believe it to be true. The quotation citer may or may not believe the proposition he quotes; if he is only quoting, his beliefs are irrelevant. The linguist may or may not believe that *all swans are white* or that *flying airplanes can be dangerous*; if his purpose is simply that of getting the sentence on the table so its syntax and semantics can be investigated, he is not expressing the belief which, on some other occasion, he might use the sentence to express. Finally, the actor's and the speech rehearser's beliefs are likewise matters of indifference from the point of view of anyone trying to understand the nature of their actions. Sir Laurence may or may not have thought that there is providence in the fall of a sparrow when he pretended to claim so as Hamlet. The audience doesn't care. And though the politician's beliefs take on importance once he starts making genuine claims and promises to his audience, they have no bearing on the question of whether or not he's rehearsing.

The ironist's beliefs, however, are crucial, and it is crucial, if the irony is to be understood, that the listener or audience understand those beliefs. Suppose that Lady E. rushes in bedraggled and soaking from the rain and Lord E. greets her with "You look positively elegant, my dear." The irony (such as it is) depends on Lady E.'s knowing full well that Lord E. does *not* believe that she looks elegant and is not genuinely purporting to believe it.

Or consider an instance of understatement. Imagine someone commenting in the foyer after a performance of *Lear*, "Things didn't quite go his way." Here the irony depends on the mutual understanding that the speaker not only believes the remark, but considers it obvious, and in fact far too tame a truth to do full justice to Lear's career. A sarcastic "Thanks a lot!" depends on a shared sense of the speaker's lack of gratitude, a joshing insult on underlying respect, a rhetorical question on everyone knowing that the questioner already knows the answer. The ironist pretends to say something, and our perception and understanding of the pretense will always depend on our awareness of the nature of the discrepancy between the beliefs, feelings, intentions, or desires that he pretends to express and those he actually possesses. To the extent that the discrepancy is complex, the irony will be also; to the extent that it is unclear, the irony will be ambiguous.

FICTION

Now, for the Poet, he nothing affirmes, and
therefore neuer lyeth.... What childe is
there that, comming to a Play, and seeing
Thebes written in great Letters vpon an olde
doore, doth beleeve that it is *Thebes*?
　　　　　　Sir Philip Sidney, *An Apologie for Poetrie*

You who　　listen　　give me life in a manner of speaking.... Where there's a voice there's a speaker.
　　John Barth, "Autobiography: A Self-Recorded Fiction"

We have described two sets of rules governing language use. The first of these is the set of rules that give words their meanings and imply certain restrictions on the ways they will be combined in sentences. The second is the set of conventions that are understood as governing speech acts and that in fact define what is involved in making a statement, asking a question, issuing an order, and so on. Pointed departures from the first set of rules may result in metaphor; pointed departures from the second, in irony.

We often use phrases like "speaking metaphorically" and "speaking ironically," but "speaking fictionally" feels strange on the tongue. Fiction is not regarded, in everyday parlance, as a manner of speaking. Nevertheless, if a listener were to overhear someone carrying on about a frog transformed into a prince or a man named Gregor awaking one morning to discover himself an insect, and if he then challenged the speaker's honesty or accuracy, the speaker might well protect himself with the characteristic disavowal: "I didn't mean it seriously; I was only telling a story." So fiction may in fact *be* a manner of speaking, though the noun is seldom adverbialized.

The question, then, is whether we can draw a clear and useful line between fictional and nonfictional speaking or writing. (The question is *not*, by the way, with fiction any more than with irony or metaphor, whether we can draw a distinction that eliminates all borderline or indeterminate cases. A distinction that works for a large number of paradigmatic cases will do, especially if it helps in showing just what is problematical about a doubtful case, or about a doubtful genre, like satire, the roman à clef, or the "nonfictional novel.") Perhaps we should think of two broad and loose categories to start with: jokes and novels, fairy tales, the fictional exemplum illustrating a point in didactic prose, detective stories, parables, fables, science fiction, and the like, on the one hand; political speeches, autobiography, newspaper stories and editorials, letters sent to and from a child at camp, history books, the *Principia Mathematica* and *Leviathan* and the like, on the other. I believe most of us will sense a difference between the two categories. If so, what is it?

Traditional answers to this question seem to fall under three general headings, and we should glance briefly at each to see why, or in what sense, they won't do:

1. *Fiction, truth, and falsehood.* It is sometimes suggested that fictional statements are false, or that they are statements the truth or falsity of which is of no importance or interest to the reader. But surely many fictional statements are true, and some are false, and it is usually crucial to the reader to know which are which. At the beginning of *Huckleberry Finn* Huck tells us about another book, *The Adventures of Tom Sawyer*, and he tells us

50

how it ended ("Tom and me found the money that the robbers hid in the cave...."[15]). He's right, and indeed most of what he tells us is true. We accept it as true because we have no reason to doubt it, though of course most of his statements are true statements about characters that we recognize as make-believe. But we must regard them as true in order to distinguish them from fictional statements that are false. Nabokov's *Ada*, for example, begins with a falsehood:

> "All happy families are more or less dissimilar; all unhappy ones are more or less alike," says a great Russian writer in the beginning of a famous novel (*Anna Arkadievitch Karenina*, transfigured into English by R. G. Stonelower, Mount Tabor Ltd., 1880).[16]

In some cases the truth remains in doubt. In John Barth's story "Lost in the Funhouse" the following sentences occur in sequence: "Naturally he didn't have nerve enough to ask Magda to go through the funhouse with him. With incredible nerve and to everyone's surprise he invited Magda, quietly and politely, to go through the funhouse with him."[17] The reader ought not to overlook such a contradiction, and though the story is silent on the question of which sentence is true, the contradiction is functional and must be both noticed and explained if the story is to be understood.

Or to choose a different kind of example, when Emma Bovary returns from an early morning rendezvous with her lover Rodolphe, she tells a neighbor whom she chances upon unexpectedly that she has been to see her daughter. She's lying, and the reader had better know it. Or again, in Iris Murdoch's *The Black Prince*, the reader believes that he is getting a true report of, if not sound judgments on, the fictional events presented until he gets to the (fictional) appendix, which calls all in doubt. Ford Madox Ford's *The Good Soldier* opens with the sentence "This is the saddest story I have ever heard,"[18] but the reader soon realizes that he must carefully assay Dowell's, the narrator's, every judgment, including that opener, for elements of self-excuse, self-deception, and simple myopia.

Fiction affords us not only deceiving and deceived characters and unreliable, teasing, and misleading narrators; it abounds in irony ("It is a truth universally acknowledged, that a single man in possession of a good fortune, must be in want of a wife"[19]), the perception of which involves judgments about the truth or falsity of statements and the intentions of the statement makers.

2. *Reference*. Fictional statements are sometimes regarded as statements made about fictional characters, places, and events. But of course many nonfictional statements refer to fictional characters (e.g., "Ishmael is the narrator of *Moby Dick*") and many fictional statements refer to people and events in the real world. Stephen Dedalus disavows eating real, not make-believe, muscatel grapes, and he cites the real, not a fictional, Thomas Aquinas as the source of his aesthetic. Pip, the narrator of Dickens's *Great Expectations*, tells us that he lived in "the marsh country, down by the river, within, as the river wound, twenty miles of the sea."[20] The river he is talking about is the real Thames, and when he later tells us of his move to London, it is the real London he refers to. When we think of him visiting Soho, The Inns of Court, or Newgate, the pretense is that he is visiting real, not imaginary places.

It is true that "fictional" is used to designate make-believe or made up or imaginary people, places, and events. That is a legitimate use of the term. But it is distinct from the "fictional" in fictional discourse, which, like nonfictional discourse, may be about fictional people, or may not.

3. *The shaping imagination*. It is sometimes noted that historians, biographers, autobiographers, even scientists, "shape" their materials, consciously or unconsciously imposing an order on them, simplifying or distorting the "facts" they purport to relate. An autobiography, for example, may be self-justifying, and a history or biography presents a version of a period or a life, not the period or the life itself. Thus the imagination may be involved in the creation of nonfiction as well as of fiction, just as real events may provide material for a novel. If that is the case, how can we really distinguish the one from the other? But while such arguments have some interest, they neither aid us nor hinder us in distinguishing, say, between Augustine's *Confessions* and *David Copperfield*. Nor should they encourage us to enlarge the concept of fiction to embrace any and every expression of an individual's perception or point of view. Indeed they simply reinforce the fact that neither truthfulness nor accuracy alone can take us very far in discovering the distinction we seek.

If we return to our earlier suggestion that fictional discourse is a manner of speaking, we may speculate that whether a piece of writing is fictional or not may have something to do with how its author intended it to be taken or understood. If, say, we were to challenge a genuine autobiographer on the accuracy of his statements, he might try to defend them by providing further evidence or argument, or he might acknowledge his mistake; he would probably *not* say, as the novelist might: "But it's only a story, a novel, fiction, not a real autobiography. You misunderstood the point of it all."

Such a definition of fiction has been advanced by John Searle in an article entitled "The Logical Status of Fictional Discourse,"[21] and as we might expect, Searle sees fiction as discourse which bears a special relationship to the conventions that govern the performance of illocutionary acts. According to Searle, the author of a novel is not "seriously committed" to the truth of the assertions he makes in the way the maker of a genuine assertion must be, for he is not making genuine assertions at all. Discussing a passage from Iris Murdoch's *The Red and the Green*, he writes: "She is pretending, one could say, to make an assertion, or acting as if she were making an assertion, or going through the motions of making an assertion, or imitating the making of an assertion." In fiction, the illocutionary conventions are "suspended." The author or storyteller does not wish what he writes or says to be taken as his own seriously meant propositions, though of course he may wish his story to be taken seriously in some other sense.

It does not follow from this position that the author necessarily disbelieves the propositions that constitute the fiction, or that the propositions are themselves untrue. Henry James may or may not have believed that "under certain circumstances there are few hours in life more agreeable than the hour dedicated to the ceremony known as afternoon tea."[22] The point is that by beginning a novel with that proposition he made no commitment regarding its truth, and we would be guilty of misunderstanding if we either questioned his sincerity or praised him for it. He was, for storytelling purposes, putting us in the presence, as it were, of a claim about the agreeableness of afternoon tea, without making such a claim.

Searle addresses the peculiar status of fictional discourse

through the notion of authorial pretense. In a third-person narrative, he says, "the author pretends to perform illocutionary acts," whereas in first-person narratives he "pretends to be someone else making assertions" (pp. 327–28). Most critics prefer to think instead of fictional narrators and fictional characters really making assertions. Thus James didn't pretend to give exquisitely qualified praise to afternoon tea; he created a fictional narrator who actually does so. Insofar as the point of Searle's "pretend" is purely negative (James himself didn't praise tea time) the two ways of describing the situation are not in conflict. It is by "going through the motions" of assertion making that James created the illusion of a narrator. But there may be some practical advantages to the critics' locution. It is awkward to think of Faulkner pretending to *be* in turn each of the fifteen characters whose narrations and reflections comprise *As I Lay Dying*. And from the reader's point of view, the notion of Faulkner pretending to be the characters is beside the point. His understanding of the work as fiction involves, first, the knowledge that the illocutionary acts are not Faulkner's, and second, the pretense that they represent the speech and thoughts of a family named Bundren and their acquaintances.

I would, in other words, prefer to compare the writer of fiction to a set designer, a sculptor, even a toy-maker—builders of occasions for others' pretenses. The set designer does not pretend to make a forest or decorate the interior of a room; he makes a pretend forest, furnishes a make-believe room. His materials are canvas, cardboard, and paint; the novelist's are words. As the audience pretends that the path through the woods leads to a castle, so the reader pretends that the sentences he reads have been said or written by someone who means them.

Given these and other minor qualifications,[23] it seems to me that Searle has offered the best formulation of the distinction we are after, a formulation in a tradition going back at least as far as Sidney. *The poet nothing affirms.* The fundamental pretense for both the writer and reader of fiction is the pretense that someone really performed the speech acts which constitute the fictional work. Nevertheless, the formulation is very broad. The wary reader will have observed that Searle's account of fiction is difficult to distinguish from the account of irony as "mock speech act" offered several pages back. (The similarity is not coincidental; the former inspired the latter.) Perhaps an understanding of the ironist's actual feelings and beliefs are more directly and particularly relevant to one's getting the point of an ironic remark than is the case with fiction; perhaps irony less centrally involves pretenses about the existence of fictional characters. But sustained irony soon becomes a fictional monologue, and a clear-cut distinction is not easy to draw.

If the definition is broad, it is because it is negative (the illocutionary conventions are not in effect) and general (fiction involves pretense). It could only be narrowed by specifying some purpose that governs fictional discourse, or some special set of positive conventions that fiction always calls into play. But this Searle wisely refrains from doing. Given the variety of overlapping subcategories within the domain of fiction, each with its own loose conventions and aims, to specify additional features common to all fiction would in all likelihood distort and oversimplify. At the end of his essay Searle rather hastily suggests that "almost any important work of fiction conveys a 'message' or 'messages' which are conveyed *by* the text but are not *in* the text." But the word "important" acknowledges that many fictional works do not convey messages: many jokes, detective stories, fairy tales, and most pornographic or science fiction fantasies do not, for example. And though we associate certain genres, such as the exemplum, the fable, the parable, and allegory with the illustrating or reinforcing of propositions not necessarily contained or performed in the text, the word "important" also betrays an unexamined didactic bias. The verdict is not yet in on *what* messages are conveyed by *Hamlet* and *Lear*, *Wuthering Heights* and *Ulysses*, *The Trial* and *Waiting for Godot*, or on *whether* they convey any messages at all. Unlike metaphor, neither irony nor fiction is necessarily an indirect way of saying something. Often they use the forms of language purely for doing things of a quite un-illocutionary sort. They may amuse, entertain, distract, and deeply move; they may express contempt, confirm a friendship, create an illusion of chaos or comfort. Wayne Booth, an adept in the analysis of both fiction and irony, delivered a lecture on irony that delightfully exhibited the nature of its own subject, beginning with an apology: "I'm afraid I'll have to disappoint you. I'm not Wayne Booth. I'm Wayne's brother George. Wayne couldn't be here tonight, but he asked me to...." What did Booth "mean"? Surely this was no indirect way of saying, "I'm really Wayne Booth, not George"! The pretense was pure play, a winning gambit, hardly a way of meaning one thing by saying something else.

How do we know when we are in the presence of irony or fiction? Of course we do not and cannot always know for sure. What we need are indicators of intent: in the case of spoken irony, tonal clues and a prior knowledge of the speaker and the situation; with written irony signs, perhaps, of an intelligence too substantial to believe the apparent content of the discourse, and some conceivable purpose that would give the irony its point. In the case of fiction we base our expectations on these and countless other generic clues. Many kinds of discourse mix fiction and nonfiction and signal the changes clearly: Jesus introducing a parable into his preaching with the "once there was a man" formula, or the domestic psychologist with *his* fictional parable ("Philip, age fourteen, accidentally spilled nails all over the floor. He sheepishly looked up at his father. Philip: 'Gee, I'm so clumsy!' Father: 'That's not what we say when nails spill'....").[24] But we are less accustomed to the intrusion of nonfiction into a primarily fictional work, for the simple reason that the novelist or storyteller often wants to sustain the illusion he has created and avoids breaking it down.

Intentions are not always apparent and univocal. The words "A Novel" on a dustjacket, like the "once upon a time" formula, may provide a hint of sorts but may conceal a trick. If it is possible to pretend to recount actual events, it is no doubt also possible to pretend to write a novel. There is nothing to prevent a writer from shifting intentions in mid-discourse, alternating between the fictional and nonfictional modes, and there is no guarantee that every author has clear intentions as he writes.

All these factors make for the possibility of genuine ambiguity, and it seems fitting to conclude this chapter by considering briefly a passage that poses problems for any reader concerned with the differences between fiction and nonfiction.

Early on in E. L. Doctorow's *Ragtime* the reader is told about Freud's 1909 visit to the United States.[25] We learn that Freud was invited to give a series of lectures at Clark University in Worcester, Massachusetts, that he sailed on the Lloyd liner

George Washington, accompanied by Jung and Ferenczi, that they were met on the dock by Ernest Jones and A. A. Brill, that the party dined at Hammerstein's Roof Garden and after the lecture series visited Niagara Falls, where Freud was hurt by the guide's motioning to the other tourists to step back and "let the old fellow go first," that Freud complained of the scarcity of toilet facilities in America, and that he later told Jones that "America is a mistake, a gigantic mistake."

Now these reports are almost entirely true, and probably as reliable as most of the reports in a biography. One might note that Hanns Sachs relates that Jones made the crossing with Freud,[26] and that Jones himself makes no mention of having been on either the ship or the dock, though he locates Jung and Ferenczi on the former and Brill on the latter. In fact Jones mentions joining the party several days later and places the meal at Hammerstein's not on the first day—à la *Ragtime*—but on the third or fourth.[27] But these discrepancies are such as may, and do, exist among biographies. Certainly if either falsehood or the fictiveness of people and events were our criteria for fiction, the reports in *Ragtime* would not qualify. Yet the dustjacket announces *Ragtime* as a novel.

A good case can be made for regarding these Freudian passages as nonfiction. Suppose that one of Doctorow's purposes was to evoke something of the flavor of an era, and that to do so he chose to tell the reader many true, many almost true, and many untrue but plausible things, shaping the narration in such a way that the reader would seldom know just where he stands. Perhaps, in other words, the novel consists of speech acts some of which are genuine, some not. And perhaps, among the pretended ones, some are intended to deceive. In every case the writing is governed by the general purpose of blurring the reader's sense of where fact leaves off and fantasy begins. Such a reading is altogether plausible, and it allows for the possibility that Doctorow was, in the section in question, genuinely telling the reader about Freud's visit, prepared to stand firm behind every sentence.

On the other hand, a case could also be made for regarding the entire novel as thoroughly fictive. Long before the reader reaches the passage describing the visit he senses that he is in the hands of a traditional omniscient narrator, the sort of narrator who can report private conversations, describe the thought processes of characters who are alone, see through bedroom walls, all without bothering to cite sources or admit to guess-work. And this narrator is intimately present in the predominantly true sections. Compare Doctorow's unhesitating "At one point, on Fifth Avenue, Freud felt as if he was being observed" with Sachs's conjectural "The ocean crossing cannot have been tedious, for Freud was in the company of his best friends." Both of these modes can be feigned, of course, and both can be used in nonfiction. But Doctorow has created a single voice for the telling of his story, a steadily reportorial, all-knowing, fictional narrator.

Yet why could not the same "voice" be heard in the seriously meant passages as in the pretended ones? Could even Doctorow himself know whether, when he wrote a sentence like "Freud arrived in New York on the Lloyd liner *George Washington*," he was making a genuine or a mock assertion, telling the reader about Freud or creating an omniscient narrator whose knowledge happens to include knowledge of real history? Perhaps the best answer he could give, were we to put the questions to him, would be that in a sense both alternatives are right. "Have it your way," he might say. If a respectable case can be made for calling such passages as we have considered either fiction or nonfiction, that is a sign that our categories overlap. But we may take comfort if they overlap for the sort of writing that would have puzzled a reader anyway, particularly if such writing raises questions that can be posed, if not answered, in our terms.

3

Writer and Reader

For books are not absolutely dead things, but do contain a potency of life in them to be as active as that soul was whose progeny they are; nay, they do preserve as in a vial the purest efficacy and extraction of that living intellect that bred them.

John Milton, from *Areopagitica*

Books are written to be read. The statement seems sufficiently obvious to serve as an axiom of literary studies. But its verbs bring to mind two agents, the writer and the reader, who have traditionally made those who describe and even some of those who do criticism nervous. Though phrases like "with all due apologies to the Intentional (or Affective) Fallacy" are happily falling into disuse, there is still apparent in much criticism an awkward and strained effort to be "objective," which is often taken to imply the avoidance of the mention of the artist and his audience.

There have been significant alternatives to this position. Freudian and phenomenological critics have with a vengeance kept the author's consciousness central to the interpretive process, and the Chicago critics initiated a healthy flowering of rhetorical criticism that seeks to understand literary works in terms of the effects they are designed to produce on the audience. But I want to show in this chapter that talking about writers and readers need not commit us to any particular critical school or approach and that in fact all interpretation rests on conceptions of the author's intent and of the reader's responses. What these conceptions need is a firmer logical footing than they have rested on in the past.[1]

Before turning to intention and response, however, let us glance briefly at two traditional versions of the author-text-reader relationship, embodied respectively in the notion of the poet as a sayer, and the notion of the poet as a maker. To think of the poet as sayer suggests that the text is what the author *says to* the reader, a model behind which stands the ordinary speech situation: "Joan said to Jane that ...," "the minister told the congregation that...." The idea of the poet as maker, however, suggests a less direct author-text-reader relationship. The author *makes* the poem and leaves it for the reader to do with it what he will: contemplate it, read it, experience it, judge it. Very nearly the same dichotomy is caught in MacLeish's famous and meaningful line, "A poem should not mean but be." As critics in the twenties and thirties became suspicious of the sayer conception and doubtful about whether poetry means something (particularly whether it means what the poet said), they returned to the maker conception and the idea of the poem as simply existing or being, an object or artifact, passive, subject to viewing, inspecting, and analyzing.

Good criticism has been written within the framework of both conceptions. Neither is wrong. But they by no means exhaust the possible relationships that may obtain among the author, the text, and the reader. Much criticism tacitly assumes, for example, that the author *does something to* the reader *by means of* the text. And doing something to someone is a broader notion than either saying something to or making something for someone. Let me give a few examples of the sort of critical comment I have in mind. The first is from Francis Fergusson's commentary on canto 5 of Dante's *Inferno*, the story of Paolo and Francesca:

> Much of the power of the canto is due to the miraculous figure of Francesca. Her delicate, generous and unthinking spirit reaches us through every little word and gesture, constraining us also to love.... She is the most seductive embodiment possible of the *primo Amore* that makes the life of the lost.[2]

The second is from Richard Poirier's observations on James's *The Portrait of a Lady*:

> The assumption behind James' own relationship with us depends, as the tone of his narrative voice reveals,

upon our feeling superior to Isabel even while we are deeply implicated in her situation and her attitudes. James is faced with the difficult task of verifying her romantic responses by making us share them, while at the same time he must in each instance reveal her inexperience by making us more sceptical of the reality of romance than she is.[3]

And finally, Erich Auerbach's contrast between the Homeric and the biblical styles:

> Delight in physical existence is everything to them [the Homeric poems], and their highest aim is to make that delight perceptible to us.... They bewitch us and ingratiate themselves to us until we live with them in the reality of their lives.... The Scripture stories do not, like Homer's, court our favor, they do not flatter us that they may please us and enchant us—they seek to subject us, and if we refuse to be subjected we are rebels.... They require subtle investigation and inter- pretation, they demand them.... Far from seeking, like Homer, merely to make us forget our own realtiy for a few hours, it [the biblical narrative] seeks to over- come our reality. We are to fit our own life into its worlds, feel ourselves to be elements in its structure of universal history.[4]

The key ideas here, in a foreshortened form, are that Dante, through his presentation of Francesca, *constrains us* to love her; that James *makes us share* Isabel's romantic responses, but also *makes us* skeptical. And the Homeric poems *bewitch*, *flatter*, *court our favor*, while the biblical stories *seek* to subject us, *seek* to overcome our reality, *demand* interpretation. All three critics speak of the author or the text as doing something to the reader and of forcing the reader to do something in return (love a character, become more skeptical, take delight in, interpret and investigate, and so on). With very little effort the list of actions that authors perform through their writings could be greatly extended to include leading, guiding, persuading, rebuking, teasing, showing, teaching, humiliating, luring, inviting, mis- leading, none of which fits neatly into the sayer or maker conceptions, though none is, strictly speaking, inconsistent with either.

INTENTIONS AND SPEAKERS

It is noteworthy that all three critics speak of what the authors do in the present tense. This is not simply a critical convention. It is testimony to the widely shared feeling that the text establishes a direct connection between the reader and the author, alive through the text as a responsible, intending agent. It is certainly true, as Wimsatt and Beardsley argued in "The Intentional Fallacy," that once published "the poem belongs to the public," and that it is then "beyond the poet's power to intend about it or control it."[5] But it is equally true that the poem remains attached to the poet, and that the public is attached to the poet by the poem. When we read a work of literature, after all, we are attached to its author because our understanding of it is always governed by a conception of his intentions. To read is, among other things, to form ideas about what a writer did and why he did it.

The fact that understanding speech involves understanding intentions should be clear from the preceding chapter. If "Don't go" can serve as an entreaty or as a command, we need more than the words themselves to know what illocutionary act a speaker is performing in his utterance of them. We need further clues, such as intonation, to understand what he is doing, or how he meant his utterance to be taken. To hesitate over whether a remark is a command or an entreaty is to be uncertain about intentions. If the sentence "Shooting hunters should be avoided" is ambiguous as a type sentence, understanding an actual use of it necessitates knowing whether the speaker intended "shooting" to be understood as a gerund or as a participle. Indeed every use of a word with more than one sense demands that we know what sense was intended. And if we are seldom aware of making choices among alternatives, it is only because such intentions are usually obvious. Referring, too, is an intentional act. (People refer; words don't.) We don't know what a speaker means by a sentence unless we know what he's referring to. We may know what the sentence "she danced until 3:00" means, but we don't know what someone means by it until we know which *she* the speaker meant to pick out from the crowd and predicate something of.

In these ways, then, intentions are involved in ordinary communication—discourse according to the rules. But we saw as well that knowing what rules are being invoked is also a matter of inferring intentions. One may say something that is ironic without intending to ("How ironic that you mentioned him just now!"), but one cannot speak ironically without meaning to. To decide whether a piece of discourse is metaphoric, ironic, or fictional is to decide how it is meant to be taken, and uncertainty about how something is to be taken is uncertainty about intentions.

How is it that we can construe intentions from sentences? The answer is very simple, though it is not always simple to construe intentions. We can do it because things that are done *for a reason* are done intentionally.[6] If from a distance we see a man slapping his thigh, we may speculate on whether he is doing it intentionally, that is, for a reason (to punish or hurt himself, to put his knee in its place), or unintentionally (out of habit or nervousness, say, or without even knowing that he is doing it). If we move closer and detect a mosquito buzzing around, we guess that he's trying to swat the mosquito. We "read" any action in the light of whatever we know of the situation in which it is performed, and that involves looking for reasons for its performance. The discovery of possible reasons for the action doesn't guarantee, of course, that it *was* done for those reasons. It is possible to misunderstand an action or a sentence. But we can come to an understanding (right or wrong) or a sentence only if the situation of its utterance (either known, or inferred from the sentence itself) is such that we can imagine reasons for the choice and arrangement of the words. That is why a sentence like "draw it faster!" is, taken alone, thoroughly ambiguous. We don't know whether the speaker is saying it to hasten the artist or the oxen. But we can understand that it is ambiguous because we can imagine his saying it for either reason.

INTENTION AND AUTHORS

What I have tried briefly to show is that understanding a sentence necessarily involves understanding its speaker's intentions. But this necessity does not speak to the question of authorial intention, since it has become commonplace in criticism to distinguish between speakers, narrators, characters on the one hand, authors on the other. We've seen that we can't understand *Hamlet* without attributing intentions to the characters speaking, but not that we can't understand it without attributing intentions to Shakespeare. There are, however, many indispensable critical terms that ascribe intentions to authors. We will see that all interpretation is either an attempt to discover the author's intentions or else assumes that those intentions are understood.

What do we mean when we say that the account of the political situation in Lilliput, in the first book of *Gulliver's Travels*, contains allusions to the political figures and incidents of early eighteenth-century England? We mean that Swift was trying to direct his readers' attention to those figures and incidents. We can't pass the buck along to Gulliver and say that *he* is alluding to the Whigs and Tories, since that sort of subtlety is quite beyond him, and since it is through his very behavior that Swift sometimes alludes to Bolingbroke and Oxford. Certainly any claim about an allusion is governed by a principle disqualifying anachronisms, and proof that the author was unaware of the events in question would force us to drop the term. It runs counter to common sense to think that a person could allude to something without intending to. If something he said just happened to remind us of something else, we would not speak of an allusion, any more than we would speak of a clock as alluding to home just because it reminds us that it's time to go there.

Similarly, if we call a work as a whole ironic or satiric or a dramatic monologue, we are describing it with an implicit reference to how its author intended it to be taken. There is an analogy between calling a particular utterance ironic and calling a fictional work ironic: in the second case, though the fictive speaker may mean what he says, the author is indicating that his attitudes are not to be identified with the speaker's. Satire, as we usually think of it, involves an attempt (and hence an intention) on the author's part to direct and alter the reader's attitudes toward something outside the work. And if these critical terms specify intentions in the very act of describing a work, so do their opposites. If we call a poem a lyric, and mean by that among other things that the feelings expressed by the poem are unqualified by any indications of their inadequacy to the situation implied by the poem, then we are drawing inferences about the poet's attitude toward his poem and about the way he intended the poem to be read.

Questions about whether a literary work is allusive, satiric, didactic, and so on, are part of the larger question of what effects a work was designed to have on its readers or audience. If we say of a particular tragedy that its catastrophe is designed to evoke pity and fear, then we are saying that its nature is such that it appears to have been intended to produce that effect. Similarly we might say of Robbe-Grillet's *The Voyeur* that it is designed to prevent the reader from developing a stable interpretation of the sequence and relationship of narrated events, or that *Everyman* is designed to teach its audience how to prepare themselves for death.

Of course it is not necessary to take a literary work in the way we assume it was meant to be taken. Our responses are controlled by our sense of the writer's intention but need not be the responses he intended. We may read a piece of poetry so bad, so sentimental, stuffy, or pretentious that we can't refrain from laughing at it. We find it very funny although and because we know it was meant to be dead serious, and if we sensed different intentions we would be amused for very different reasons or perhaps not at all. Take the case of an ambiguous piece of writing where we are not sure whether the intentions were ironic but we feel that somehow it would be a better work if *viewed as* ironic. Whether we can "choose" to view the work as ironic in spite of our remaining unconvinced that it is in fact so is an interesting question. Even here our response would appear to be governed by our sense of the writer's intentions, for unless we actually forgot our uncertainties a certain pretense or make-believe would be involved that would be absent in the case of what we considered to be clear-cut or full-fledged irony.

Finally, notions of intention are involved in the appraisal of a work of literature and in judgments of the success or failure of its parts. Wimsatt and Beardsley declared that the "intention of the author is neither available nor desirable as a standard for judging the success or failure of a work of literary art," and that "we have no excuse for inquiring what part is intended or meant."[7] These statements are simply untrue. In fact our judgments of the success of a work (and often our liking or disliking it as well) depend on our sense of how it was intended to be taken. To take an obvious example, one's favorable judgment of a Browning monologue, or of Blake's "The Little Black Boy" from *The Songs of Innocence*, or of many of Donne's love poems is dependent on assumptions about the poet's stance vis-à-vis the voice in the poem. One *might* retain a high esteem for "My Last Duchess" on the assumption that it was intended as a confessional lyric, but the grounds for such esteem would be very different from our present grounds for admiring it.

To take a more complicated example, but one which seems to me to be very typical of much critical judgment, consider David's marriage to Agnes Wickfield at the end of *David Copperfield*, a marriage which is widely regarded as disappointing and a flaw in relation to the reader's sense of David's needs and wishes. On this marriage, Q. D. Leavis comments as follows:

> We all feel—though the Victorian public didn't for the most part—that the schematic marriage to Agnes, theoretically the right wife, is hollow and unconvincing, that all the reality is in David's feelings for Dora.... Agnes is only a willed concession to the Victorian ideal—seen always as the angel on the hearth, in the light from a stained glass window, 'pointing upward,' or with her 'patient smile.' Moreover, she has been established as in essence a sister-figure to David, and there is an unpleasant suggestion in the Sister-and-wife combination corresponding to the "O my father and my husband" of the Strongs' marriage, neither of which Dickens at bottom found appealing, we can see, for he can't make them either attractive or plausible.... We must admit therefore that Dickens in *David Copperfield* is not able to provide an adequate answer to the question of Victorian man's happiness that he set out to tackle.[8]

Mrs. Leavis treats the novel as in some sense a problem-solving or question-answering labor, and that is a common way of construing something when we judge its success or failure. The problem is both "artistic" and also "personal" in the sense in which every artistic problem is personal for the artist. Though she has an extremely high regard for the novel as a whole, she avers that the ending fails to give a satisfactory answer to a question that has been implicit in the novel from the beginning. Her terms are clearly and properly intentional: "a willed concession," "can't make them attractive," "not able to provide," "set out to tackle." The assumptions on which her appraisal rests, put somewhat schematically, are as follows:

1. David himself has been presented as having certain needs which must be met if he is to gain maturity and self-fulfillment.
2. Dickens intends us to accept Agnes as answering to those needs.
3. She does not in fact answer to them.

If Mrs. Leavis is right about Dickens wanting us to accept Agnes as the perfect wife for David, it is because that is the likeliest reason for his having dwelt upon her radiant virtue, on David's unalloyed pleasure, and so on. Could the same judgment be issued in nonintentional terms? To say only that Agnes is an unsuitable wife for David is to make no judgment on the artistry of the novel at all. Furthermore, if the first and last assumptions listed above are accepted, the only way to disagree with Mrs. Leavis would be with a counterappraisal postulating a different intention. The marriage would appear to be a flaw only on the premise that the novel is the achievement of a purposeful agent. We might say—with that manner of sidestepping intention that has become a trademark of some critics—that the *novel*, rather than Dickens, invites us to accept Agnes as a good wife, but, unless we think the novel somehow "just grow'd," that is a metonomy for an appraisal based on inferred authorial intentions.

ABANDONING THE AUTHOR

There have been many attempts to show that the author can or should be dispensed with in interpretation and criticism, and that we can make sense of a text without considering him, but none of them will do. Jonathan Culler, for example, is an advocate of "structural analysis," which, he says, offers "a particular type of explanation":

> It does not attempt, as phenomenology might, to achieve empathetic understanding: to reconstruct a situation as it might have been consciously grasped by an individual subject and hence to explain why he chose a particular course of action. Structural explanation does not place an action in a causal chain nor derive it from the project by which a subject intends

a world; it relates the object or action to a system of
conventions which give it its meaning and distinguish
it from other phenomena with different meanings.
Something is explained by the system of distinctions
which give it its identity.... Not only does structural
analysis abandon the search for external causes; it
refuses to make the thinking subject [i.e., the speaker
or author] and explanatory cause.... Even in the case
of a single work, how could the author be its *source*?
He wrote it, certainly; he composed it; but he can write
poetry, or history, or criticism only within the context
of a system of enabling conventions which constitute
and delimit the varieties of discourse.[9]

This is by no means a peculiar method of explaining something. We do not always explain actions by placing them in a
causal chain or by deriving them from a subject's intended
project. If you are watching a baseball game with a friend who
knows something but not everything about the game and he asks
you why the batter went to first base after being hit by the ball,
you explain the action precisely by "relating it to a system of
conventions which give it its meaning and distinguish it from
other phenomena with different meanings." Being hit by a
thrown object means something different depending on whether
you're batting (you go to first), playing second base (you're
clumsy), or walking through a dark alley. In the first case we can
explain the action of walking to first base easily by referring it to
one of the rules or conventions that constitute the game of
baseball. In the same way one can explain why a certain sentence
is grammatical or ungrammatical by referring to the linguistic
rules that constitute the language.

It is important to recognize that structural explanations of this
sort, though they have their uses, eventually run into a dead
end. It is essential, for example, that our friend knew "something
but not everything" about the game. For if he had not known
how runs are scored, and if he had not known that the team that
scores the most runs wins the game, telling him that batters who
get hit by a pitched ball get to go to first would have availed him
very little. (And if he did not know why one would want to win
the game, our difficulties would be increased even further.) In
other words, the meaning of the individual action is hardly
comprehensible without an understanding of the point of the

game, a point which renders the actions on the field intelligible and lets us see what the players are trying to do. The system of conventions alone does *not* give meaning to the action unless we know the purpose (or in the case of language and literature the many, many conceivable purposes) of the system.

It is no doubt true, as Culler says, that an author "can write poetry, or history, or criticism only within the context of a system of enabling conventions." And it is useful to study the system. But the system will never be sufficient by itself to explain the actual meaning of what somebody says or writes.

Linguistics, defined as a description of the rules and conventions that constitute a language, is limited in the same way. An adequate linguistic theory can explain why the sentence "Flying airplanes can be dangerous" is ambiguous out of context. ("Flying" may be used either as an adjective or noun, and "can" can take either a singular or plural subject.) But it does not speak to the question of how a hearer or reader of an actual utterance of the sentence determines the meaning the speaker or writer meant. The "enabling conventions" can't explain the point of a remark or a poem because they don't tell us what the speaker or poet is *doing* with the conventions, what he is using them *for*.

A good example of what happens when you try to leave the author out of account is Culler's analysis of a translation of a Chinese fragment:

> Swiftly the years, beyond recall.
> Solemn the stillness of this spring morning.

I will quote the analysis in its entirety:

> Reading poetry is a rule-governed process of producing meanings; the poem offers a structure which must be filled up and one therefore attempts to invent something, guided by a series of formal rules derived from one's experience of reading poetry, which both make possible invention and impose limits on it. In this case the most obvious feature of literary competence is the intent at totality of the interpretive process: poems are supposed to cohere, and one must therefore discover a semantic level at which the two lines can be related to one another. An obvious point of contact is the contrast between 'swiftly' and 'stillness,' and there is thus a primary condition on 'invention': any inter-

pretation should succeed in making thematic capital out of this opposition. Moreover, 'years' in the first sentence and 'this morning' in the second, both located in the dimension of time, provide another opposition and point of contact. The reader might hope to find an interpretation which relates these two pairs of contrasts. If this is indeed what happens it is no doubt because the experience of reading poetry leads to implicit recognition of the importance of binary oppositions as thematic devices: in interpreting a poem one looks for terms which can be placed on a semantic or thematic axis and opposed to one another.

The resulting structure or 'empty meaning' suggests that the reader try to relate the opposition between 'swiftly' and 'stillness' to two ways of thinking about time and draw some kind of thematic conclusion from the tension between the two sentences. It seems eminently possible to produce in this way a reading which is 'acceptable' in terms of poetic logic. On the one hand, taking a large panoramic view, we can think of the human life-span as a unit of time and of the years as passing swiftly; on the other, taking the moment of consciousness as the unit, we can think of the difficulty of experiencing time except discontinuously, of the stillness of a clock's hand when one looks at it. 'Swiftly the years' implies a vantage point from which one can consider the passage of time, and the swiftness of passage is compensated for by what Empson calls 'the answering stability of self-knowledge' implicit in this view of life. 'This morning' implies other mornings—a discontinuity of experience reflected in the ability to separate and name—and hence an instability which makes 'stillness' the more valued. This process of binary structuring, then, can lead one to find tension within each of the lines as well as between the two lines. And since thematic contrasts should be related to opposed values we are led to think about the advantages and disadvantages of these two ways of conceiving of time. A variety of conclusions are of course possible. [Pp. 126–27]

This account is certainly relevant to one's reading of the fragment, and I don't mean to deny its utility. But it is radically incomplete and misses the point in precisely the way I suggested.

Culler's analysis would obtain equally well for a poem that went, "Solemn the stillness of this spring morning. / Swiftly the years, beyond recall." There is nothing in his account to explain the order of the lines, the sense in which the second is read as the coming to rest or closing of a thought process, a commentary on or "placing" of the first line rather than the other way around. And as a corollary of this omission he has also neglected the expressive value of the poem: the pause between "swiftly the years" and "beyond recall" that stresses the regret attendant upon a sense of loss; the way the word "solemn," by affirming the importance of what is to follow, transcends the loss without denying it; the way the three consecutive stressed syllables (this´ spring´ morn´ ing) signal the concentration of the speaker's attention, at the end, on the present moment.

I am not merely offering a "different interpretation" of the fragment. What is at issue is the question of what a reader must assume, and what kinds of knowledge he must have, in order to read at all. I am claiming that the reader, if he is to make sense of a poem, must conceive of the whole utterance as speakable, or of the whole train of thought as thinkable. And he must assume that there was some point in publishing the words as a poem. That is, the words have been ordered by the poet according to some intention, and the reader understands them when he grasps the principle according to which they have been ordered. It is only in the light of such a principle that one can decide which of the "binary oppositions" are important or functional and what their importance or function is. One suspects that Culler was able to put the lines together as successfully as he did only because he, too, tacitly assumed a person speaking. Why Culler speaks of an acceptable reading in terms of *poetic* logic is hard to say, for what he offers us is not a poem but a set of contrasting items that we may use as cues for intellection. ("We are led to think about the advantages and disadvantages of these two ways of conceiving of time. A variety of conclusions are of course possible.") One is not convinced that his logic is more applicable to poems than, say, to a small pebble and a large stone, or, more fairly, to any two statements offering different ways of conceiving of the same thing.

One might think that all Culler has left out is a "fictional speaker." But there is more to it than that. For my analysis also assumes that the author intended us to imagine just this fictional

71

speaker (e.g., to see the second line as a reaction to the first) and that he intended us to take the poem straight—not as a parody. The fact that the two lines are translated from the Chinese complicates the situation, but not greatly. We seek the feelings that the poem must be presumed to express in order for it to make sense. The translator of course may have misconstrued or misrepresented the original; the fragment might have occurred originally in a context that would alter our sense of what it expressed, and so on.

It is important to recognize that one can, intentionally or unintentionally, express feelings, attitudes, beliefs, and intentions by acting in certain ways and by doing certain things, and that the ways and things need not be verbal. Furthermore, one can express one's attitudes (etc.) in language without directly naming them, reporting on them, or announcing them. Dickens expressed his feelings about *David Copperfield* very directly in his preface. "Like many fond parents, I have in my heart of hearts a favorite child. And his name is DAVID COPPERFIELD." In the novel he indirectly expressed many other attitudes, toward different kinds of behavior and institutions, for example, by *doing* things: things like making some characters admirable and others despicable and having them interact in certain ways, or like giving David the narrator those qualities he possesses so that one's understanding of events is filtered through a certain point of view; in short, by writing the novel as he wrote it.

When we say that a poem expresses an attitude, whose attitude are we talking about? The attitude must be *somebody's*, since we would certainly be confused if we said, and meant it literally, that the *poem* admires, approves, resigns itself to, or dislikes something or other, just as we would be confused if we spoke literally of a poem fearing, hoping, or believing something.

Let me try answering this question by referring to Frost's "West-Running Brook," a dialogue spoken by a man and his wife as they reflect upon a nearby stream that runs west "when all the other country brooks flow east / To reach the ocean," and upon a white wave thrown back against the current by a rock. The man and the woman make a good deal of the brook and the wave, interpreting their significance. Each expresses certain attitudes toward them, toward each other, and toward life and the passage of time. They do not always see eye to eye, though they reach accord if not agreement at the end. After a long and rather inflated philosophical harangue by the husband, the wife replies with lovely tact, "Today will be the day / You said so." To which the husband, now down off his high horse, replies, "No, today will be the day / You said the brook was called West-running Brook." And the wife has the last word: "Today will be the day of what we both said."[10]

We can speak here of attitudes expressed *in* the poem by the two fictional speakers, just as one speaks of the attitudes expressed in a play by the various characters. But it is not clear that in doing so we have spoken of the attitudes expressed by the poem, or that by describing the significance of the attitudes expressed by the man and the woman we have reached the significance of the poem, any more than Culler had comprehended the fragment by comprehending the significance of each line and the contrasts between them. For Frost, by creating these characters, has expressed certain attitudes (wry good humor and approval) toward them and the sort of relationship they have, and any interpretation that failed to move beyond the characters would be incomplete. The speeches in the poem are mostly about the brook and the wave, living and dying; but the poem, while it is a poem about these things, is also a poem about marriage, about human bonds, about the differences between the ways people see things and how those differences may be bridged by love. As Reuben Brower says: "What the drama of the poem means is not what the man alone says, but what they 'both said,' the marriage of two visions of the brook and of reality. In explaining why the brook runs west, the wife had given her husband the metaphor that has shaped all the rest of his thinking. . . ." The poem is "characteristic of Frost in that the total attitude expressed arises through a dramatic movement, through the arrival at a new relation between 'the two.' "[11]

One sometimes hears it said that even this Robert Frost to whom we attribute certain ideas, attitudes, and intentions is a "fictional construct." One can accept the word "construct" if it implies that it is the reader who constructs the interpretation. Of course it is. But the word "fictional" is preposterous if it implies that we are not trying to figure out what the *real author* was trying to do. If we see tracks and other signs in the woods and conclude that an animal must have been foraging for berries there, we are constructing an interpretation to the effect that a real animal, not a fictional one, was foraging. The fact that our interpretation of something may be wrong—that Frost, say, may not have admired and wished us to admire the marriage he portrayed, or that the Chinese writer of fragments may never have regretted the passing of the years—has nothing to do with the reality of the person to whom we attribute those feelings. You may think I am pulling your leg right now. If you do, you think it is the real me doing the pulling, whether you are right or wrong.

Unconscious Intentions

One further word of clarification is perhaps in order at this point. To say that our understanding of a work relies upon a conception of the author's intention is not to say that interpretation reconstructs some private thought process that the author engaged in while writing; nor is it to say that all the qualities, relationships, and meanings that we may correctly attribute to a work were intended.

To speak to the first and more obvious qualification first: the mosquito swatter need never have said to himself, "I will (or I intend to) swat that mosquito," or performed any other mental act, for his swatting to be regarded as intentional. Nor do we, when we choose our words, do something called "intending" in addition to the choosing. We simply choose them for a reason—for example, to get the oxen to draw the cart faster. If we are writing with care, we may deliberate what words are best for doing what we want to do, but deliberating isn't intending. The interpreter is not trying to recover a mental event; he's after, rather, the reasons for the author's having written what he wrote.

As for the second qualification, there is no question but that we often do things unintentionally, and that not everything in a work can be explained by reference to the author's reason for putting it there. A work may have a design which we decide did not come about as a result of the author's intentions. And we would base our conclusion that certain designs or effects were unintended on evidence suggesting that the author didn't do what he did for some reason—evidence, for example, that the possible reasons for his doing it contradict our sense of what his intentions in fact were. Such unintended effects may be the result of any number of factors, from ignorance or prejudice or ineptness to habits of verbal or conceptual association of which the author was unaware and which were therefore not in his control.

But at my back I always hear several well-intentioned colleagues begging some allowance among these factors for the author's "unconscious intentions." Perhaps the previous paragraph makes sufficient allowance for them. It would be disingenuous not to admit, however, that for me the phrase "unconscious intention" has at least the appearance if not the reality of paradox about it.

There are certain facts about one's self that one discovers by examining, or being confronted with, evidence. One learns that one is running a fever by noticing that one feels hot and shivery and by taking one's temperature; one discovers that one is developing a nervous tic by catching oneself repeatedly in the act of twitching. But it seems to be the case that we do not infer our intentions by scrutinizing ourselves or our behavior in this way. (We infer the intentions of *others* by observing their behavior, but we are considering here the agent himself and how he understands his own actions.) Intentions are like emotions in this respect. You don't discover that you wanted a pair of shoes by reflecting that you spent your last penny on them, or that you were afraid of the dog by noticing that you avoided it. Nor do you discover that you intended to avoid the dog by noticing that you walked on the other side of the street.[12]

This would seem to be a defining characteristic of intentional actions. That is, there are certain things we do for which a reason may be assigned but which we would nevertheless call unintentional—actions like blinking, shivering, and sneezing. (We blink to lubricate the eye, shiver to keep the body at a constant temperature, and so on.) But our doing these things is generally independent of our knowing why we're doing them, and we would not know why we do them, or understand the reason for our doing them, without being told or else figuring it out. Intentional actions, then, are distinguished from these other actions done for reasons by virtue of our not having to discover what the reasons were by observation and inference after the fact.

Yet unconscious intentions are usually defined or illustrated in a way that directly contradicts this fact about intentions. For they are always cases where a person, to be convinced of his "real" intentions, must have certain patterns or repetitions in his behavior described to him and persuasively connected with other facts about him. He comes to believe that he was doing something for a certain reason only after retrospection, observation, and inference.[13]

This extraordinary difference between intentions and "unconscious intentions" *may* simply be an analysis of what the latter phrase means. Perhaps unconscious intentions simply *are* intentions of which the subject has to be persuaded or convinced by evidence. On the other hand, this analysis does away with one of the very criteria by which we determine whether an act is properly thought of as intentional. It is as if unconscious intentions are defined in such a way as to make them not intentions at all. If "intentions" in the derivative sense means something quite contradictory to what it means in the primary sense, then we should stop pretending that unconscious intentions are a kind of intention.

Readers

As we reached the end of our discussion of intention we were brought face to face, in Mrs. Leavis's commentary on *David Copperfield*, with the reader. And not just any reader, but the nineteenth-century reader and the twentieth-century reader. And if we hark back to the quotations from Fergusson, Poirier, and Auerbach, we will remember that the reader figured prominently in their commentaries too. If there has been one primary reason for the hesitation that some critics have felt about readers, it has been the multiplicity of actual readers, readers who no doubt understand and respond to a work of literature differently and whose own responses to a single work will change from reading to reading. Yet critics persist in talking about the reader, about ideal readers, informed readers, seventeenth-century Puritan readers, contemporary readers, readers "implicit in the text," "us," and so on. And naturally so; the reader is the author's and the critic's audience, and the value of literature can hardly be understood or appreciated if the reader is left out of account.[14]

In the following pages we will consider two questions: What

sorts of responses to literature can the critic talk about? And how can we talk about the reader's responses to a literary work without talking about any particular reader's actual responses? I will propose that the most useful and fundamental question we can ask about a literary text and its readership is the question: How *ought* the reader (and by "the reader" I mean *any* reader) respond to the text? Since the word "ought" sticks in some throats, I will offer the further assumption, or bias, that a reader ought to respond to a work on the basis of a correct understanding of it. (In the next chapter we will consider more closely the difference between misunderstanding a work and understanding it correctly. For now we will simply assume that a reader who misunderstands a work cannot respond to it as he ought.)

Formulating the topic as a matter of how a reader ought to respond to a work has certain advantages over other formulations. It depends not at all on an abstract characterization of an ideal or informed reader arrived at prior to consideration of the text at hand. It is not predictive of any actual reader's or group of readers' responses, and hence it is not vulnerable to counter-examples or charges of oversimplification. ("But not all Victorians were like that!" or, "But most of the people who saw the play laughed!") At the same time it can incorporate the best of what those other formulations have to offer: the ideal reader for a particular text will be the reader sufficiently informed to understand *it* correctly and hence respond to it as he ought. Finally, the question speaks to the educative function of criticism, for if criticism cannot guide us toward better responses and make us better readers, it is surely of little worth.

The first admission to make, however, is that the notion of a reader's response to a literary work covers a great deal of ground, not all of which can be surveyed through our question. It includes whatever the reader experiences as a result of reading the work, whatever the work makes him think, feel, or do, whatever happens to him as a result of the reading. There is no reason to narrow the reference of the term, and certainly no reason to prejudge the sorts of responses that may or may not be of value or interest to some given individual reader. But at the same time we have to recognize that certain kinds of responses naturally lie beyond the critic's ken and interest. I assume that the critic is not interested in everything that goes on in all readers' minds when they read and that he is interested primarily in those responses that are responses *to* the text and about which he can in some way generalize. I am pointing at a rough distinction between all the experience that may grow out of the reading, and the experience that *is* the reading, a distinction between everything we may think or feel as we read on the one hand, and what we think and feel about what we read as we read it on the other. To make this distinction more precise will be one of our tasks, considering first some possible responses to literary works which, however much we may value them, are only contingently related to the nature of what we read and hence do not and cannot occupy a central place in critical argument.

FEELINGS

One reason why this distinction is difficult to make is that certain typical and natural "response" words are vague. The term "feeling," for example, is used in such a variety of ways that it hardly constitutes an isolable category of response. That is, we can feel a chill, feel the pain of a sprained ankle, feel tired, angry, superior. We can even feel that everything will come out all right or that honesty is the best policy. Feelings, in short, include physical sensations, emotions, attitudes, and beliefs. There is no reason not to use the word, since what is involved is usually clear in context. But its shifting uses should remind us that not all things that go by the name of feelings have something important in common.

SENSATIONS

Physical sensations like chills along the spine, gooseflesh, and sinking feelings in the pit of the stomach hardly need concern us. Though such sensations may accompany some reading experiences, critics simply do not talk about them except occasionally in a loose and metaphorical way. To call a tale chilling is usually a way of suggesting not that it will cause actual chills, but that it is frightening, and fright is not a sensation but an emotion. A reader who reads a frightening tale has responded appropriately if he feels frightened by it, whether his fright is accompanied by chills, or by an increased pulse rate, or by a tingling scalp, or by none of these. But if he feels his scalp or his spine tingle *without* experiencing fright, he has had a peculiarly inappropriate response, and one might suspect that it was a draft or an internal bodily condition rather than the story that gave rise to the sensation.

REMINISCENCES AND REVERIES

Some responses, including sensations, are rather haphazardly related to the nature of the work being read. Others are idiosyncratic in the sense that they would be possible for only one or at most a very few readers. A character in a novel may remind me of my cousin, but I would have a hard time justifying the claim that the character reminds *the reader* of my cousin, or that he *ought* to be reminded of him. It is this sort of response that I. A. Richards characterized as a mnemonic irrelevance. To point out that personal associations, physical sensations, and the like are only contingently related to the text and cannot be arbitrated by critics is not to say that they are uninteresting or blameworthy. Personal associations may explain why we value a certain poem highly and return to it again and again. And a tingling scalp, an outburst of tears or laughter, may certainly be signs of a work's power over us. Only an obsessive anti-sentimentalist would want to deny a reader's right to such experiences or to such reasons for treasuring his favorite books.

Similarly, something in a work may prompt a stream of reverie or fantasy. Gaston Bachelard, who is widely known for his writings on reverie, values certain passages of poetry highly for their power to initiate daydreams in him, and he regards poetry as a valuable cue to reverie. Commenting on his response to a poem by Verlaine, he observes:

> In my room in Paris, far from the land of my birth, I carry on Verlaine's reverie. A sky from another time spreads out over the city of stone. And through my memory hum the bars of music that Reynaldo Hahn wrote to accompany Verlaine's poems. A whole layer of emotions, reveries and memories grows up out of this poem for me.[15]

The critic has no business denying the daydreamer his delight, unless, of course, he wants to argue that there is greater value in attending to the text than to one's own fantasies. But as Bachelard points out, each reader will dream "in his own way" (p. 15). The daydream is a response directed away from rather than toward the work. In Bachelard's words, "I think I am reading; a word stops me. I leave the page" (p. 17). Or, in another fine phrase, the daydreamer "is led to liberate himself from the teleology of the sentence" (p. 49). It is his understanding of the privacy of reverie that gives Bachelard's studies their distinctive flavor. He is a master at reporting daydreams and cites a wealth of commentary by poets who foreshadowed his own ways of thinking about reverie. He can also point to reverielike qualities in a poem or descriptive passage, but there is no necessary connection between such qualities and a reader's response to them, no reason to think that a passage that reads like a daydream will stimulate daydreaming. And if it did, as Bachelard would be the first to point out, it would mean the end to reading for the time being.

Cognitive Responses

If it is not possible for the critic to argue that one ought to get gooseflesh at a certain point in a story, or to be reminded of his (the critic's) great aunt, or to have a daydream, it *is* possible to argue about appropriate cognitive and emotional responses. Whatever else he may do as he reads, it is certain that a reader will form ideas and opinions about the work in question. He may *learn* that certain people in the poem, novel, or play say and do certain things; he may *discover* that Mrs. X is the guilty party, that Miss Y is clever, and that Mr. Z lives beyond his means. He may *draw inferences* about causal relationships among events, about characters' motives, or about the point or significance of an episode. He may *make judgments* about characters and their behavior. He may *expect* certain things to happen, and he may from time to time experience confusion, certainty, doubt, or suspicion. And in all these cases he may be right or wrong. One might read *David Copperfield* with or without being reminded of a near relative, but to read it without at some point recognizing that Micawber lives beyond his means would constitute a failure in reading.

Since these cognitive responses occur as one reads, judgments formed at a certain point may be correct on the basis of the information thus far presented but later be proved incorrect. Confusion may be the appropriate response if the information provided is confusing, and certainty is inappropriate if it arises from neglect of information that would make for confusion.

In recent years this ongoing temporal experience of the text, particularly as it involves expectations fulfilled or disappointed, has received much attention, generating a sort of Aristotelian analysis of more and more minute segments of the reading process. Stanley Fish, for one, has been a most persuasive spokesman for the notion that one ought to ask what a literary work (or scene or passage, paragraph or sentence) *does* to the reader as he reads. In his most theoretical treatment of the question, he illustrates it with the following analysis of a sentence from Browne's *Religio Medici*:

> "That Judas perished by hanging himself, there is no certainty in Scripture: though in one place it seems to affirm it, and by a doubtful word hath given occasion to translate it; yet in another place, in a more punctual description, it maketh it improbable, and seems to overthrow it."
>
> Ordinarily, one would begin by asking "what does this sentence mean?" or "what is it about?" or "what is it saying?", all of which preserve the objectivity of the utterance. For my purposes, however, this particular sentence has the advantage of not saying anything. That is, you can't get a fact out of it which could serve as an answer to any one of these questions.... The strategy or action here is one of progressive decertain- izing. Simply by taking in the first clause of the sen- tence, the reader commits himself to its assertion, "that Judas perished by hanging himself" (in constructions of this type "that" is understood to be shorthand for "the *fact* that").... He knows ... that this first clause is preliminary to some larger assertion ... and he must be in control of it if he is to move easily and con- fidently through what follows; and in the context of this "knowledge," he is prepared, again less than con- sciously, for any one of several constructions:
>
> That Judas perished by hanging himself, *is* (an example for us all).
>
> That Judas perished by hanging himself, *shows* (how conscious he was of the enormity of his sin).
>
> That Judas perished by hanging himself, *should* (give us pause).
>
> The range of these possibilities (and there are, of course, more than I have listed) narrows considerably as the next three words are read, "there is no." At this

point, the reader is expecting, and even predicting, a single word—"doubt"; but instead he finds "certainty"; and at that moment the status of the fact that had served as his point of reference becomes *un*certain. (It is nicely ironic that the appearance of "certainty" should be the occasion for doubt, whereas the word "doubt" would have contributed to the reader's certainty.) As a result, the terms of the reader's relationship to the sentence undergo a profound change. He is suddenly involved in a different kind of activity.... The natural impulse in a situation like this, either in life or in literature, is to go forward in the hope that what has been obscured will again become clear; but in this case going forward only intensifies the reader's sense of disorientation. The prose is continually opening, but then closing, on the possibility of verification in one direction or another. There are two vocabularies in the sentence; one holds out the promise of a clarification—"place," "affirm," "place," "punctual," "overthrow"—while the other continually defaults on that promise—"Though," "doubtful," "yet," "improbable," "seems"; and the reader is passed back and forth between the alternatives—that Judas did or did not perish by hanging himself—which are still suspended (actually it is the reader who is suspended) when the sentence ends (trails off? gives up?).[16]

I take it that what both Fish and I are concerned to show is that one can talk objectively about what happens to a reader, or about what a reader *does* as he reads. If I can show, then, that Fish is wrong in his analysis of the effect of this sentence, I will have lent credence and support to his general thesis. It seems clear, then, that a reader *ought not* to respond to the sentence as Fish says he will, because such a response is based on a misunderstanding of the sentence.

Fish asserts that the sentence is progressively decertainizing or disorienting. It is not. The first part of the sentence, up to the colon, makes a very definite claim: namely, that the Scriptures are unclear on the question of whether Judas hanged himself. The reader's expectation of clarification following the first comma is fulfilled. The rest of the sentence repeats, reaffirms, and slightly particularizes the initial claim by asserting that one passage from Scripture seems to affirm Judas's death by hanging and that another seems to deny it. The sentence *does* say something, and a reader who understands it as he ought will be able to say what it means, what it is about, and what it is saying. We could go still further and point out that the second part of the sentence suggests that Scripture makes a stronger case against the hanging than for it, since the affirmation is based on a "doubtful word," the overthrow on "a more punctual description." In short, while the first clause, like any introductory dependent clause, leaves the reader hanging, the sentence completes itself in a normal grammatical way and thus fulfills the reader's expectation.

Fish is correct in saying that any reader who knows English ought to be prepared, following the first clause, for any of a limited number of possible constructions. Just so, a reader who reads an "if" clause will expect some sort of a "then" clause, and a reader who comes upon a "they" will expect a plural verb. It is also true that "there is no . . ." limits the range of constructions. It *may* also be correct that most readers will expect "doubt" rather than "certainty." This, however, is a matter of probability; one certainly couldn't say that a reader *ought* to expect "doubt." Nevertheless, whether or not he is surprised by "certainty," its appearance should not be the occasion for doubt! He will have understood the clause correctly whether or not he is surprised. He will have misunderstood the sentence if, after reading the word "certainty," he remains in doubt about the alleged status of the proposition about Judas or about the meaning of the sentence to that point.

It is important to recognize this distinction between predictions about how readers are likely to respond and assertions about how any reader who understands what he reads will respond. It is easy to predict that a reader will have trouble sorting out the "its" in Fish's example, that a reader unaccustomed to archaic syntactical order will have more trouble with the sentence than a literary historian. These predictions *do* reflect something in the style of the sentence, and they have hypothetical validity. One could say, for example, that *if* a reader knows only the modern meaning of "translate," then he will be baffled by the clause in which the word occurs. But one can also say how the sentence will affect the reader sufficiently informed and patient to understand it. Thus, the two vocabularies that Fish finds so cluttered would only disorient a grammarless reader who forms an impression of a sentence on the basis of the connotations of terms. A set of terms, abstracted from a syntactical context, can neither promise clarification nor default on that promise. For the reader who realizes that the sentence asserts the absence of certainty, the two vocabularies will be expected and clarifying.

What I have tried to demonstrate, in concurrence with Fish's overall thesis, is that there are ways of talking about what a sentence will do to a reader that do not deny the divergence of actual responses but are not hindered by it either. Fish's way, as I understand it, is to hypothesize a "construct, an ideal or idealized reader," and that method can be extended to include the constructing of hypothetical readers with particular limitations or qualifications, from the hypothetical cannibal reading "A Modest Proposal," to the reader who knows only one meaning of "translate," to the reader who is certain that Scripture affirms Judas's death by hanging, of whom we could say, with certainty, that if he understands our now overanalyzed sentence he will disagree with it. Similarly, one might try to distinguish the effect of a story on someone who knows how the story ends from its effect on someone who doesn't.

My way, on the other hand, is to assign to the reader only so much knowledge as is necessary to understand what he reads correctly, in which case the critic's search for a true understanding of the nature and shape of the passage or text is itself a search for the response the reader ought to have to it. The kind of response I am talking about actually constitutes correct understanding.

We have dwelt, for demonstration purposes, on some small units of discourse—the reader's developing discovery of the meaning of a sentence, expectations not of death or marriage or apocalypse but of possible grammatical constructions. To show that one can also debate rationally how one ought to understand and respond to large-scale elements will be part of the purpose of the next chapter. For now, let us turn to a different but closely related aspect of the reading experience.

EMOTIONS AND ATTITUDES

As several writers have pointed out, one distinction between emotions and attitudes on the one hand and sensations on the other is that the former are object directed whereas the latter are not. We fear someone, something, or some event. We feel superior or inferior toward particular people. We might feel superior toward everyone, or no one, but if we say we feel superior and someone asks "toward what?" we can hardly answer, "toward nothing," for that would be tantamount to confessing that we don't really feel superior at all.[17]

Furthermore, emotions and attitudes are directly and logically dependent on our perception or judgment of their objects. Pity is directed toward someone whom we believe to be suffering, unhappy, or unfortunate beyond his desert. Fear is directed toward what we deem to be threatening to us or to someone else whom we care about. This is true whether what we fear is an imminent physical danger or future events like the effects of the population explosion. It is not that the mind is somehow programmed to feel certain emotions in the face of certain situations; one can't imagine the wires getting crossed in such a way that we would feel anger toward a sufferer or fear of good fortune. It is rather that anger and fear and the other emotions and attitudes are defined and explained by the nature of the situations toward which they are directed. Dictionaries define an emotion or attitude by offering synonyms for it and then specifying its object. Hence a description of a person's misfortune is always a reasonable answer to the question "Why do you pity him?" And it would always be nonsense to say "I pity him because he's happy (or well-fed, intelligent, or lucky)," unless I also feel his happiness to be in danger of destruction or see it as a hindrance to some greater good.

If these remarks are true, then one *always* feels the emotion appropriate to one's understanding of a situation. But one's understanding of a situation may be wrong or incomplete. I may feel anger toward what I take to be an effrontery, and later learn that I had misconstrued the act. A neurotic may fear people whom he has no reason to fear, but he will not fear them unless he *thinks* they pose a threat. The person who is incapable of feeling pity may mistakenly appraise every instance of suffering he perceives as fully merited—the just retribution for the wrongs the world has perpetrated on *him*. Or he may find the sight of others suffering so pleasurable that he loses sight of the fact of suffering altogether.

These two aspects of emotions and attitudes—their object-directedness and their dependence on one's understanding of the object—suggest why critics would naturally take more interest in them than in sensations and private associations. It is possible to argue rationally about the emotions or attitudes appropriate to a literary situation, and to say what one *ought* to feel about it. One can provide reasons for adopting an emotion or attitude, and if the reader accepts the reasons he will undergo a change of heart. This is certainly so in real life, where we argue that someone is more to be pitied than despised by pointing out the facts that make pity rather than scorn the appropriate response. Consider the way your feelings change when you discover that the person you thought had snubbed you when you passed on the street is in fact very nearsighted and had not seen you. Or consider the way Gulliver's feelings toward the immortal Struldbruggs changed from envy to pity and horror when he learned that they were not immune to the physical and mental ravages of aging. We can hardly change our sense of what something is without changing our feelings toward it.

When Aristotle discriminated between the sorts of actions that would inspire pity and fear and those that would not, he was not offering or relying upon a general psychological law based on empirical evidence. He was simply reminding us of what we mean by "pity" and "fear." R. S. Crane offers an Aristotelian rhetorical account of *Macbeth* that concludes:

> Our responses, when this part of the action is before us, are such as are clearly dictated by the immediate events and the poetic commentary: we desire, that is, the complete success of the counter-action and this as speedily as possible before Macbeth can commit further horrors. We desire this, however—and that is what at once takes the plot-form out of the merely retributive class—not only for the sake of humanity and Scotland but also for the sake of Macbeth himself.... If we are normal human beings we must abhor his crimes; yet we cannot completely abhor but must rather pity the man himself.[18]

We desire what we deem to be good (for ourselves or for someone else); we abhor what we deem to be criminal or blameworthy; we pity him who suffers. Again, these are not discoveries made by observing how people respond in different

situations; they are analyses of the concepts of desiring, abhor-
ring, and pitying. Hence, Crane's job is to show that Macbeth's
and Scotland's situations are such as to render these the
appropriate responses. And the reader who would refute Crane
must do so by showing that the situations are otherwise, perhaps
by casting doubt on the goodness of Macbeth's enemies, or by
showing a possible alternative end for Macbeth that would be
better for him than death. Note that the accuracy of Crane's
account doesn't really depend on our ability to define "normal
human beings," or even on a large number of people having
responded in the way he claims to be appropriate. If no
spectators or readers ever really responded in the way Crane
prescribes, that would constitute good grounds for looking back
to see if his description of the play was inaccurate or omitted
some important considerations. But it would not by itself refute
the original claim. Indeed critics often argue in behalf of a
response that no reader ever had. And this is not surprising,
since the critic may well be displaying relevant aspects of the
situation that had previously escaped attention.

We have been considering emotional responses to literary and
nonliterary events, and to fictional characters and real people, as
equivalent insofar as the reasons that can be given in support of
them are descriptions of the nature of the situation toward which
the response is directed. A word should be said about the
sometime differences between them. For there are reasons that
might be brought forth in behalf of a response to a literary work
that have only remote analogues in life: it is after all a relevant
aspect of Macbeth's situation that he is a character in a tragedy.
Not only is the spectator or reader in no position to influence the
course of events (by no means a purely literary predicament!), a
fact which itself qualifies and complicates our response. But the
spectator or reader is aware that he is in the hands of an author
who has planned an outcome and whose very style of presenting
characters and events is itself a part of the situation which moves
us. There are reasons for pitying Desdemona and fearing her
death as we approach the end of act 4 of *Othello*, and there are
reasons for pitying the hero and fearing his death as we
approach book 16 of *Tom Jones*; but in the latter case our
potentially painful feelings are greatly attenuated by all those
comic elements that reassure us, as we read, about the likelihood

of Tom's success: the character of the narrator, the ineffectual and ridiculous nature of Tom's enemies, Sophia's frequently demonstrated quickness to forgive Tom, and Tom's own brushes with disaster, from which he repeatedly emerges unharmed.[19]

Finally, there are no doubt people who fail to respond emotionally to fictional events just because they are fictional, just as there are people who have difficulty becoming involved spectators of an athletic contest because it's only a game. One can imagine a reader responding to Crane's analysis of *Macbeth*: "I can see that Macbeth's predicament is such as you describe, and if he were real and alive, no doubt I would feel the emotions you mention. But after all, he's not a real person, and hence I neither care about him nor take any interest in him." To such a challenge there is no easy reply, for it reminds us that the willing suspension of disbelief, the active relaxing or letting go into the pretense that constitutes fiction, is learned and must be nurtured. While it has its origins, no doubt, in childhood play and make-believe, perhaps even in a time when the distinction between fiction and nonfiction is not clearly perceived, there is no question but that responding fully to more sophisticated literary forms is the product of literary experience and the gradual development of the capacity for imaginative sympathy. Since caring for and being interested in are themselves emotions, one can provide reasons for or against caring for or being interested in *this* character or *that* poem, referring as usual to the situation of the character, the nature of the poem. But when the question is why one should be interested in literature, the truest answers, as with the question why should one care about people, will be, though obvious, too general to persuade the diehard adult.

What I have tried to show is that there is a necessary connection between a reader's understanding of a situation and the emotions and attitudes he will feel toward it and that his understanding cannot change without his emotions and attitudes changing as well. It is this connection that permits the critic to talk about how a reader ought to respond to a passage or work by talking about the text. This is why Wimsatt and Beardsley were able to say, and they were right, that

> The more specific the account of the emotion induced by a poem, the more nearly it will be an account

of the reasons for emotion, the poem itself, and the more reliable it will be as an account of what the poem is likely to induce in other—sufficiently informed—readers. It will in fact supply the kind of information which will enable readers to respond to the poem.[20]

A NOTE ON IDENTIFICATION

One term that is widely used in talking about responses to literary works is "identification." As D. W. Harding pointed out in a shrewd and persuasive essay, it is a term used in a large variety of ways:

> The great difficulty about the term 'identification' is to know which one of several different processes it refers to. The reader may see resemblances between himself and a fictional persona only to regret them. . . . He may long enviously to be like a fictional character so different from himself that he discounts all possibility of approximating to him. . . . He may adopt the character as a model for imitation. . . . Or he may be given up, for the duration of the novel or film, to absorbed empathy with one of the characters. The fact is that we can avoid all this uncertainty and describe each of the processes accurately by speaking explicitly of empathy, imitation, admiration, or recognition of similarities. We sacrifice little more with the term 'identification' than a bogus technicality.[21]

The distinctions Harding makes are useful and merit more detailed investigation than I will give them. All that I wish to consider is the last of Harding's definitions of "identification" ("absorbed empathy with one of the characters"). Many people who seriously subscribe to identification as an important aspect of literary responses are thinking of empathy, but unfortunately the one term is about as vague as the other, so Harding's definition hasn't taken us very far. Nor do most definitions of either term, which tend either to take us back to empathy as a recognition of similarities between oneself and the character or else to be highly metaphorical. For example, Walter Slatoff distinguishes between two "forms of identification": *empathy*, which "is essentially a lending of oneself to the character," and *projection*, which "is a substitution of the self or part of the self for the character."[22] But these definitions won't do, for one is left with phrases that are as mysterious as the original terms. What is it to "lend oneself" to a character? How can we distinguish between *lending ourselves to* and *substituting ourselves for* a character? The only hope, it seems to me, is to try to translate the terms back into the vocabulary of understanding and emotion. What happens, literally, if and when we empathize?

Most discussions of either term hint at the reader's experience becoming identical with that of some character or characters in the story being read. Now in one sense this happens frequently in both literary—and life—responses. As I watch the melodrama, both the heroine and I may hate the villain, feel outraged by his threats, hope that bankruptcy can be avoided, and so on. Our feelings, so described, receive the same name. Or in a public forum a whole audience may be swept up in fervid admiration for a speaker addressing them. They share the same feelings and attitudes and are, in this weak sense, identifying with each other. I call it a weak sense because if all that is involved is sharing some feelings and attitudes, two people can identify with each other without even knowing of each other's existence. These cases are easily encompassed by our previous account of the emotions, and it is not surprising or mysterious that our feelings should concur with those of others—fictional or alive—who are similarly perceiving a single situation.

It might be argued that having any emotional response whatsoever to a character depends upon such sharing of feelings and perceptions, or that it depends upon having been in a similar situation. The first of these claims is untrue. We may fear for a character, for example, because we know what is about to happen to him, when he hasn't the faintest notion of the danger he is in. Nor need we feel some temporary equivalent of the person's feelings in order to understand and respond to them. We do not have to feel ashamed to understand what it would be like to be caught red-handed, and we can understand what it feels like to have accomplished something difficult without feeling proud of ourselves. As for the claim that we can't respond to a character without having at some time been in a similar situation, it may be true but it is vague. I may not be able to understand what it is to feel pain or grief without having experienced either, but on the other hand, I don't have to have experienced a toothache or the loss of a favorite pet to pity the toothache sufferer or the grieving child.

Sometimes identification-as-empathy is presumed to involve imagining being in a character's situation or imagining being a character and experiencing what he experiences. It is of course possible for anyone who knows a work well to imagine being one of the characters. If you know *Othello* you can sit back, in the absence of any performance or text, and imagine being any one of the characters in any conceivable situation whatsoever. And perhaps, if one's imaginings are especially vivid, one will actually experience the emotions of the person one imagines oneself to be. Perhaps it is even possible to *think that you are* one of the characters, though it is doubtful that one can do so at will. The question is, what do such imaginings have to do with literary responses? Can they be regarded as appropriate responses to a literary work? Can one "have" them while one is attending to the work?

It is important to see that some of our feelings in such a case will be at odds with whatever feelings would be appropriate toward that person as an "other" person separate from ourselves.[23] For example, the heroine who fears for her safety and who perhaps feels a degree of self-pity will call forth pity, not self-pity, from someone who understands her situation. And though she and we may both concur in "fearing for her safety," there is a significant difference between fearing for someone else's safety and fearing for one's own. Yet if I literally imagine myself to be the heroine, surely that suggests that my feelings are directed toward myself, and not toward some other person. Is it possible, under such an illusion, to sustain my pity *for the heroine*?

The strongest and clearest presentation of such a view is that put forth by Simon Lesser in *Fiction and the Unconscious*.[24] Lesser wrote that "when we are engrossed, a great deal of evidence indicates, *we imaginatively experience the entire action, ourselves act out every role*" (p. 201). This happens, he claimed, not just with characters we admire, or characters in whom we see some special resemblance to ourselves: "Other studies of response to fiction also indicate that if we can understand and empathize with some of the characters in a story, with varying degrees of candor and completeness we can usually identify with them all" (p. 202).

In reading a Shakespearean tragedy, or *Anna Karen-ina* or *The Idiot*, we identify with the principal protagonist and, as we know, in most cases with other characters as well, and covertly secure the full satisfaction the various roles provide. We err with the characters and vicariously secure the instinctual gratification their errors entail. We share the subsequent experiences to which their course commits them and the emotions aroused by those experiences. [Pp. 248–49]

I frankly do not know how to tell whether this actually happens when we read. Let us explore instead the question of what it would mean if it did happen. What would it mean, say, if we responded to *Othello* according to Lesser's model? Among the thoughts and feelings that the major characters experience in the course of the play are the following:

1. At certain times in the play Othello trusts Iago, becomes convinced of Desdemona's guilt, and suspicious of Cassio's relationship with her. He wishes to kill both Desdemona and Cassio. When he kills Desdemona, he feels that he is committing an act of justice.

2. Desdemona (who is of course certain of her own fidelity to Othello) wonders why Othello is behaving strangely toward her. She becomes fearful and apprehensive.

3. As for Iago, though his motives, if they exist, are notoriously hard to pin down, perhaps we can say at least that he wishes to destroy Othello and Othello's relationship with Desdemona.

Now it seems to me that the notion that the spectator "imaginatively experiences" these thoughts and feelings is patently absurd. Absurd, first, because the play offers the spectator no reason (a) to trust Iago, (b) to become convinced of Desdemona's guilt, or (c) to be puzzled, as Desdemona is, about Othello's reasons for baiting her. At least so far as Othello and Desdemona are concerned, the audience, at every stage of the game, knows more than they do about their situations, and what the audience knows is often directly at odds with what they think. Second, our feelings are therefore often quite contrary to the feelings of the characters: when Othello is most confident, *we* suspect him guilty of excessive pride; when he feels remorse, we feel pity; when Desdemona thinks "*I* will be killed," we think "*she* will be killed." We could not feel what the protagonists feel without an experience of illusion or mistaken identity so strong that it blotted out all the information that the play provides about the characters' situations.

As for Iago, if we identify with him in Lesser's sense as he soliloquizes, that would mean that we sometimes suspect Cassio and Othello of having leapt into *our* seats and worn *our* nightcaps, and though I can imagine that he would think so, I have more trouble believing that any attentive spectator ever imagined it to be so. We may share, to a degree, some of Iago's desires. We may harbor some envy of Othello's success, some resentment of his overweening self-esteem. We may, in short, have some grounds for disliking him or wishing him ill, and experience some satisfaction—mingled, one hopes, with other feelings—at Iago's success. We may wish to see him get his comeuppance, but then draw back in horror at the extremity of what follows. This indeed is a perfectly ordinary emotional response of the sort we have already discussed, and a critic might argue for or against the appropriateness of such a response, citing act, scene, and verse. But such feelings have no necessary connection with identification in Lesser's sense. While Iago may think to himself, "*I* want to destroy *my* general," *we* think (if we deeply resent Othello) "I want *him* to destroy *his* general." And those are very different feelings.

What I have been at pains to suggest is that if we take identification in Lesser's strong sense seriously, it asks us to respond to a work in ways that are quite inconsistent with the information that the work provides and with the feelings that are appropriate to that information. Unfortunately (from my point of view) Lesser has a neat and easy answer to such an objection. It is that identification takes place on an unconscious level. And of course if there is an altogether separate level of response, disconnected from our perceptions, emotions, and attitudes, all that I have said about our responses may be irrelevant to what is going on on this other level. In fact Lesser writes of the unconscious in terms that protect him from the charges I am making:

> Of one or two of the characteristics of unconscious response we can also speak with reasonable assurance. If only from glimpses we occasionally catch of the unconscious in operation, we know that it often works at lightning speed. We know, too, that it is unbelievably perceptive, and prodigal in supplying us with impres-

sions and associations.... Unburdened by the need
to be coherent or consistent, employing the most slap-
dash kind of shorthand, the unconscious can easily
outspeed and out-produce the painstaking conscious
intelligence. [P. 196]

Given this impressive set of qualities, it is easy to see why it is
hard to refute the notion that we do in fact identify with
characters as we read or watch. If the unconscious works with
lightning speed, and without regard for consistency or coherence, perhaps we do indeed on one level bypass the information that the text provides and mistake ourselves for the
characters, even as on a conscious level we respond with intense
feelings based on our observations of them and the situations
they are in. Lesser assures us that "all the empirical evidence [he
has] been able to gather indicates that most people have a wide
capacity for identification" (p. 203). Perhaps it does. But it need
not concern us here, for if identification does occur, the critic
can hardly talk about it as a response of *the reader* at all. If
consistency and coherence are thrown to the wind, if it is not
linked directly to our understanding of the work, the notion of
an *appropriate* unconscious response must go by the boards. If
there is such a process, one suspects that, like mnemonic
irrelevancies, private associations, and reveries, it is highly
idiosyncratic, recoverable perhaps on the analyst's couch, but
not deducible from the nature of the text and an understanding
of the objects of human emotions.

One final word: implicit in our discussion of responses to
literature is a view of the reader as an observer, someone who
learns about and responds to the dilemmas, successes, and
failures of *other people*. I suspect that the real motive for seeking
some other sort of response such as those adumbrated by Slatoff
and Lesser is the desire to testify to the strength and depth of the
feelings that literature can evoke. One is drawn to words like
"empathy," perhaps, when one's feelings are especially intense.
But to think that strong feeling can come about only when the
distinction between ourselves and others is ignored is to sell
human nature short. And it is unnecessary. Surely there is no
limit to the intensity of feelings that another person, in a
situation different from our own, can arouse. We can pity,
admire, despise, or rejoice for another as intensely as we can

pity, admire, despise, or rejoice for ourselves. The role of an observer is not a passive, unemotional role. Nor is it a role that precludes being swept up by, drawn into, or emotionally involved in the action of a work. Being emotionally involved in a situation, literary or otherwise, has nothing to do with confusion about who one is or with being able to alter the course of events. Slatoff, who is generally aware of this fact, nevertheless postulates that "when one sees one's own child being hurt ... one feels the pain as though it were one's own and is ... as fully involved emotionally as it is possible to be" (p. 50). I not only doubt that one feels the pain as though it were one's own; I suspect that doing so would be nothing but a distraction from the burning desire to help, and (perhaps) the anguish of being unable to do so, that would constitute genuine emotional involvement.

4

Understanding and Misunderstanding, Or: What to Do with a Bad Student

A DIALOGUE

GEORGES POULET: When reading a literary work, there is a moment when it seems to me that the subject *present* in this work disengages itself from all that surrounds it, and stands alone. Had I not once the intuition of this, when visiting Scuola di San Rocco in Venice, one of the highest summits of art, where there are assembled so many paintings of the same painter, Tintoretto? When looking at all these masterpieces, brought there together and revealing so manifestly their unity of inspiration, I had suddenly the impression of having reached the common essence present in all the works of a great master, an essence which I was not able to perceive, except when emptying my mind of all the particular images created by the artist. . . .
It seems then that criticism, in order to accompany the mind in this effort of detachment from itself, needs to annihilate, or at least momentarily to forget, the objective elements of the work, and to elevate itself to the apprehension of a subjectivity without objectivity.

LUCIEN GOLDMANN: I would ask what is the criterion of falsity in this knowledge? To put it very simply and naively from an outsider, if a bad student of Poulet

A portion of this chapter is a modified version of "Description and Explanation in Literary Criticism," which appeared in *The Journal of Aesthetics and Art Criticism* 28 (1969): 281–82. Copyright © 1969 by The American Society for Aesthetics.

goes to the Scuola di San Rocco, has the impression that he is identifying, and finds what he takes to be an essence of Tintoretto—but he is mistaken. How could we in this case know that he is mistaken, while in another case, such as you have so magisterially analyzed, the identification has a creative, critical value? . . . If an answer is possible it would give me considerable clarification of the status of your critical activity.

GEORGES POULET: What would Poulet do with a bad student of Poulet? In reality, what I should try to do with any writer, or with Tintoretto in the case of painting—I would try to identify with my bad student and I would not be able to do it; I would fail in this effort of identification. The sole criterion that I would have that Poulet's student was a bad student of Poulet would consist in the fact that Poulet could not identify with this student.[1]

The subject of this chapter is what is variously called the truth, correctness, plausibility, or validity of interpretations. Can two interpretations of a single work be distinguished in these terms, and if so how? Can two mutually incompatible interpretations both be right? What sorts of evidence substantiate an interpretation? How can we tell, if we can, whether we are misunderstanding a work?

I will argue, as I think most readers would, that it is possible to misunderstand something; I will also argue that it is usually possible, when two interpretations are actually in conflict, to adjudicate between them (when it is not possible, the work or passage in question is ambiguous); and that of two conflicting interpretations the better is the one that accounts for the words of the text more completely, simply, consistently, and coherently. I will take up several challenges to these views along the way. At the same time, E. D. Hirsch is surely right when he says that in interpretation "certainty is always unattainable."[2] We can never be sure that new facts won't turn up to invalidate our interpretation, or that someone won't conceive of a new and better interpretation of the facts at hand.

What do these criteria (completeness, consistency, simplicity, coherence) mean? I do not think that they are easy to define in the abstract or in such a way as to provide easy solutions to critical dilemmas, yet I am quite sure that we all employ them as rules of thumb. They are intricately related to each other, and as a group they are derived from what we mean by making sense of something, understanding something, seeing how the parts of something are related to each other. They are in no sense purely literary, and indeed they are the same criteria we use to establish an understanding of a "real life" utterance, act, or situation. They are explained best through examples, and if they come clear, it will be through using them and seeing them used in the pages that follow.

For a starter, then, we demand logical consistency of an interpretation: we expect the critic not to contradict himself or base his interpretation on contradictory assumptions. For example, Ernest Jones, in his psychoanalytic study of *Hamlet*, distinguishes between the character traits of a man whose infantile attraction for his mother had been excessive and insufficiently repressed and those of a man whose infantile attraction had been intensely repressed. He then ascribes to Hamlet some traits that belong in the first category (e.g., a "tender feminine side") and others that belong in the second (e.g., misogyny and an attraction to a woman very unlike his mother). Indeed at times he describes Hamlet as having received from Gertrude, from his childhood on, "passionate fondness" and "the warmest affection," while elsewhere he speaks of Hamlet's sexual repression as "highly pronounced," his feelings for his mother as having "always been firmly dammed." Now Jones regards the play as complicated, but not as confused or self-contradictory. The inconsistency is in the interpretation; one simply cannot make sense of and accept two contradictory assumptions: that Hamlet's affections were both insufficiently and intensely repressed.[3]

To take another sort of example, Samuel Holt Monk, in a well-known essay on book 4 of *Gulliver's Travels*,[4] points out that Swift was strongly opposed to:

> Rationalism, especially Cartesianism, with its radical tendency to abstract truth into purely intellectual concepts and its bold rejection of the experience and wisdom of the past. Swift doubted the capacity of human reason to attain metaphysical and theological truth. A safer guide in this life seemed to him to be . . . the time-approved wisdom of the race.

Later on in the essay he writes that:

> in every sense Houyhnhnmland is a rationalistic Uto-
> pia. The Houyhnhnms are the embodiment of pure
> reason. They know neither love nor grief nor lust nor
> ambition. They cannot lie, indeed they have no word for
> lying and are hard put to it to understand the meaning
> of *opinion*. Their society is an aristocracy. . . .

Ergo, according to Monk, Swift was strongly opposed to the
Houyhnhnms.

The problem with this argument is simply that the rationalism
defined in the major premise is not the same as the rationalism
defined in the minor premise. What do "the radical tendency to
abstract truth into purely intellectual concepts" and "the rejection of the experience and wisdom of the past" have to do with
"knowing neither love nor grief nor lust" or with the inability to
lie or with aristocracy? The argument, quite apart from the truth
claims it makes, is inconsistent.

Completeness, on the other hand, has to do with fitting all the
relevant parts of the text accurately. To cite disconfirming
evidence, or to quarrel with the accuracy of the ways the text or
characters or events are described is to point to the incompleteness of an interpretation. We will explore several examples of
incompleteness later. (Inaccuracy and the ignoring of evidence
are common failings.) But imagine for now that Monk still
wished to claim that Houyhnhnmland is a rationalistic Utopia in
the sense embodied in his major premise. In that case we could
challenge his interpretation if we could cite passages in which the
Houyhnhnms resist abstraction, shy away from metaphysics or
theology, or accept the experience and time-approved wisdom of
the race.

As for the tricky criterion of simplicity, consider Wallace
Stevens's poem "Anecdote of the Jar":

> I placed a jar in Tennessee,
> And round it was, upon a hill.
> It made the slovenly wilderness
> Surround that hill.
>
> The wilderness rose up to it,
> And sprawled around, no longer wild.
> The jar was round upon the ground
> And tall and of a port in air.

It took dominion everywhere.
The jar was gray and bare.
It did not give of bird or bush
Like nothing else in Tennessee.[5]

Yvor Winters, in his commentary on the poem, quotes two critics who agree in interpreting the jar as a symbol of man's superiority to, or dominion over, nature. Winters then comments as follows:

> If the poem ended with the fourth line, there might be an imperfect justification of the interpretation offered by these writers, for in the first four lines the wilderness is not only dominated by the jar—as, in fact, it is dominated throughout the poem—but it is called slovenly. If we examine the next two lines, however, we see that the phrase, "the slovenly wilderness," is in fact a slovenly ellipsis. The wilderness is slovenly after it has been dominated and not before: it "sprawled around, no longer wild."... The poem would appear to be primarily an expression of the corrupting effect of the intellect upon natural beauty, and hence a purely romantic performance.[6]

Winters wants to argue, in other words, that the jar is a corrupting intrusion on a previously beautiful natural landscape. But not only is there no clear evidence that the wilderness was beautiful before the jar was placed in it; the third line is a positive embarrassment to Winters's reading, a potentially disconfirming bit of evidence. So Winters can save the theory only by postulating, not an epicycle, but an "ellipsis." Stevens did not *mean* that the jar made the slovenly wilderness surround the hill. He meant that it made the wilderness surround the hill and *then* the wilderness became slovenly.

Winters could be right, of course. An interpretation can be *too* simple to account for the facts, and must be complicated enough. But if there were an interpretation of the poem which accounted for all the facts without having to introduce a complication, we would, I suspect, prefer it.[7]

The criterion of coherence stands apart from the other three but embraces them all. Interpretation proceeds, though it does not finally rest, on the assumption that the *text* is coherent, that its parts are related in a perceptible way, that as a whole it makes sense. Hence an interpretation that makes sense of and is consistent with the whole text is preferred to one that must ignore or treat as extraneous some part of it. It is this criterion which allows us to use "disconfirming evidence" from some passage in the work which the author did not treat, or which allows us to prefer, other things being equal, a simple interpretation to a complicated one. One proceeds on the assumption that the text is coherent though one knows that it may not be so. For the only way to discover that a text does not cohere is to fail in every attempt to make it do so.[8]

The fact that critics employ these criteria and rebut each other by pointing out inconsistencies, unexplained data, unnecessarily complicated explanations, and the like, shows that we tacitly treat the work as the act of an intending author doing what he does for reasons that he trusts will be apparent and make sense. Without such an assumption the criteria would be groundless, and without it there would be no way to talk about unintended effects.

Textual and Extratextual Evidence

Let us at this point attempt to put asunder what has too often been joined together: What the critic is looking for and how he can tell when he's found it are two different matters. The fact that reading and interpreting involve the postulation of intentions says nothing about the relevance or irrelevance of so-called extratextual evidence. The assumption that "intentionalist" criticism must go hand in hand with historical-biographical research has led to bogus disagreement and real confusion.

Among the chief confusions has been that between the kinds of information we seek in an effort to formulate an interpretation and the kinds of criteria we use to test it once it has been formulated. This distinction is parallel to the distinction in the sciences between the skillful guesswork employed in imagining an explanatory hypothesis and the methods used to validate the hypothesis. Wimsatt and Beardsley illustrate the distinction nicely, but unintentionally. The literary text at issue is a quatrain from Donne's "A Valediction: Forbidding Mourning":

> Moving of th' earth brings harmes and feares,
>   Men reckon what it did and meant,
> But trepidation of the spheares,
>   Though greater farre, is innocent.

They catch Charles Coffin out in a misreading of the phrase "Moving of th' earth" as a reference to the movement of the earth around the sun, a movement which, according to Coffin, was the most radical principle of the new astronomy. Wimsatt and Beardsley agree that Donne was "deeply interested" in the new astronomy. But as they point out, reading "moving of th' earth" as a reference to earthquakes makes for a much more coherent interpretation of the passage: an earthquake can be referred to as a singular, past event ("men reckon what it *did* and *meant*"), while the earth's orbiting of the sun cannot; and earthquake is more consistent with the "tear-floods" and "sigh-tempests" of the preceding stanza, and so on. So far so good. But Wimsatt and Beardsley confuse the *source* of Coffin's interpretation with the grounds for rejecting it. They accuse him of "disregarding the English language," of preferring "private evidence to public, external to internal."[9] But what *they* disregard is the fact that the "earthquake" reading apparently had not occurred to Coffin, who never even attempted to show that Donne intended one meaning rather than the other. The inadequacy of his interpretation stems from a failure to have thought of earthquakes; it has nothing to do with the fact that the new astronomy is private, esoteric, or external to the poem. Earthquakes are as external to the poem as orbits are, and sometimes the right interpretation of a passage includes a meaning that is private and esoteric. The encouragement to shy away from information that might lead to a sound reading simply on the grounds that it is not common modern knowledge is clearly misleading and, if taken seriously, would put an end to efforts to read the literature of the past or of other cultures with understanding. Wimsatt and Beardsley's reading makes good sense of the passage because it is simpler, more complete, and more consistent than Coffin's. What this means, in the light of the connection between intentions and reasons, is simply that it is hard to imagine a reason for Donne's having chosen the words *did* and *meant* as predicates for a continuing rather than a completed motion. The door is always open, of course, for the discovery of one. It also means that, given what he does elsewhere in the poem, he had several good reasons for referring to earthquakes.

We recognize the fact that a writer, like anyone else, may fail to achieve what he tried to achieve. We don't always say what we mean or even what we mean to say. It is conceivable that the interpretation of a poem that makes the best sense of the poem may be at odds with what, for other reasons, we suspect the poet's intention to have been. For example, E. D. Hirsch suggested that one can make equally good sense of the text of Wordsworth's "A Slumber Did My Spirit Seal" on the assumption that Wordsworth was expressing invincibly affirmative feelings and on the contrary assumption that he was expressing pessimistic and unconsoled feelings.[10] Let us suppose that Hirsch is right, and let us suppose further that he is right when he says that evidence drawn from Wordsworth's other writings of the period indicates the great likelihood that Wordsworth intended to convey the former sorts of feelings. On these suppositions would it not be reasonable to say that Wordsworth intended to convey one attitude, but that the poem conveys neither attitude clearly? An unnecessary confusion is forced upon us by the assumption that in such a case a choice or preferential decision has to be made. Hirsch argues that the correct interpretation of a work is the one which the author is most likely to have intended and that extratextual evidence will always be decisive in making the determination. But even if this latter proposition were true, a statement to the effect that Wordsworth expressed affirmative feelings in the poem would be a misleading and inaccurate description of it. We need to distinguish between an ambiguous poem and another poem that expresses some attitude or feeling clearly and unambiguously. If the poem is ambiguous but was not meant to be, that is an interesting fact, a fact that the literary historian or biographer might want to try to explain.

To repeat: if the intentions we infer from the text are at odds with other signs of the writer's intentions, the solution lies in granting the discrepancy. Those "other signs" may bring to mind a new way of interpreting the work that makes better sense of it; in that case the discrepancy no longer exists. But as long as the discrepancy remains we have a problematical and ambiguous situation which cannot be wished away. The textual evidence may be very strong, the extratextual evidence weak, or vice versa; in either case a problem remains. This is true, but not cause for alarm. There are startlingly few cases in criticism of clear and serious descrepancies of the sort we are considering.

Wimsatt and Beardsley offered none, and Hirsch's Wordsworth example had to be considered hypothetically because most readers seem persuaded that actually the biographical and textual signs point in the same direction.[11]

A word here about the word "evidence." We sometimes complain that a critic or a student has failed to provide enough evidence, and we demand more of it, meaning by more evidence more quotations from or references to the text. But calling the language of a text *evidence for* an interpretation is a potentially misleading shorthand; the text is the data which the interpretation attempts to explain or make sense of. The evidence or "proof" that an interpretation is a good one is that it fits the data well—more simply, completely, and coherently than its competitors. In the case of discrepancies between textual and extratextual "evidence," then, what we actually have is two sets of data that can't be made sense of in the same way, or with a single interpretation. If we try to explain both sets of data with a single hypothesis, it will necessarily be a hypothesis that includes an explanation of the discrepancy. This is another way of saying that it will acknowledge the presence of a problem.

DOES THE COHERENCE CRITERION WORK?

Hirsch has argued more powerfully than anyone else for the view that evidence drawn from the writer's milieu and other writings should take precedence over the "fit" of an interpretation to the work. I have already urged that there is something phony about the whole question of precedence. But Hirsch's argument contains a further premise which, if it were granted, might make us give up the whole enterprise. Let us assail the premise:

Hirsch's strongest argument for preferring historical evidence to coherence and fitness is that the coherence-completeness-simplicity criterion "cannot, in fact, either reconcile different readings or choose between them. As a normative ideal, or principle of correctness, it is useless" (p. 227). Again, it "cannot suffice to validate a single expert reading I know of at the expense of its expert rivals" (p. 192). That is, Hirsch claims that all competing expert readings, like the two readings of Wordsworth's poem, fulfill the coherence criterion equally well. It is on these grounds that Hirsch urges criticism to set its sights on a different target—not on the interpretation that makes the most sense of the passage, but on the interpretation of the author's probable intention inferred from as much relevant historical evidence as possible.

This is partly an empirical claim, the sort of claim one can imagine arising out of repeated experiences (which of us hasn't had them?) of inconclusive debates about the significance of this or that particular passage from a poem or play or novel. One can imagine wanting to escape from such inconclusiveness to firmer ground. The empirical side of the claim is hard to refute, for to offer instances that seem to me to demonstrate that the coherence criterion can convincingly discredit some expert readings is to run the risk of making interpretive mistakes that would seem to reinforce Hirsch's skepticism. In that case nothing would have been proven except my ineptness. Nevertheless, before objecting to Hirsch's claim on more theoretical grounds, let me say that he is confusing human fallibility with logical necessity, and let me run the risk, trusting that if the reader is not convinced he will come up with persuasive examples of his own. Let us look at misreadings of two works that have been subjected to much scrutiny. I have chosen my examples, by the way, from critics to whom most of us would grant the title "expert" with no hesitation. (By "expert" Hirsch can only mean "performed by an acknowledged expert," since if he meant by it "highly coherent and adequate" his claim would have been tautological.)

In an essay on *Antony and Cleopatra* Kenneth Burke considers the function of the eunuchs in the play:

> At first glance, one might assume that the lines on eunuchs belong in the play sheerly because of their "entertainment" value, since they allow for the kind of "dirty" wisecracks that many people regret in Shakespeare. But are not subtler kinds of persuasion involved here?
>
> At the very least, such references serve (and are explicitly used) to emphasize by contrast the virility of the hero. But is there not a still subtler operation? Without the eunuchs, there would be a much greater risk in the mighty buildup of Antony's sexual prowess, including Cleopatra's envy of his "inches." Add the many telling references to eunuchs' shortcomings, and the drama

sets up a terministic situation implying that practically all the men in the audience were *in the same class* with Antony. Such classification-by-contrast enabled Shakespeare to accentuate Antony's exceptional amative prowess without risk that persons of more moderate resources in this regard might lose their sense of "identification" with him.[12]

But consider the following facts:

Philo's opening speech in the play concludes with a description of Antony as having become "the bellows and the fan / To cool a gypsies lust." This description is followed immediately by the stage direction, "Enter Antony, Cleopatra, her ladies, the train, with Eunuchs fanning her." The audience sees the eunuchs performing an action in fact that Philo has attributed to Antony in metaphor. This juxtaposition is reinforced by Caesar: Antony "is not more manlike / Than Cleopatra, nor the Queen of Ptolemy / More womanly than he" (act 1, scene 4, lines 5–7).

In act 2, scene 5, after some jesting at Mardian's expense ("As well a woman with a eunuch played / As with a woman"), Cleopatra recalls a delicious episode in their past in terms that highlight her pleasure in playing the man to Antony's drunken and emasculated weakness:

> That time—oh, times!—
> I laughed him out of patience, and that night
> I laughed him into patience. And next morn,
> Ere the ninth hour, I drunk him to his bed,
> Then put my tires and mantles on him whilst
> I wore his sword Philippan.
>
> [Lines 18–23]

Again, while the battle is going badly, Enobarbus clearly suggests that Antony and the eunuchs have traded places: "He [Antony] is already / Traduced for levity, and 'tis said in Rome / That Photinus, a eunuch, and your maids / Manage this war" (act 3, scene 7, lines 13–16). Later in the same scene, Canidius says, "So our leader's led, / And we are women's men" (lines 70–71). One might go further and question whether Antony's behavior is *ever* presented as being unambiguously virile except in some of Cleopatra's imaginings, especially in those that occur after Antony's death. But these passages are sufficient to show that Burke's interpretation leaves unexplained many of the details which it specifically claims to explain. We may put the question this way, bringing out its intentional nature: If Shakespeare had wished to use the eunuchs to emphasize Antony's virility, why would he have so stressed Antony's kinship with them? Or we can say that, compared to an interpretation that accounts for these passages, Burke's is incomplete. To say this is not to insist upon an equally simple but opposite interpretation; it is true, for example, that some of the judgments of Antony may be made by speakers with an unreliable point of view. It is simply that Burke's reading does not fit the facts very well. It might be revised and expanded in order to fit them better, but then it would be a new interpretation, with the revisions made in accordance with the coherence criterion.

For a second example, consider Dorothy Van Ghent's interpretation of Joe Gargery's behavior in *Great Expectations*.[13] Van Ghent's thesis is that:

> Some of the most wonderful scenes in *Great Expectations* are those in which people, presumably in the act of conversation, raptly soliloquize; and Dickens' technique, in these cases, is usually to give the soliloquizer a fantastic private language as unadapted to mutual understanding as a species of pig Latin.

This technique, she claims, "is an index of a vision of life that sees human separatedness as the ordinary condition, where speech is speech *to* nobody and where human encounter is mere collision." Her primary witness is Joe Gargery, the humble blacksmith, whose bumbling attempts to articulate his thoughts are apparent in countless scenes in the novel.

Van Ghent cites, first, the following exchange between Joe and the aggressive lawyer Jaggers:

> "Now, Joseph Gargery, I warn you this is your last chance. No half measures with me. If you mean to take a present that I have in charge to make you, speak out, and you shall have it. If on the contrary you mean to say—" Here, to his great amazement, he was stopped by Joe's suddenly working round him with every demonstration of a fell pugilistic purpose.
> "Which I meantersay," cried Joe, "that if you come into my place bull-baiting and badgering me, come out!

Which I meantersay as sech if you're a man, come on!
Which I meantersay that what I say, I meantersay and
stand or fall by!"

Second, she cites the scene in which Miss Havisham discusses
with Joe the question of Pip's wages. "For each question she
asks," writes Van Ghent, "Joe persists in addressing his reply to
Pip rather than herself, and his replies have not the remotest
relation to the questions."

Third, there is the scene in which Pip, who has been struggling
to learn to write, composes a letter to Joe (who is sitting next to
him at the time). Joe, who cannot read, regards the letter as "a
miracle of erudition" (the phrase is Pip's), and in response to
Pip's question whether Joe is fond of reading, Joe replies:

> "On-common. Give me," said Joe, "a good book, or a
> good newspaper, and sit me down afore a good fire,
> and I ask no better. Lord!" he continued, after rubbing
> his knees a little, "when you *do* come to a J and a O,
> and says you, 'Here, at last, is a J-O, Joe,' how in-
> teresting reading is!"

"There is, perhaps," Van Ghent assures us, "no purer expression of solipsism in literature. . . . Dickens' soliloquizing characters, for all their funniness . . . suggest a world of isolated
integers, terrifyingly alone and unrelated."

Dorothy Van Ghent's criticism is ordinarily keen and observant, but surely she misconstrued the significance of Joe's
illiterate speech. In the first scene Joe's pugilistic response is a
highly communicative and expressive counter to Jagger's unnecessary "badgering" (a pretty good word to describe Jagger's
belligerence), and the fact that Joe communicated his feelings
clearly is shown by the fact that the lawyer immediately rose,
backed up to the door, and delivered his final remarks "without
evincing any inclination to come in again."

As for the scene with Miss Havisham, though it is true that Joe
in his embarrassment speaks to Pip, his replies bear, every one of
them, a direct relation to that strange and intimidating lady's
questions. For instance:

> Miss H.: "You are the husband of the sister of this
> boy?"
> Joe: "Which I meantersay, Pip, as I hup and married
> your sister."

Miss H.: "And you have reared the boy, with the intention of taking him for your apprentice; is that so, Mr. Gargery?"

Joe: "You know, Pip, as you and me were ever friends, and it were looked for'ard to betwixt us, as being calc'lated to lead to larks."

Miss H.: "Has the boy ever made any objection? Does he like the trade?"

Joe: "Which it is well beknown to yourself, Pip, that it were the wish of your own hart."

Miss H.: "Have you brought his indentures with you?"

Joe: "Well, Pip, you know, you yourself see me put 'em in my 'at, and therefore you know as they are here."

Furthermore, Joe's behavior succeeds in communicating to Miss Havisham not only his answers to her questions, but also something of his essential sweetness of spirit, as is indicated by Pip's comment and her delicately tactful reply to Joe's disavowal of any desire for additional remuneration:

Miss Havisham glanced at him as if she understood what he really was, better than I had thought possible, seeing what he was there; and took up a little bag from the table beside her.

"Pip has earned a premium here," she said, "and here it is. There are five-and-twenty guineas in this bag. Give it to your master, Pip."

As for Joe's limited reading skills, Van Ghent has simply confused illiteracy with solipsism. The entire scene is one in which the conversation demonstrates warm, compassionate understanding. If their conversation is tainted at all, it is not by Joe's illiteracy but by Pip's callously high regard for the superficial merits of linguistic facility. The progress of the novel as a whole might suggest that solipsism and the inability to communicate are the product not of failures of language but of social pretensions and self-interest.

We might ask at this point what sort of evidence drawn from Shakespeare's or Dickens's other works or from other writings of their times would establish the author's intentions more persuasively than the coherence criterion. Is it not at least as likely that extratextual documents themselves will support multiple competing interpretations as that the text will? Or again, once Hirsch has selected his relevant extratextual documents, how will he determine *their* meaning? By drawing upon documents still more remote? And then?

If it were true (in spite of my effort to demonstrate the contrary) that the coherence criterion can never choose between competing readings, and can never invalidate an expert reading, then all literary works for which competing interpretations have been proposed are *radically* ambiguous. If every text of consequence can support competing readings equally well, then no author of such texts has succeeded in conveying what he meant to convey. The ambiguity I am referring to is not the sort of low-level ambiguity, intentional or unintentional, with which we often deal. The sort of ambiguity that follows from Hirsch's thesis—we might dub it meta-ambiguity—is far more destructive of communication than that. It issues in a profound skepticism about the possibility of any understanding of a difficult text being achieved. That seems to me to be a skepticism refuted by every reader's common experience, by the vast amount of agreement that underlies even the most divergent interpretations of a text, and by the occasional happy event when two critics who differ sharply discuss their differences and succeed in educating each other to a sounder view of a work than either had held before.

FACTS

We have used rather freely in this exposition certain notions that stand in need of further explication. I am thinking of the related notions of *the facts, data,* and (once again) *evidence.* Among the facts, data, and evidence I have referred to are the following:

> Cleopatra took pleasure in recalling having drunk Antony to his bed;
>
> Antony is sometimes presented as being no more virile than the eunuchs;
>
> Joe Gargery succeeds in communicating his indignation to Jaggers;
>
> Joe's answers are related to Miss Havisham's questions;
>
> Joe possesses an essential sweetness of spirit.

I want to make it clear at this point that while I think each of these statements is true and does constitute a fact, I also believe that they must be regarded as interpretations of others facts and finally subject to challenge and reassessment. Statements like these are neither the reader's last resort, nor, finally, the bedrock data he is working with.

Two philosophers, Morris Weitz and Joseph Margolis, have attempted to define the line between fact and interpretation in criticism.[14] Their results are similar, useful, but finally unsatisfactory. Weitz characterizes the distinction as one between descriptive and explanatory statements, Margolis as one between descriptive and interpretive statements. We must realize, however, that they are using the term "descriptive" in a special way, for a great many statements that we make about people's (and hence about characters') physical and verbal acts simultaneously describe, interpret, and explain. If you describe someone as taking a nap, resisting arrest, stealing a book, or pleading for mercy, you are saying *what* they are doing at the same time that you are saying what the point of their doing it is. You are describing their actions in a way that also explains them.

But Weitz and Margolis mean something quite different by "description." For Margolis, " 'Describing' suggests a stable, public, relatively well-defined object available for inspection" (p. 71). For Weitz a descriptive statement is one that is "true or false, verifiable, and logically independent of explanation and evaluation" (p. 244). He asks, "Can we find anything in *Hamlet* about which there can be no doubt or about which if there are doubts and debate, these can be resolved by a direct appeal to the various elements, characteristics, and relations of the play?" "What are the *données* in *Hamlet*?" (p. 228). Describing, then, is apparently a matter of saying what these elements, *données*, or objects are, and of characterizing them but not interpreting or explaining them. And both critics agree in their lists of what these elements are. Without hesitation Weitz announces that:

> Among the elements, distinguishable if not in all instances separable from each other, are the various characters, their traits, speech, and actions; the dialogue, soliloquies, versification, prose, and language; and the plot, with its individual episodes. [P. 229]

Characters, their traits, speeches, actions, the plot—these, according to Weitz, are the data of the play, about which critics can make verifiable, true statements, and to which further statements of an interpretive or evaluative nature would have to appeal as evidence. A descriptive statement is one which reports these elements either truly or falsely, and only descriptions can rightly be called true or false.

And for Margolis:

> In all the arts, furthermore, there is an indisputable range of comments that will be descriptive in the narrowest possible sense. . . . In the literary and dramatic arts, plot, action, characters, vocabulary, rhythm, rhyme, style of language, and the like are said to be described. [P. 82]

But there is something peculiar about these accounts. Neither of them makes it altogether clear whether describing is defined by the nature of its referent (an "object" or "element") or by the nature of the kind of statement being made. The fact that a statement is *about* one of these elements excludes very little. The propositions that the plot of *Hamlet* is intricate, that it is based on patterns of ancient ritual, and that it is the best plot ever are all statements about the plot. And the more one ponders these assortments of givens, the more aware one becomes of the lack of any apparent rationale for them. Why are characters and character traits included while themes, say, are not? Why is the plot included but not the intended effect of the work upon the audience?

Perhaps it's not a matter of what descriptive statements are about, but of their being verifiable. But if they are to be verified by inspecting certain objects or appealing directly to certain elements, then the question of *which* objects or elements becomes crucial. Perhaps we could determine what the objects or elements are by asking what it is that we can inspect or appeal to.

But "direct appeal" and "inspection" are slippery metaphors in this context. What do we do as readers when we "appeal directly" or "inspect" something? A description of a painting might be verified by looking at the colors and shapes, by seeing similarities among them, and so on; and Weitz sometimes uses "look" and "apprehend" instead of "appeal." But clearly we do not test a statement like "Hamlet is melancholy" or "Hamlet delays," which Weitz accepts as both descriptive and true, by literally looking at Hamlet. (We look at Hamlet behaving in a performance, but the actor may choose not to play him as, or interpret him as, a melancholy delayer.) Suppose someone makes a statement of what he takes to be a theme of the play—the theme, say, of evil begetting evil. When we question him, he says, "look at the way the characters behave." Is this really any different in kind from "Hamlet is melancholy; look at how he behaves"? A claim to the effect that Hamlet is melancholy is different from a statement like "there's a blotch of red in the upper left corner of the canvas." For one thing, pigment can't pretend to be red, but a man can pretend to be melancholy. The eyes have it in one case, but not in the other. I don't mean to imply that one can't be fooled or wrong about what one sees; the point is simply that you can't just look and see whether someone is melancholy.

Is there a way of separating the verifiable critical statements from the nonverifiable ones? Perhaps we can at least accomplish the less ambitious goal of providing a rule for *dis*qualifying certain kinds of statements and arrive at a list of *données* by a process of elimination. It seems to be true of Weitz's explanatory or interpretive propositions that they are logically related to other propositions about the work, while descriptions are "logically independent of explanation." And the plausibility of explanatory statements depends on the validity of the logic and the plausibility of the other propositions themselves. Thus, to choose an obvious example, the statement "Hamlet delays because he is melancholy" depends not only upon the truth of the two substatements but also upon the relative inadequacy of other explanations of his delay, the absence of evidence to the contrary, and so on. Surely any statement so dependent on other propositions, themselves tentative at best, could not be considered as reporting a piece of raw data. Let us make it our rule, then, that a descriptive statement is one that is not logically dependent on the truth of other statements about the play. This seems as good a way as any of finding out what it is that we can inspect or appeal directly to.

Let us return, with this notion in mind, to Margolis's and Weitz's lists. Are the characters in a work describable "in the narrowest possible sense"? Are character traits—the attitudes, temperaments, motives, and so on—of the characters in *Hamlet données*? Are Hamlet's alleged madness, his melancholy, pessimism, obscenity properly regarded, as Weitz regards them, as things of which, once we understand how to use those terms, there can be no doubt whatsoever? Surely mental traits and attitudes are no more given in a play than they are in real life. The ascription of traits to the characters does indeed rest upon further assumptions about the play, and such ascriptions are properly regarded as explanations, incapable of verification. We do not, after all, observe attitudes and states of mind. We observe behavior and infer the reasons or causes for it.

Consider, for example, Ernest Jones, who builds his Freudian interpretation of Hamlet's behavior on several alleged facts in the play, one of the chief among which is Gertrude's "passionate fondness for her son."[15] How do we know that Gertrude was passionately fond of Hamlet? Jones directs our attention to act 4, scene 7, where Claudius says of Hamlet, "The Queen his mother lives almost by his looks." But Jones's interpretation of Claudius's remark depends for its plausibility upon the assumption that Claudius means what he says. And that assumption, since Claudius is in the process of thinking up reasons to allay Laertes's suspicions as fast as he can, is a rather dubious one. We do not even know that Claudius *thinks* Gertrude passionately fond of Hamlet.

Or again, consider the many critics who use the famous "What a piece of work is man" speech as direct evidence for Hamlet's past and present traits, his former optimism, his present disenchantment. But that speech, too, occurs in a context. Hamlet is talking to Rosencrantz and Guildenstern, whom he knows to have been sent to spy on him and discover what is really on his mind!

I am not arguing that Gertrude is not fond of Hamlet, or that Hamlet is not an optimist *manqué*. I am simply pointing out that the process of arriving at such conclusions, or any conclusions about what is going on in a character's mind, involves interpretation, not direct appeal. *Hamlet* is an excellent example of the necessity of regarding any statements made about the characters and their thoughts and actions as interpretive as well as descriptive, for it is a play which constantly invites the reader to reinterpret earlier speeches in the light of subsequent ones— Claudius's first speech to the court, say, in the light of the ghost's later revelations, or Hamlet's treatment of Ophelia in the nunnery scene in the light of his behavior at her funeral.[16] And as a play which deals persistently with deceit, there is hardly a line in it the interpretation of which does not depend upon our sense of its speaker's sincerity and rhetorical purposes.

It seems clear that the facts of a literary work are, to borrow a phrase from Hamlet himself, "words, words, words." One can say that Laertes said this, Ophelia that, Gertrude such and such, filling in the predicate with a quotation. These are facts in the sense that they constitute the text we are interpreting. This does not imply (harking back to our earlier discussion) that one can prove or substantiate an interpretation by citing them. You can't say, "of course Gertrude is fond of Hamlet; just look at what Claudius says to Laertes." It implies only that reading is an interpretive process through and through and that words are what we interpret when we read.

This conclusion should not come as any surprise, given the fact that words are the medium of literature. We do not understand words or sentences merely by looking at or hearing them. If we did, we would not have to learn a foreign language in order to understand it. The text—the sequence of words we choose to talk about—is the datum.

If that is so, then "the facts" about Antony, Cleopatra, and Joe Gargery that I cited earlier, as well as such banal truisms as that Hamlet sometimes behaves rashly, that he saw the king at prayer, or that Ophelia went mad, are themselves interpretations of the text. We call them facts, perhaps, because they seem true enough to serve as the basis for higher-level interpreting or as evidence with which a more sweeping interpretation may be refuted. There is no harm in so regarding them, and indeed we could hardly get along in reading or in living without assuming many of our low-level interpretations as true. But we must recognize that they are subject to challenge or refutation and that we may at times be called upon to justify them.

THE PROBLEM OF INTERPRETIVE PLENITUDE

Anyone familiar with the history of criticism, or more particularly with the current plethora of literary reviews and periodicals, knows that most great works of literature, and many less-than-great ones, have been interpreted in many different ways. There are many interpretations of *Hamlet, Great Expectations,* and "Anecdote of the Jar." This fact has been taken as a threat to my view—regarded as hopelessly naive in some quarters and as authoritarian in others—that one can understand a literary work correctly, be right or wrong about it, and so on. I want now to examine this threat and show how empty it is. In the course of the examination we shall see how misused the extraordinarily vague phrase "there are many interpretations of" has been.

Let me begin by sketching Margolis's view of what he calls "the logic of interpretation." On the basis of nothing more than the obvious fact that there are Freudian, Marxist, Jungian, and Catholic interpretations of literary works, Margolis concludes that "the philosophically most interesting feature of critical interpretation is its tolerance of alternative and seemingly contrary hypotheses." "In principle, plural, non-converging, and even incompatible, critical hypotheses may be defended as interpretations of a given work of art." Interpretations may be thought of as plausible or implausible, but not as true or false, and "the statements 'P is plausible' and 'Q is plausible' are not contraries." Hence critical interpretations "are, in principle, logically weak" (pp. 89–93).

It would be easier to assess this position if Margolis had given some examples of incompatible or contrary interpretations of a single work. Since he does not, one must look at the argument itself, which turns out to be correct only where it is trivial. It is trivial, for example, to say that "incompatible hypotheses may be defended." Today, fifty years after the Scopes trial, incompatible explanations of the origin of man are, and hence may be, defended. The Ptolemaic cosmography may be defended, and so, no doubt, may the proposition that Shakespeare was Bacon. The question is not whether an interpretation may be or has been defended, but whether it may be defended well, or whether, more precisely, there are ways in criticism of arbitrating between incompatible interpretations.

Margolis's word "plausible" is not objectionable. Suppose that P and Q are equally plausible interpretations of a poem (that is, in our view they meet the coherence criterion equally well), and suppose furthermore, that P and Q are incompatible (Q contains a not-P within it somewhere). On the basis of this evidence, the correct interpretation of the work would be that it is ambiguous, and that neither P nor Q alone is correct. Margolis speaks of critical interpretation being "tolerant" of contrary hypotheses.

What can this mean? If it means that one can find incompatible interpretations of a work if one searches the bookshelves doggedly enough, he may be right, but the fact has nothing to do with the logic of interpretation. Does it mean that there are some critics who knowingly hold two mutually contradictory interpretations of a work? If so, there are very few of them, or those who do are reluctant to admit it. (I am not talking here about mere manners of speaking, like "Well, it's a tragedy, and yet in a sense it isn't really tragic," or about cases where a single interpretation attributes ambiguity to a work. If *King Lear* dramatizes unambiguously the presence of ambiguities in the world, it would not require two incompatible interpretations of the play to say so.)

After testifying to criticism's tolerance for contrary hypotheses, Margolis writes that, in contrast:

> We should not allow incompatible descriptions of any physical object to stand: at least one would require correction, else we would find that the disparities were due to the different purposes the descriptions were made to serve or the different circumstances under which they were rendered. But given the goal of interpretation, we do not understand that an admissable account necessarily precludes all others incompatible with itself. [P. 92]

How the goal of interpretation differs from the goal of describing a physical object Margolis never says. I assume that the goal of interpretation is a correct understanding of the work. But the comparison of our treatment of texts with our treatment of physical objects is instructive and can serve to show, I believe, why careless readers leap from the plurality of interpretations to the strange notion that criticism can tolerate inconsistency with logical impunity. I have before me a pencil.

1. It is on my desk.
2. It is cylindrical in shape, tapering to a point at one end.
3. It is mostly black.
4. It was made by a machine in Danbury, Conn.
5. It was designed for writing, and it writes well.
6. Its lead is softer than that of the yellow one next to it.
7. It's shorter than the yellow one, because I prefer writing with it.
8. It reminds me of my cousin, who chews pencils.

The point (of this list) is that one can say many very different things about something without running into incompatibilities. Each statement is a response to a different question about the pencil. Each refers to a different aspect of it, or a different relationship it has with something other than itself. (Perhaps we have the beginnings of structural, genetic, evaluative, affective, and generic "approaches" to pencils here.) Before one generalizes about the acceptance of incompatible interpretations of a literary work, one must be sure that the critics are not merely talking about different aspects of the work or different relationships that it has with something else.

Morris Weitz tried to do just that by looking at a large number of interpretations of *Hamlet* in detail, but he spoiled his own effort by assuming what he ought to have demonstrated: namely, that the different interpretations he reports on are "competing" interpretations. Weitz's position is that "there is no true, best, correct, or right explanation, reading, interpretation, or understanding of *Hamlet*, nor can there be as long as debate and doubt are possible on the categories of explanation and on what is primary in the play" (p. 258). It is a position based on the assumption that all interpretations of the play are in competition for the same prize, a prize to be awarded for "the best interpretation of *Hamlet*." Consider, for example, the following characteristic passage, which comes after Weitz's summary of the interpretations of E. E. Stoll, L. L. Schücking, and Theodore Spencer:

> Spencer offers his explanation of *Hamlet* as the best one. Other critics disagree. Indeed, each of the historical critics already discussed disagrees: Stoll claims that the best explanation of *Hamlet* is as a revenge tragedy with an ideal hero; Schücking says that it consists in *Hamlet*'s being understood as a revenge tragedy with a fashionable melancholy hero; and so on. Clearly, now, if there is the best interpretation of *Hamlet*, not *all* of these competing ones can be it. [P. 75]

But are these three interpretations properly regarded as competing, as incompatible, or mutually exclusive? One first becomes suspicious when one rereads Spencer and discovers that he nowhere makes any claim to the effect that his is the best interpretation of the play. In fact he is engaged in answering a rather special question: How can we account for the increase in what he calls the "largeness" or "universality" of the characters and events of *Hamlet* compared to those of the earlier plays?[17] And he attempts to account for it by postulating that Shakespeare in *Hamlet* brought into the foreground of the play certain conflicts in the Elizabethan views of the nature of man in a way that he had not before.

There would seem to be a conflict, however, between Stoll's "ideal hero" and Schücking's "fashionable melancholy hero." But then one opens the pages of Stoll and comes upon the statement: Hamlet "is melancholy . . . like the other Elizabethan revengers."[18] As Stoll uses the terms, there is no contradiction in regarding Hamlet as both ideal and melancholy, and there is no disagreement between Stoll and Schücking, at least on this score.

I confess that I see no reason for thinking that there cannot be several, different, correct interpretations of the same play, employing different "categories of explanation," none of them incompatible with or competing against any other. They could only be regarded as incompatible if they were all seen (as Weitz sees them) as answers to the single question: What is the best interpretation of *Hamlet*? If one returns to the critics, one finds, even when they claim to compete, that their interpretations are answers to very different questions.

Here, in brief, are the data on which Weitz bases his skeptical conclusions:

a) "For Robertson . . . *Hamlet* is an adaptation of a double play by Kyd."

b) "Stoll offers a full-fledged reading or interpretation as well as the meaning and understanding of *Hamlet* in his explanation that *Hamlet* is a revenge tragedy."

c) "Spencer explains *Hamlet* as the dramatization inside the hero's consciousness of the Elizabethan conflict between optimism and pessimism."

d) "Miss Campbell explains *Hamlet* as a study in the passion of grief."

e) "For Fergusson, *Hamlet* is a series of analogues, a multiple plot, on the major *donnée*, the theme of the attempt to find and destroy the hidden imposthume that threatens Denmark."

f) "Miss Spurgeon explains *Hamlet* in terms of its predominant imagery, as a tragedy of the inevitable natural condition of man, which is his infection and decay" (pp. 250–52).

Now this list is like the inventory of pencil descriptions in one important respect: none of the explanations is, on the face of it, incompatible with any of the others. (I am not claiming that all these interpretations are sound, or that critics never contradict one another; merely that an abundance of different interpretations proves nothing about the "logical weakness" of interpretation.) Weitz's claim that not all of them can be the best means very little. Best for what? Surely each of them is better than all the others for answering the question it sets out to answer. The same holds for our alleged inability to determine what is "primary" or "most important" in the play. Primary or most important for what? Osric may be most important for the critic who is curious about the function of fops in the play.

Even a single question about a literary work may receive several correct answers. Though the proposition is so vague that one hardly knows what is being asserted, let us assume that Hamlet delays. We are then confronted with the question, if we think it important, "*why* does he delay?" Consider the following possible interpretations or explanations of the delay:

1. He delays because he wants to make sure the ghost was truthful.
2. He delays because the mere thought of the deed arouses intense guilt feelings in him.
3. He delays because he is melancholy.
4. He delays because Shakespeare wanted to create suspense.
5. He delays because it is Shakespeare's point that our designs are not always within our control, rough-hew them how we will.

A single question, particularly a *why* question, may be several questions and may admit of several different compatible answers.

A possible objection could be raised to the effect that we have been talking about interpretations of different parts or aspects of the play, but that if one is talking about interpretations of the play *as a whole*, different interpretations must be incompatible. But let us say that "the whole play" is a revenge tragedy, that it exemplifies the consequences of grief, that it is designed to evoke pity, fear, and wonder. Have we made incompatible statements? Not necessarily, any more than when we say that the whole pencil is long and that the whole pencil was made in Danbury. Any proposition about a whole *is* a proposition about one of its aspects, some of its parts or relationships, and so on.

Turning the objection slightly, it could be pointed out that none of the interpretations Weitz cites is complete; each leaves much out of account. That is true, but it is true of any description of anything. One can't finish the job of describing something, because one can't exhaust the number of things it may be like or the number of relations it may have with other things. But then one seldom wants or needs to. Books that tell you everything you've always wanted to know about a subject never tell you everything you could know, and they usually give you more information than you wanted. An interpretation arises out of a desire to answer certain questions or to convey an understanding of what one considers, for some reason, to be important.

It is of the utmost importance to see that Weitz and Margolis defend their skeptical position on the grounds only of the existence of allegedly incompatible interpretations of the same work, never getting within striking distance of the sort of careful comparison of two such interpretations that would support their view. Once one looks hard at what two critics are saying, one will find either that their views, though different, are complementary (they're talking about different aspects of the work), or that they are incompatible and susceptible of being adjudicated according to the criteria I have sketched in this chapter. To the extent that one disavows procedures for discriminating among interpretations, one is driven into the solipsism represented by Georges Poulet's share in the dialogue at the chapter's head, where all you can say to someone who doesn't see things your way is "I don't identify with you."

Weitz's and Margolis's Anglo-American vocabulary is the vocabulary of logic and scientific method; their emphasis is on the relationship between the critical statement and the literary work it describes or explains. The French version of their skepticism, currently much in vogue, tends to be cast in the language of ontology and epistemology, but the grounds for the position are the same. If for us "There are so many interpretations of *Hamlet!*" for them "There are so many Racines!"

Roland Barthes once posed the rhetorical question: "How

could we believe, in fact, that the work is an object exterior to the psyche and history of the man who interrogates it?"[19] I would answer, how could we *not* believe that the work is an object exterior to the psyche and history of the man who interrogates it? One wants to know the antecedent and referent of that "it" that stands as the object of interrogation. It is possible, of course, even desirable, for a critic to interrogate his perception of the work. He may then arrive at a perception of his perception of.... Of what? Of the work, that object exterior to him, the very *same* object, by the way, which others may perceive differently. The fact that two critics may have different interpretations of a work seems to me to have no bearing on the ontological status of that work. One sometimes hears it said, as a manner of speaking between two readers who disagree, "Well you and I just aren't talking about the same play." But they are, and they know it. They just understand it differently. If what each of them understands in his own way is something "interior" to each, then they don't disagree at all, since they're not talking about the same thing. Nothing but confusion can result from taking the fact that something can be seen from different perspectives as indicating that there is nothing out there to be seen.

As an example of such confusion, take the slogan, "A literary work changes through time." I am not certain what the slogan means, but I know I would not want to see it on a true-false test. On one metaphorical level, the slogan is harmless enough, perhaps. For example, there are certain things we might be able to say about a work now that couldn't have been said when it was written: that it was written three hundred years ago, that it influenced Blake, that it wouldn't make a good movie, that it has a message for our time. A poem's relations with other things change and are no doubt inexhaustible. Furthermore, it is true that we may express our understanding of a work in idioms of our own and that our experience and our beliefs will influence what we notice or fail to notice in a work. But critics with a penchant for saying that works change, or that they are "voids" that each reader fills in his own way, or that the reader "creates" the work in the process of reading it, have something more in mind; namely, that there is no *Hamlet*, but only one age's *Hamlet*, and then another's, or one reader's *Hamlet*, and then another's, and so on. We, "knowing" what we "know," will see things in *Hamlet* that neither Shakespeare nor his contemporaries could have seen: we read a different play. And once these self-contradictions are admitted, of course, talk about understanding the play correctly becomes silly.

Let me offer two examples of this subjectivist confusion from critics writing under the influence of Barthes:

Edward Wasiolek writes that if we "turn a Marxist semiology" on the "overtly Christian system in [Tolstoy's] 'The Death of Ivan Ilytch,' " it "raises in our consciousness a distinctly different tale, so that Barthes is partly right when he speaks of criticism 'creating' the literary work."[20] First, Wasiolek interprets the story as Christian Parable:

> Ivan Ilytch lives his life badly, does not heed the biblical injunction of loving one's neighbor, thinks more about his material pleasures than his soul, and through a trivial accident is brought to the consciousness of how badly he has lived his life, to the subsequent consciousness of his sin, to contrition, and presumably in the last hours to some form of redemption. It is the tale of a man who has lost his soul.... In the humanist-Christian-philosophic vocabulary that we are most familiar with, we tend to read literature as if men lived only with ideas, souls, hearts, and other abstractions, unimpeded by the material world about us.

But Marx has led us to "new perceptions about our relations with things, especially things that we make, exchange, and own." Hence the reader acquainted with Marx reads a different tale. At this point, and at some length, Wasiolek convincingly demonstrates the importance of status and material possessions in defining Ilytch's career and bringing about his fall. "It is to things, too, that his memory returns when he attempts to recapture the uncorrupted Ivan Ilytch, when he was small and his relationship to the world was not the set of abstractions, manipulations and profit-and-loss exchanges that it becomes later."

I have no quarrel with Wasiolek's commentary on the story. What strikes me as odd is the notion that the Christian and Marxist readings result in "distinctly different," or even in *slightly* different tales. First, it is hard to see why a reader versed only in the humanist-Christian vocabulary ("Lay not up for yourselves treasures upon earth"; "I have seen all the works that are done under the sun; and, behold, all is vanity and vexation of spirit"; "a rich man shall hardly enter into the kingdom of heaven") would ignore the importance of *things* in the story, or find anything shocking or even unfamiliar in Wasiolek's "Marxist" reading. Second, if the objects in the story function as Wasiolek says they do, then they did so before he transformed the story "into a Marxist semiological system." One's acquaintance with a "system" *may* open one's eyes to things one wouldn't otherwise have noticed (it's a chancy business); on the other hand, it may also lead one to see things that aren't there; if so, so much the worse for the acquaintance.

To illustrate a similar point about how the meaning of a text changes, Frank Kermode writes of *Wuthering Heights* as follows:

> [Heathcliff] stands between a past and a future; when his force expires the old Earnshaw family moves into the future associated with the civilized Grange, where the insane authoritarianism of the Heights is a thing of the past, where there are cultivated distinctions between gentle and simple—a new world in the more civil south.... Cathy's two cousin-marriages, constituting an endogamous route to the civilized exogamy of the south—are the consequence of Heathcliff's standing between Earnshaw and Linton, north and south; earlier he had involuntarily saved the life of the baby Hareton. His ghost and Catherine's, at the end, are of interest only to the superstitious, the indigenous now to be dispossessed by a more rational culture.[21]

It's a safe bet that neither Emily Brontë nor her contemporaries would have *said* this of the novel, that it is Kermode's acquaintance with the categories of structural anthropology that allowed him to say it in this way, and that he might not have noticed the pattern he describes if the anthropologists had not taught him to look for such patterns. My point is simply that if Kermode is right, the pattern was there from the start.[22] I would suggest, further, that if he is right, he could have educated the novel's first readers to see the pattern. Indeed, it may even be the case that, if Kermode's paragraph were paraphrased in nontechnical language, we would see that it describes a pattern so fundamental that even those early readers perceived it, though they would have described it in different terms. We are likely to render or articulate an interpretation in our own idiosyncratic language, our own favored categories, and it is useful to do so. But the implication of our capacity to do so is that our way of putting things changes, not that novels change.

SUMMARY

What we interpret when we read, then, is a composition of words arranged by an author. We assume that he arranged them as he did for some purpose, though we acknowledge that his reasons may not always be apparent or recoverable, nor his aims achieved. We test our interpretations of parts of the composition against our developing understanding of the whole, and we prefer an over-all hypothesis that explains the whole as consistently, completely, and simply as possible. (The "we" here, if it is not universal, is nearly so. Few critics, whatever method they preach, willingly propound an inconsistent interpretation, or prefer an elaborate explanation when they know a simpler one would do as nicely, or feel comfortable in the face of evidence that clearly disconfirms their reading.)

Of course we bring many kinds of "extratextual" knowledge and information to bear on our interpretation of a text. No text "speaks for itself," though it exerts a power over what we may reasonably say about it by virtue of its being a complex arrangement of certain words (rather than others) in a certain order (rather than some other conceivable order). The knowledge and information we bring to the text includes linguistic knowledge, knowledge of literary genres, conventions and aims, and knowledge of human behavior. It may also include specific information about the author, his environment, his beliefs, his stated aims. We do not *deduce* our interpretation from such information. Rather we use it as a source of possibilities that the text may have actualized. In a sense we subject our knowledge to the complexity of the text, letting the composition filter out the irrelevant and the unlikely, letting it bend or complicate whatever is too rigid or simple in our expectations.

To the extent that a given work *is* complex, there will be many things we may want to say about it, both about its internal relations and its relationships to history and to its readers. The work will foster different interpretations, some of them much truer to it than others, many of them different though harmonious. However modern or technical the terms in which an interpretation is cast, if it explains the work well in the light of the criteria we have considered it will have laid bare a form, a meaning, or a fictional world which the work possessed, asserted, or dramatized from the beginning.

5

Theories of Literature

At the beginning of his and Austin Warren's *Theory of Literature* René Wellek wrote: "The first problem to confront us is,
obviously, the subject matter of literary scholarship. What is
literature? What is not literature? What is the nature of literature?"[1] It indeed seems obvious to think of these as first
problems. How can we talk intelligently about literature if we
don't know what it is that we are talking about? But the
questions have proven to be problem ridden; the history of
criticism would suggest that it has not been easy for anyone to
come up with answers that satisfy a wide audience over a long
period of time.

In this chapter we will consider several recent attempts to
answer Wellek's question, as well as the very similar question,
"what is poetry?" I have divided literary theories into three
distinguishable but closely related kinds: first, attempts to *define*
literature; second, attempts to specify its *function*; third, attempts
to describe the *institution* of literature. The first sort of theorist
is primarily interested in isolating those qualities or properties
which all literary works, and only literary works, possess.
He proceeds by classifying literature and then distinguishing
it from other members of the class. The second asks instead
what function, purpose, or need literature has fulfilled for
society or its members. The third looks to the reader and
seeks to discover what he does when he reads something

Parts of this chapter are from "Monroe Beardsley and the Shape of
Literary Theory," which appeared in *College English* 33 (1972): 558–70.
Copyright © 1972 by The National Council of Teachers of English.

as literature. Recognizing that society thinks of certain writings as being literary, and assuming that it deals with them in a special way, this sort of theorist tries to discover the conventions or implicit cultural rules that comprise the literary institution.

DEFINITIONS

Often the question "what is literature?" is taken as a call for a definition; not a simple lexicographer's synonym, or a report on the various meanings of the term, but a so-called real definition, proceeding in the traditional way through classification and differentiation, genus and species. Wellek's first two questions seem to indicate such a demand: what *is* literature and what is *not* literature? And together the answers should give us the nature of literature.

I propose to consider first Monroe Beardsley's *The Possibility of Criticism* because Beardsley's book illustrates with great clarity one of the major goals of literary theory: a determination of how to interpret and evaluate literature as literature, poetry as poetry.[2] Beardsley, adopting Austin's terminology, defines a poem as an imitation of an illocutionary act. But this, as he points out, "is to give a genus, not the differentia." So the class must be narrowed:

> Not all imitations of illocutionary acts are poems: for example, to mimic what someone has said, to tell a joke, to say something for the purpose of testing a public address system. What makes a discourse a literary work (roughly speaking is its exploitation to a high degree of the illocutionary-act potential of its verbal ingredients—or, in more usual terminology, its richness and complexity of meaning. And what makes a literary work a poem is the degree to which it condenses that complexity of meaning into compact, intense utterance. [P. 61]

In other words, poetry is distinguished from other imitative utterances by virtue of its richness and complexity, and from the rest of literature by virtue of its compactness and intensity. This, says Beardsley, is what poetry "essentially is."

The first problem that confronts us is the primary act of classification. Do poems actually belong to the class of imitation illocutionary acts? Before we can answer that question, we need to know more about the concept of imitation, a concept which Beardsley elucidates in the following two passages:

> The so-called "poetic use of language" is not a real use, but a make-believe use.... The writing of a poem, as such, is not an illocutionary act; it is the creation of a fictional character performing a fictional illocutionary act. [P. 59]

> Now, if a poem (as I argued earlier) is the imitation of a complex illocutionary act, then three fundamental and universal things can be said about poems: first, that every poem has an implicit *dramatic speaker*, whose words are the words we read or hear; second, that every dramatic speaker is confronted with some kind of *situation*, however broadly described; and third, that one of the fundamental axes on which the poem turns is the speaker's *attitude* toward that situation— how he purports to feel about it, his emotions and reflective thoughts. [P. 101]

Let us also have before us, in order to test these propositions, something we would presumably agree to call a poem; for example, Robert Frost's "Nothing Gold Can Stay":

> Nature's first green is gold,
> Her hardest hue to hold.
> Her early leaf's a flower;
> But only so an hour.
> Then leaf subsides to leaf.
> So Eden sank to grief,
> So dawn goes down to day.
> Nothing gold can stay.[3]

Beardsley assimilates poetry to fiction. According to his view, "Nothing Gold Can Stay" must be comprised of a fictional illocutionary act performed by a fictional character. But what reason is there for calling Frost's poem fictional, or for thinking that he did not mean precisely what he wrote? Certainly none of the references is to fictional or make-believe things. Frost was referring to the world we live in: to the green gold of early spring, to the shape of new leaves, to the loss of innocence, the brevity of dawn, and so on. The verse is carefully wrought, obviously not a spontaneous outpouring of first impressions, but then many speeches, letters, and essays are carefully wrought and subjected to intensive revision. Care in expression, attention to details of sound, rhythm, and metaphor may be exhibited in many good poems, but they hardly signal fictiveness. In short, the propositions in Frost's poem are true, he probably believed them, and their appearance in a poem gives us, in the absence of further evidence, no reason to think that he did not mean them.

The novel has always been so closely associated with fiction that perhaps the mere presentation of an extended piece of prose as a novel assures that readers will approach it as fiction and that intrusions of nonfiction in a novel will be occasions for initial puzzlement. But such is not the case with poetry, a genre as often associated with versification as with fictiveness. It is by no means uncommon to find sophisticated readers of poetry inter-preting the statements in a poem as what the poet said, as the following brief excerpts from Cleanth Brooks's *The Well-Wrought Urn* will show:

> "Keats meant what he said and he chose his words with care" (p. 155).
> " 'What men or gods are these?' the poet asks" (p. 156).
> "The poet [Donne] points out to his friend the infinite fund of such absurdities . . ." (p. 13).
> "The only way by which the poet could say what "The Canonization" says is by paradox" (p. 17).
> "The poet is saying: 'Our death is really a more intense life' " (p. 16).
> "But if Herrick is confused about what he is saying in the poem, he behaves very strangely for a man in that plight" (p. 69).[4]

Brooks was highly influential in popularizing the notion that a poem has a dramatic speaker, but *dramatic* is not tantamount to *fictional*. What Brooks directed us to attend to was the speaker, a man or woman with purposes and feelings, implicit in, or inferable from, the style and structure of a poem. But such a speaker is inferable from any discourse. As we saw in chapter 2, the very act of interpreting language involves the construction or projection of an intending speaker behind the speech. At the same time, Brooks and other New Critics also reminded us that the speaker *need* not be the poet and that just as there may be fictional prose, so there may be fictional poetry, ranging from the ironic to the fully fictional forms like the dramatic monologue and the prosopopoeia, which is to poetry what the history play is to drama.

Just as there may be borderline cases in prose, so may there be in poetry. Consider, for example, the disagreement between R. S. Crane and Yvor Winters over the proper way to read and judge Gray's "Elegy Written in a Country Churchyard." For Crane the poem is "an imitative lyric of moral choice rather than of action or of mood, representing a situation in which a virtuous, sensitive, and ambitious young man of undistinguished birth confronts the possibility of his death. . . ."[5] For Winters, however, such a way of construing the poem puts it "beyond the reach of [evaluative] criticism" and "outside of history." The poem, he claims, is "a meditation on death and on certain aspects of life, spoken not by a hypothetical young man dramatically rendered, but by Thomas Gray and to the best of his ability."[6] Crane's view is perfectly consistent with his definition of poetry as imitation, and Winters's with his own definition of poetry as statement. Winters, in other words, took what one might call the poetry of statement as his paradigm for all poetry and regarded the dramatic monologue as a rather deviant form. The Chicago critics, with their stress on mimesis, and the New Critics, in their severing of the poem from its biographical roots, took the monologue as paradigm.

It would appear, then, that some poems are imitation speech acts and that others are not (the poet-as-maker and poet-as-sayer dichotomy again) and that Beardsley's initial act of classification is wrong. But suppose he had been right. Suppose all poems were fictional. What inferences could we draw from such a fact? Beardsley claims to be giving a definition of poetry that tells us "what it essentially is." What can one mean by such a phrase, or by the notion of a definition which tells us the "true nature" of something? Let us remember that the history of criticism is replete with a variety of definitions of literature and poetry, many of them claiming to be "essential" or "real" definitions. Some of these definitions have been offered in a rigorous, some in a casual spirit. But all begin by placing literature in a class wider than itself. And they often proceed analytically to specify some of the differences between it and other members of the class. Meyer Abrams's now familiar scheme for categorizing literary theories is a useful summary of some of the broad classes most often used in defining literature, and all of them are thriving in our own time.[7] He speaks of "mimetic" theories, which treat literature within the class of imitations, copies, representations, and the like, and then proceed to differentiate it in terms of the manner or object or purpose of imitation; and of "expressive" theories, which differentiate it from other expressive activities according to what it expresses, or how it expresses it, and so on; and of "pragmatic" theories, which treat it within the class of effect-producing things, and then differentiate it according to the kinds of effects which it has or ought to have.

Any act of classifying expresses or embodies the classifier's preoccupations and interests. It is a way of construing, either consciously or unconsciously, the subject under consideration; it reflects a decision or predilection for treating literature *as* something—namely, as a member of the class to which one assigns it. And if the initial act of deciding what class literature belongs in reflects interests and values, so, of course, do the various ways of differentiating it from other members of the class. No doubt the two classes in terms of which literature has been defined most persistently in our century are *language* and *art*. R. S. Crane has pointed out the tendency of modern critics to treat poetry under the genus language and then to differentiate it by contrasting it with scientific or philosophical or ordinary language.[8] If the language of science is literal, poetry must of course be metaphorical. If the language of science is univocal, that of poetry is essentially ambiguous or paradoxical. If ordinary language is used for making statements, poetry must make pseudostatements. As if the essence of a thing consisted in whatever qualities it possesses that are least like, or even directly opposite to, qualities possessed by other members of its class!

One of the dangers of this definition by contrast method is that it will inevitably suit some poems better than others. And the "essence" singled out for attention will be different depending on which class we begin with and which features of that class we use for contrast. Beardsley's procedure is a case in point. "Richness," "complexity," and "intensity" seem like harmless enough terms; but why do they receive the spotlight rather than "truth," "universality," "simplicity," or "persuasiveness"? Is Beardsley telling us what poetry is? Or has he buried in an allegedly objective definition his view of what good poems are like? What about all those simple or expansive or not quite unified works that we would nevertheless agree to call poems?

Because literature is composed of language, and because, since the late eighteenth century, there has been a strong tendency to see it as one of the arts, these two classes "feel right"—so right that they are taken for granted. The chaotic variety of definitions that have followed even from these two categories is partly a function of the fact that language and art are themselves not easy to define. It is also a function, however, of the protean nature of what we call literature. The heart of the matter is this: Works of literature belong to many classes, can be construed as many things. They are interesting to us for many reasons and in many ways. That is why literary theory, when it involves the search for the proper or real or essential nature of literature, is always fruitless. To say that literature belongs to a certain class is to say no more than that it is similar to certain other things and that those similarities may provide insight into it or suggest new ways of asking or answering questions about it. But to talk about *the* class to which it belongs is, so far as I can see, to misunderstand the nature of classification. Given a single, well-defined goal of inquiry, a single classification system may prove especially fruitful and come to dominate a given discipline for a long period of time, so that the class seems to have some natural sanction for it. But that is a result of human interest, and interests in literature not only change in time but also vary considerably at any one time.

The position I have been urging here—and it has been urged by others in other ways[9]—runs directly counter to one of the major aspirations of twentieth-century criticism—the search for ways of interpreting and evaluating literature that are uniquely suited to its nature and that do not employ "nonliterary" methods and criteria. This search has been so widespread that it led Abrams to include a fourth sort of critical theory in addition to the expressive, mimetic, and pragmatic theories. This "objective" sort of theory, he points out, "on principle regards the work of art in isolation from all these external points of reference [author, world, and reader], analyzes it as a self-sufficient entity constituted by its parts in their internal relations, and sets out to judge it solely by *criteria intrinsic to its own mode of being*" (p. 26, my italics).

As instances of the search for an "objective" theory, Abrams quotes Eliot's dictum that "when we are considering poetry we must consider it as poetry and not another thing," and John Crowe Ransom's call for recognition of "the autonomy of the work itself as existing for its own sake." We could add, among countless such rallying cries, A. C. Bradley's desire "to consider poetry in its essence" and to stress its "intrinsic," "*poetic* value,"[10] or Northrop Frye's advice to the critic "to make an inductive survey of his own field and let his critical principles shape themselves solely out of his knowledge of that field."[11] When Frederick Crews argued in *PMLA* that literary works might usefully be regarded from sociological and psychological viewpoints, he was answered in a subsequent issue by Morton Bloomfield, who scolded him for slighting the "autonomy" of literature which has "its own structure and rules," and by Lawrence Hyman, who appealed to the importance of "genuinely literary value."[12]

If my argument is correct, however, an "objective" theory of literature is a will-o-the-wisp. To read or interpret or assess a work of literature is to read or interpret or assess it *as* something—as an expression of thought or feeling, as a complicated statement about life, as a subtly persuasive piece of rhetoric, or whatever. If we say that we ought to read it *as literature*, we are at best advocating special attention to the complexities of the work and to its possible individual differences from other things of its kind; at worst we are deceiving ourselves, claiming an undeservedly privileged status for our way of reading.

Beardsley's theory illustrates this aspiration, and the ways in which it is futile, very nicely. In his opening attack on Hirsch's intentionalist position, he avers that "the proper task of the literary interpreter is to interpret textual meaning." Conversely, "the *general* and *essential* task of the literary interpreter cannot be the discovery of authorial meaning." Why is this the case? Why is it somehow "unliterary" to worry about authors and their intentions? Because "the primary purpose of literary interpretation" is "to help readers approach literary works from the aesthetic point of view." But the aesthetic point of view turns out to be, *by definition*, simply the point of view that is interested in the text itself (pp. 32–34). Apparently aware of this circularity, Beardsley admits that a full answer to the question must be deferred until the "nature of literature" has been defined. As we have seen, however, little help can come from that corner. The definition fails to distinguish clearly between literary and non-literary writings.

What about his attempt to establish purely literary criteria for judging poetry?

> To be artistically good, a poem must bring together some different meanings and include elements of contrast or opposition or tension. It must unify them so that its tension is contained within a whole that possesses a notable degree of integrity and independence. And it must take on, as a whole, a pervasive quality, or set of qualities, which I call regional qualities: its melancholy, its irony, its wit, its vigor, its vitality, etc. The more complexity it enfolds, the more thoroughly it is unified, the more intense its qualities, the better it is as a poem. [Pp. 91–92]

How can such a claim be justified? Beardsley does not pretend that it is a conclusion derived from the study of a large number of good poems, and of course he could not do so, since the good poems could not have been separated from the less good ones until the criteria for poetic goodness had been formulated. He suggests rather that it follows from the differentiae of his definition. (What makes a discourse literary is "its richness and complexity of meaning." What makes it a poem is "the degree to which it condenses that complexity of meaning into compact, intense utterance.") But even if one were to accept the notion that complexity, unity, and intensity are the differentiae of poetry, ignoring the suspicion that they were normative criteria to begin with, does it follow that poems that possess these qualities to a high degree are better than those which do not? Are mammals better mammals for being very hairy?

But Beardsley's logic is not too clear on this point. If being a poem is a matter of degree, so that the more complex, unified, and intense an imitation discourse it is, the more of a poem it is, then it is still unclear in what sense a poem that is "more of a poem" is *better* than one that is "less of a poem." Why not settle for saying simply that this poem is more of a poem than that one, whatever that would mean? If he claims, on the other hand, really to distinguish poems from nonpoems, then he seems to assume that the possession to a high degree of the qualities that differentiate a species make a member of the species *good*. It might be true that possessing those qualities would make the poem a good *example* of poetry—for illustrative purposes, say. But that is surely a more trivial sort of goodness than most critics or Beardsley himself want to be talking about when they praise poems.

In his earlier work, *Aesthetics: Problems in the Philosophy of Criticism*, Beardsley tried to provide grounds for this definition of goodness, but in fact only enlarged the circle of his theory, by claiming that it is a functional definition. A good work of art is *good for* producing "aesthetic experience." What is an aesthetic experience? One which is unified, intense, and complex. But the only justification given for this claim seems to be that "these are points on which, I take it, nearly everyone will agree."[13]

Beardsley's definition of poetry, like most, fits some poems better than others—complex dramatic monologues with a clearly fictional speaker, say, better than simple lyrics like Frost's. It would appear that the more specific a definition is (that is, the narrower the class and the more precise the differentiae) the more likely it is that the definition will fail to include many poems. Conversely, if the definition is sufficiently broad and flexible to include all poems, it is likely to cover a great deal of language and human behavior that is not literary. Unfortunately, because of our desire to treat art *as art*, poetry *as poetry*, and so on, one of the dominant modes of argument in contemporary aesthetics has been to reject as trivial or illogical any characterization of literature, poetry, or art which fails to distinguish clearly between art and nonart, poetry and nonpoetry, literature and nonliterature.

For example, the so-called expressive theory of art—the notion that works of art express or reveal the feelings, attitudes, talents, or ideas of their creators—is patently true, however banal it may seem when described in such general terms, and however subject it may be, like all truths, to misunderstanding and misuse. And on the basis of such a general notion a great deal of excellent and subtle criticism rests. But it has become a veritable philosopher's tic to reject the expression theory out of hand on the grounds that any other, nonartistic product of behavior, or behavior itself, is also expressive. Thus Joseph Margolis calls the theory "trivial" because "whatever one does 'expresses' one's own self." (Of course Margolis's own definition, "A work of art is an artifact considered with respect to its design," is likewise trivial, since any artifact may be considered with respect to its design.[14]) And Eliseo Vivas writes: "In order to expose their flaw, let us ask defenders of theories of expression what function does expression perform that cannot be performed by any other means? ... Emotion can be expressed by non-artistic means."[15] (Needless to say, Vivas's own definition, "A poem is a linguistic artifact, whose function is to organize the primary data of experience that can be exhibited in and through words,"[16] falls by the same wayside.)

Similarly, Suzanne Langer writes, in *Feeling and Form*, that "all drawings, utterances, gestures, or personal records of any sort express feelings, beliefs, social conditions, and interesting neuroses; 'expression' in any of these senses is not peculiar to art, and consequently is not what makes for artistic value."[17] But by the time her own criteria for defining poetry and art have been fully developed, we discover that they hold true not only for prose fiction, but also "for the essay and for genuine historical writing" (p. 257); we discover that argumentative, discursive language can embody a "feeling pattern," just as nondiscursive language and nonverbal art forms do (p. 302); and finally, we learn that we may perceive "emotional forms"—the distinguishing feature of art works—in "actual experiences" and in natural objects like birds and mountains (p. 395). The line between art and nonart has broken down. In fact one begins to suspect that the more important the feature of art or poetry that a theory tries to draw our attention to is, the greater the likelihood that it will be a feature found outside of art as well.

What we are watching, I think, is a group of aestheticians running on something of a logical treadmill. Convinced that the proper task of the theorist is to define "literature" and "art," and taking definition very literally as the discovery of exact and uncrossable limits, they have little trouble exposing the flaws of other theories, while inevitably exposing their own to the same objections. In other words, the fact that the aspect of literature singled out for attention by a literary theory is an aspect shared by nonliterary things is not a flaw at all. The only flaw occurs when the theorist makes excessive claims for his theory—claims about its unique or privileged appropriateness to the subject matter. No self-respecting scientist would make such claims for his discipline: neither the biologist's, the chemist's, the landscape architect's, the ecologist's, or the botanist's way of understanding a tree is *the* way; and no way is exclusively "arboreal."

THE FUNCTION OF LITERATURE

In Dryden's *Essay of Dramatic Poesy*, Lisideius offers a definition of a play as "a just and lively image of human nature, representing its passions and humours, and the changes of fortune to which it is subject, for the delight and instruction of mankind." But his friend Crites, always somewhat fussy, twits him and raises "a logical objection against it; that it was only *a genere et fine*, and so not altogether perfect."[18] That is, Lisideius's definition gives the class to which plays belong, and their purpose or final cause, but fails to distinguish plays from other members of the class. In the same spirit we might note that Beardsley's definition is only *a genere et specie*. It attempts to specify those qualities or attributes the possession of which qualifies something as poetry, but it ignores the end, purpose, or function of such attributes. As we saw, this lack prevented Beardsley from offering any reason for accepting unity, intensity, and complexity as criteria of literary value and thus lent an arbitrary quality to his entire argument. Other recent theorists, particularly those aware of the very problems entailed in "real definitions" that we have been considering, have sought to ground their theories on some notion of the *function* of literature for the individual reader or for society as a whole.

One of the most interesting, original, and provocative of such theories is that put forth by Morse Peckham, first in a book entitled *Man's Rage for Chaos: Biology, Behavior, and the Arts* (1965) and later in several essays that have been reprinted together in *The Triumph of Romanticism* (1970).[19] Peckham's argument is intricate, and it encompasses not only literature but also painting, music, and architecture. While I cannot begin to do full justice to its details and its scope, I believe that a summary can reveal the shape of the literary aspect of the theory in an instructive way.

For Peckham, "the ultimate question about any kind of human behavior is a question about why any human being should trouble to do it. That is, what is its *function* in biological adaptation?" The only way to approach the matter, he claims, is "to consider artistic activity as a mode of biological adaptation," "an adaptation of man to the environment" (*MRC*, p. x). Since he is interested primarily in the behavior of the art audience, he naturally enough begins with a general description of art in terms of that behavior: "*A work of art . . . is any artifact in the presence of which we play a particular social role, a culturally transmitted combination of patterns of behavior*" (*MRC*, p. 49). This role involves, among other things, a neglect of the object's "possibilities as a tool for manipulating the environment." And it is accompanied by a certain "framing" of the object which isolates it from the rest of the environment (on a mantelpiece, in a museum or auditorium, within a garden, in a comfortable chair in a quiet room) in order to "subdue distraction of other perceptual fields" (*MRC*, p. 65). For any given art, the perceiver's role is very demanding. It "requires long training, involves an unusual degree of self-criticism" (*MRC*, p. 66).

Peckham is perfectly aware that this definition excludes very little. As he says, any object, from a landscape to a stone to a wall covered with books, may be a work of art so long as it is a "perceptual field which an individual uses as an occasion for performing the role of art perceiver" (*MRC*, p. 68). But one can distinguish between what one might call a casual from a cultural work of art by taking a broad historical perspective. If, over a long period of time, a kind of functional object—a pot, an ax handle, a church—exhibits no change that cannot be attributed to a more efficient performance of its utilitarian function, then it did not serve generally as an art object. If on the other hand, the historical sequence reveals changes in "style" that are not explainable in utilitarian terms, then the objects *did* serve, in part, the cultural function of art. "Stylistic dynamism," or the tendency toward "rapid stylistic drift," is characteristic of all the arts (*MRC*, pp. 26, 71). Such objects, and literature is one of them, thus have at least two kinds of function: the utilitarian function (storing wine, splitting wood, enhancing religious worship) and another, artistic function signified by the fact of changes in style. In literature, the utilitarian functions may vary from period to period and may include such things as teaching, entertaining, reinforcing old truths or inculcating revolutionary ones. These "semantic" functions of literature are utilitarian, not artistic (*MRC*, pp. 128–29).

The question is raised, then: "*Why* is art—a term we can now safely use—characterized by stylistic dynamism? Why does the social role of perceiving art demand it? Why does the poor artist have to sweat and toil to provide it? Why is the perceiver of art so greedy?" (*MRC*, pp. 72–73). At this point Peckham redescribes stylistic change as the violating of the rules, either explicit or implicit, of the previous stage of the art. The changes in style become ways of "presenting the unpredictable." "It would appear that the artist's primary function is executed by offering a problem, but *not* a problem to be solved. He simply presents the unpredicted; he offers the *experience* of disorientation" (*MRC*, p. 79).

Peckham mentions four general methods by which literature provides its readers with the experience of disorientation. Poetry, for example, affords violations of our expectations of regular rhythms and natural subject-verb-object sentence patterns (*MRC*, pp. 202–23). Dramatic and narrative fiction offer us "plot," which "consists of problem exposure and solution postponement." (The "real motive" for Shakespeare's portrayal of Hamlet's early failures to kill the king was simply to present sustained discontinuity. "Expectation is built up for revenge, and then it doesn't happen" [*TR*, pp. 305–7].) They also offer us characters whose behavior is unpredictable. For Peckham, "the importance of a character is defined by the amount of discontinuity he displays" (*TR*, p. 314). Though these particular applications of the theory deserve close examination,[20] let us concentrate instead on the general shape of the theory and the nature of functional explanations.

Peckham concludes, then, that disorientation or "discontinuity" is "the distinguishing or differentiating attribute of artistic behavior." "The distinguishing character or attribute of the perceiver's role is search-behavior focussed on awareness of discontinuities." Though the artist, however, is rewarded for "breaking or violating rules, for offering discontinuous experience," "all other human activity is normally rewarded for offering a continuity of experience, for following rules" (*MRC*, p. 220). And it is this disjunction between the artist's function and that of other occupations, and between our ordinary and our art-perceiving roles, that introduces the "biological" and functional explanation of artistic behavior, an answer to the question, "What, then, is the function of art that makes us live better, that adapts us better to the biological-perceptual situation we find ourselves in?"

> Man desires above all a predictable and ordered world, a world to which he is oriented. . . . But because man desires such a world so passionately, he is very much inclined to ignore anything that intimates that he does not have it. And to anything that disorients him, anything that requires him to experience cognitive tension he ascribes negative value. Only in protected situations . . . can he afford to let himself be aware of the disparity between his interests, that is, his expectancy or set or orientation, and the data his interaction with the environment actually produces. [*MRC*, p. 313]

The art-perceiver's role, Peckham concludes, is just such a situation:

> Art is rehearsal for those real situations in which it is vital for our survival to endure cognitive tension. . . . Art is the exposure to the tensions and problems of a false world so that man may endure exposing himself to the tensions and problems of the real world. [*MRC*, p. 314]

The shape of the whole theory, then, looks something like this: certain data are laid out which seem to call for an explanation. They are (*a*) the presence of discontinuity in the "insulated" experience provided by art for anyone who has learned to play the art-perceiver's role, (*b*) the human tendency in other kinds of behavior to seek order and continuity, (*c*) the necessity of encountering and enduring "cognitive tension" in real life situations. Then a hypothesis is offered to explain the data: the hypothesis, namely, that art behavior persists and has the character it has because it allows people to rehearse the endurance of cognitive tension.

This is, as far as it goes, a perfectly respectable procedure. But something is missing. The hypothesis, though it is adumbrated at the beginning of the study, is not described in detail until the end, and what is missing is nothing short of some kind of evidence or set of reasons for accepting the hypothesis. Peckham is quite right in not supposing that his data lends support to the hypothesis; it merely raises the question for which the hypothesis provides a possible answer. (If this failure to go beyond the hypothesis to reasons for believing it to be true seems surprising, it should not; most literary theories stop abruptly at this point. Peckham's theory is remarkable not for its shortcomings, but for its unusually systematic exposition, which renders its shortcomings more apparent.)

What, then, *might* support the hypothesis? I would suggest that one cannot even say what sort of evidence would count in its favor until a prior step is taken. What is needed is some consideration of other possible explanations for the same data. Only in the light of such consideration can one test the hypothesis at all. We shall see, however, that when the theory is exposed to a rival what happens is not so much a confirmation or refutation as a collapse of both rivals into something much less than full theoretical or explanatory status.

One of the most striking facts about Peckham's theory, after all, is that the facts about literature and life on which he dwells have been explained in an altogether different fashion by a traditional theory that seems antithetical to his own. Sir Philip Sidney was echoing a well-established tradition when he wrote that poets offer us a golden world in exchange for our brazen one, and so was Bacon when he spoke of poetry as affording to the spirit of man "a more ample greatness, a more perfect order, and a more beautiful variety than it can anywhere (since the Fall) find in nature." In Frost's laconic phrase poetry offers us not an immersion *in* but "a momentary stay *against* confusion." And Eliot wrote that "it is ultimately the function of art, in imposing a credible order upon ordinary reality, and thereby eliciting some perception of an order *in* reality, to bring us to a condition of serenity, stillness, and reconciliation."[21] The tenacity of the view that literature offers us an experience *more* ordered than the experience of life makes one suspect that Peckham must be looking at a very different set of data, thinking of different novels and poems, or talking about hitherto unnoticed aspects of the literary canon. But that, as we shall see, is by no means the case.

One of the most eloquent modern spokesmen for the traditional view is Frank Kermode. In a published series of lectures, Kermode described our need for, in the words of his title, *The Sense of an Ending*—the sense that one's evermoving present is significant by virtue of its relationship to an anticipated conclusion.[22] Even in this skeptical age, he writes, "in 'making sense' of the world we still feel a need ... to experience [a] concordance of beginning, middle, and end" (p. 35). And it is the function of literary fictions to satisfy this need, satisfy it by offering a world in which, as we read, we sense the ending, though we know not how it will be achieved, as immanent in the moment.

Kermode's book is very different from Peckham's. Tentative, somewhat meandering, it makes little pretense to system. Yet Kermode, too, explains literary fictions by reference to "some basic human 'set,' biological or psychological. Right down at the root, they must correspond to a basic human need, they must make sense, give comfort" (p. 44). "Biology and cultural adaptation require it" (p. 58). Yet fictions change. Old patterns, old ways of tying plots together, are discarded. And something like Peckham's stylistic dynamism appears as Kermode speaks of literary history. For novels are also shaped by another need, the need to accommodate our skepticism, our understanding of how the world really is. It is because of this "pressure of reality" that epistolary novels give way to historical novels, novels to antinovels, tragedy to grotesquery, and so on. And it is this pressure too that makes us reject routes to the end that seem too pat, too direct. "Peripeteia ... is present in every story of the least structural sophistication":

> Peripeteia depends on our confidence of the end; it is a disconfirmation followed by a consonance; the interest of having our expectations falsified is obviously related to our wish to reach the discovery or recognition by an unexpected and instructive route. It has nothing whatever to do with any reluctance on our part to get there at all.... The more daring the peripeteia, the more we may feel that the work respects our sense of reality; and the more certainly we shall feel that the fiction under consideration is one of those which, by upsetting the ordinary balance of our naive expectations, is finding something out for us, something real. [P. 18]

Granting Kermode's primary interest in fictions, both dramatic and narrative, it is nevertheless clear that on many matters he is in fundamental agreement with Peckham. Both men acknowledge the basic human need for order, for making sense of experience, as well as the tension or cognitive dissonance attendant upon our failure to achieve it. Both acknowledge the presence in the reader's experience of peripeteia and denouement, discord and resolution. (Peckham does not argue that fiction denies resolution, only that it postpones it.)

Nevertheless, on the crucial question of the function of literature and the causes of historical development in literature the two theories are radically opposed. Wherein then do the differences lie? Kermode attributes the shapes of fiction to a tension between two forces, our need for order and our skepticism, rather than to a single force. That is an attractive feature of his theory, recognizing as it does the significance of knowledge and belief in the literary experience. Peckham sees the arts, including literature, as performing a unique function, different from other products of human behavior by virtue of the high value placed on discontinuity. Hence the apparent need for a unique explanation. Kermode, on the other hand, explains literary phenomena by fitting them into a broad pattern of activities. For him, literature is a response to the same needs that also give rise to theology, history, and science. Though it is different from them (largely because its fictions are generally recognized as fictional), it nevertheless manifests many of the same characteristics, and for Kermode the history of the various arts and sciences are roughly parallel.

The antithetical or polar terms of this debate, the descriptive categories accepted by both parties—order and disorder, continuity and discontinuity, expectations fulfilled and unfilled, making sense and failing to make sense—are useful critical terms, sufficiently clear and distinct when employed in the context of a discussion of a particular piece of art or literature. But certain muddles arise when they are used in a theoretical context—in the context, say, of questions about whether the experience that literature offers is necessarily or fundamentally ordered or disordered. We seem to be in a situation where, finally, if one were asked whether one agreed with one theory or the other, the only proper answer would be a hesitantly proffered "yes and no."

No one who had read or watched the opening lines or scenes of *Lear* or *The Way of the World*, *Pride and Prejudice* or *The Trial*, *Paradise Lost* or "Prufrock," would be baffled by the suggestion that they raise problems and questions; or that certain characters in them appear to be disoriented, and the audience with them; or that as the work proceeds some of the questions raised get answered, others do not. Perplexities arise, expectations are created, frustrated, satisfied. Any given work of art, no doubt, can be seen as being ordered in some respects, disordered in others. Kilmer's "Trees," as its detractors enjoy pointing out, is highly chaotic with regard to the spatial analogies it presents between trees and women. Yet just as surely it is highly unified with respect to the attitude or feeling it expresses. It also appears that these antithetical qualities are qualities that a given work may possess in greater or in lesser degree. Consider Kermode's term "consolation," for example. It may be that works like *Lear* or *La Nausée* (which Kermode comments upon very shrewdly) reach conclusion, or bring about a degree of satisfaction. But it is not at all clear that the relationships that order the world of either work are really very consoling or more coherent than the relations through which even the most disenchanted among us experience the passing of time in our sublunary and nonfictional worlds.

This point is made with some force by Peckham's and Kermode's fundamental agreement that both halves of the order-disorder continuum are needed to describe any work of art worth discussing. The agreement is not surprising, for at either pole boredom sets in. Kermode argues passionately and well against avant-garde theorists who propose or predict a future for the novel from which plot, cause-effect relations, character, and all the other unifying devices of the tradition will be eradicated, imitating, as it were, a world of pure haphazard contingency. His point is that without some semblance of relationship between its parts the novel will cease to satisfy our deep need for making sense of things. But he also recognizes another way of describing the situation—a way that speaks not at all to the question of the function of fiction. There is a relationship between the orderliness of language (syntactical, semantic, narrative, or whatever) and the reader's ability simply to understand it. When one realizes that a string of words or of narrated events is intended to resist the understanding entirely, then one stops reading altogether—not because the strings are not consoling, but simply because after the very few minutes it takes for the novelty to wear off, one gets bored. Our reading need not be directed always by a single point, but we won't endure reading that is altogether pointless. There are more engaging activities awaiting us elsewhere.

Having considered two theories of the function of literature, we may meet the notion of *function* itself head on. We use this notion in more ways than one and must recognize the differences between them. Peckham speaks, for example, of the function of wine jugs as the storing of wine and of the function of teapots as the brewing of tea. This is a very common use of the term: the function of something is the use for which it has been designed, or the use to which it is put. If you ask the potter about the function he intends his pot to serve, he will be able to tell you what that function is. In this sense the idea of function occasions little difficulty. Of course an object can be used for a function for which it was not designed, or for more functions than one. The wine jug may hold matchsticks in front of a fireplace; the concrete block, wedged under the tire, may function to prevent the car from rolling downhill. The mirror in its ornate frame may serve as an attractive decoration even as it allows for last-minute primping and covers up the chink in the wall. In each case, the function is a readily understood answer to the question "What is it used for?" An object's function is relative to someone's use of it, and it may serve different functions for different people. A recent philosopher of science rejects out-of-hand the notion that "the function of long hair on dogs is to harbour fleas," but that rejection is clearly due to his inability to take the flea's point of view.[23]

This familiar sense of "function" is not the one upon which Peckham and Kermode centrally rely, however. Though Peckham acknowledges that literature has served different purposes for different people at different times, he considers these not as "primary" but as contingent, "extra-poetic" functions. He is perfectly willing to assign a "primary" function to every work of art which neither the artist nor his audience would have hit upon if they were asked why they were making, viewing, listening to, or reading the work of art in question. Nor would they necessarily agree after having been told by Peckham why they were doing what they were doing. Peckham's view of the artist and perceiver, after all, is highly deterministic. The artist does what he does because he is "rewarded" for doing it. His "role *requires* him to create occasions in which the perceiver's predictions will be frustrated, and the receiver's role *requires* him to look for them" (*TR*, p. 262, my italics). This is a notion of function, then, that is not related to the purposes of either maker or user. The function of works of art is "to provide occasions for the rehearsal for the endurance of cognitive tension" (*TR*, p. 265), and the function of the artist, whether he knows it or not, is to produce such works.

As for Kermode, though his theory grants both writer and reader a good deal of creative and cognitive freedom and though he is developing a traditional conception of the function of literature, his notion is likewise independent of the avowed purposes of those who design and those who use novels; independent, that is, of such frequently expressed purposes as teaching, delighting, inspiring virtuous action, and so on, as well as of the disconsolatory or expectation-frustrating purposes of those modern writers with whom he takes issue.

Now there are cases where we speak of the function of something quite apart from some maker's or user's purposes. One can say that the function of the heart is to circulate and restore the blood, or that the function of blinking is to keep the eyes moist. In this case function is simply the contribution something makes to the operation of some system. On the other hand, it is easy to confuse these two meanings of "function." Peckham, for example, introduces his theory with the following pair of questions: "To me, the ultimate question about any kind of human behavior is a question about why any human being should trouble to do it. That is, what is its *function* in biological adaptation?" But the two questions are not at all equivalent; many appropriate answers to the first question, including statements of purposes or goals, would be foolish as answers to the second, and vice versa.

How seriously can we take Peckham's stress on biology and on adaptation to the environment? If he were making the sort of claim that biologists sometimes make about the *original* adaptive function of some physiological features (like the claim that man's erect posture enabled him to see over the tall grasses when he had been driven from the forests), his argument would have had to take a very different direction, and it would have a very different significance. Yet in a sense Peckham is in the predicament of a biologist trying to tell us what the "primary," but not the original, function of our erect posture is. Obviously the original adaptive function of our posture is not its primary present function. What can be meant by "primary" in such a situation? Opposable thumbs serve a great variety of functions, though no specific one of them is primary. And the claim that their function is to assist in holding things is not analogous to Peckham's artistic function, since it is a general description that includes most of the specific uses, whereas Peckham's artistic function *excludes* most avowed, specific artistic purposes.

Would the removal of the arts from a society produce a citizenry unable to endure cognitive tension? The mere raising of the question seems a bit ludicrous. How would one know, given the many qualities of works of art (including orderliness as well as disorderliness), which one or ones it would be whose absence gave rise to whatever symptomatic disturbances we might detect?

Peckham seems to want to argue instead that the rehearsal function is primary in the sense that all art and only art provides it. But this is highly dubious. Neither poems with perfectly regular rhythms, nor difficult poems we are very familiar with, provide much of it, and philosophical treatises and daily life often provide a great deal of it.

There is another use of "function" which lies outside the domain of expressed purposes and which has some bearing on arguments about the function of literature. (I am indebted here to an example that has been similarly employed by A. R. Louch.[24]) One might ask an anthropologist for an explanation of the institution of marriage and receive answers like the following: The function of marriage is to preserve the species, to provide protection for the young, and to insure the possibility of determining an individual's lineage by assigning a status to the new members of the society. But these answers hardly tell us why individuals "trouble" to marry, except in the case, perhaps, of a couple with an overdeveloped social conscience. Sometimes, indeed, there are no children in need of protection and none anticipated or desired. Now it so happens that these functions are often performed within a marital framework. One can observe married adults providing, with varying degrees of success, for their offspring, and so on. But this is dependent on whether a society's definition of the institution, embodied in its laws and ceremonies, includes these activities. If another form of marriage were adopted in which the children were turned over nameless to the state or commune, then marriage would not perform these functions. And conversely, species preservation and childrearing would not be absent from a society that lacked marriage altogether unless one simply *meant* by marriage any institution that included those functions. Thus, to say that the cultural function of marriage is so-and-so, disregarding individuals' reasons for marrying, is circular in so far as so-and-so-ing is part of what is entailed by marrying in that culture.

There is a loose analogy between the anthropologist's talk about marriage and Peckham's talk about the function of literature and art, and both should be viewed as subject to the same restrictions: The best that can be said for either is that it designates a function or functions that an institution may serve from time to time. But just as there may be highly valued childless marriages, so there may be highly valued literary works that produce a sense of calm stability rather than disorientation. (Peckham's theory, like Beardsley's, describes some works better than others.) The analogy is weak, however, at a crucial point: many societies do in fact explicitly associate childrearing with marriage and one might expect a member of such a society to say, if asked, that indeed childrearing is an activity that the society locates within the institution of marriage. But our society can hardly be said to conceive of the institution of literature reading or art perceiving in terms of the function Peckham assigns to them. There are words in our language that connote a function; words like "awl" and "barometer," "baptism" and "raindance," "medicine" and "fungicide," "market researcher" and "exorcist." *Literature* is not among them. There are certain objects and activities, like the kidneys and sneezing, whose functions have been discovered and can be tested. Literature is not among them.

It is possible, then, having conceived of some desired goal, to ask whether or how well an institution serves it. One might, that is, assess a particular marriage, or marriages in a particular social group, in the light of any of several conceivable functions. And one might do the same for a literary work or genre, asking whether it is well designed for whatever purpose one has in mind, be it Peckham's or Kermode's or any one of the variety of functions that have through the ages been mistakenly put forth as *the* function of literature in general. To broaden our horizons a little: John Dennis claimed that the function of literature is "to instruct and reform the World, that is, to bring Mankind from Irregularity, Extravagance, and Confusion, to Rule and Order," and Tolstoy claimed that it is to join men together in mutual feelings. The Russian formalist Victor Shklovsky claimed that the function of literature is "to make one feel things, to make the stone *stony* . . . to impart the sensation of things as they are perceived and not as they are known," while Frederick Crews claimed that it is to reconcile competing conscious and unconscious psychological pressures.[25] I see no way to make sense of these or any other claims as to *the* function of literature except by seeing them as claims about the function that literature *ought* to serve, a formulation which we will discuss in the next chapter.

It would be consoling but illusory to think that the function of literature will be clarified for us if only we wait patiently for the biologists, anthropologists, psychologists, or philosophers to discover the last word about human nature. Though new developments in these fields will provide us with new questions to ask about literature, they cannot determine *the* function of literature at all. It is not that the sciences are deficient, but that literary works are too varied, written and read for too many reasons, to permit the definite article. One can no more talk about the function of literature than one can talk about the class to which it belongs.

Institutional Theories

Let us turn now to a third and rather different approach to literary theory, an approach similar to Peckham's but favored by critics who are aware of the difficulties one faces in trying to establish the *essential nature* or *function* of literature. These critics raise a new set of questions: What do people *do* with a text when they treat it as literature? How does reading literature differ from reading nonliterature? Recognizing that observable differences between literary and nonliterary language are hard to discover, but that there nevertheless must be reasons for the persistence of the concept of literature, they turn their attention on literature as a social institution, a set of conventions that are brought into play when one regards something as literature.

John Ellis's *The Theory of Literary Criticism*,[26] like Beardsley's *The Possibility of Criticism*, is an attempt to set critics straight on a wide variety of matters: on the proper way to analyze literature, on the evaluation of literary works, on the aims of literary study, and on the usefulness for criticism of other disciplines. And as was true for Beardsley, the matter of definition is crucial for Ellis: from it all else follows. But Ellis approaches the matter of definition from an apparently new direction:

> When we seek a definition, what we are seeking is not a statement of the features held in common by the members of the category, but the appropriate circumstances for the use of the word and the features of those circumstances that determine the willingness or unwillingness of the speakers of the language to use the word. Factual research into such a definition is possible, but it will be research not into the common features of the category, but into the responses of speakers of the language to appropriate and inappropriate uses of the word. [Pp. 34–35]

> Literary texts are not defined as those of a certain shape or structure, but as those pieces of language used in a certain kind of way by the community. They are used as literature. [P. 42]

This last sentence, as Ellis points out, may sound circular, but it is not. The way to discover what literature is, he argues, is to discover what people do with those objects they call literature. What are people doing when they use something "as literature"? In answering this question Ellis resorts to the standard New Critical ploy: he contrasts the literary use of language with the "ordinary," "utilitarian" use:

> We ordinarily use language as a means to a specific end, to achieve given purposes in our everyday lives. We find out things we need to know and tell others things we need to communicate to them. We use such

language for a purpose that is relevant to the immediate context of the utterance of that language. It is
a specific context in which a specific person addresses
others for specific reasons to do with that context.
After the purpose is achieved, the language can be
forgotten; its purpose is over. . . . When, on the other
hand, we treat a piece of language as literature, we characteristically do something quite surprising: we no
longer accept any information offered as something to
act upon, nor do we act on its exhortations and impera-
tives. We do not generally concern ourselves with
whether what it says is true or false, or regard it as
relevant to any specific practical purpose. In sum, we
no longer respond to it as part of the immediate context
we live in and as something to use in our normal way
as a means of controlling that context; nor do we
concern ourselves with the immediate context from
which it emerged, and so are not taking it up to learn,
in our normal way, something about that actual everyday context. [Pp. 42–43]

And so, with the aid of a deceptively simple contrast, we
arrive at "the *definition* of literature":

literary texts are defined as those that are used by the
society in such a way that *the text is not taken as
specifically relevant to the immediate context of its
origin.* [P. 44]

The definition is not easy to get a handle on. The key terms
get switched around from passage to passage. The statement
quoted above, for example, reads "the text is not taken as
specifically relevant to the immediate context of its origin," but
elsewhere we read that "the original context of origin is not
relevant to literary texts" (p. 46), or that a literary text is not
referred to its "original context . . . or to any other" (p. 44). But
one is justified in suspecting the presence of a vague but very
strong antihistoricist bias. Ellis proceeds to use the definition to
bludgeon any and every sort of attempt to make the context of
the origin of a work relevant to our understanding or evaluation
of it. He rules all such attempts out of bounds "by definition."[27]
Remember that Ellis invited us to look to the community of
language users for our definition of literature. How do *they* use

the word? What uses of the word do they deem appropriate and inappropriate? But Ellis's definition did not grow out of any such research. It appeared as if by conjuration out of a contrast with ordinary, everyday, utilitarian speech. But it so happens that one language community to which Ellis refers very frequently in his book is comprised of literary historians (the confused enemy) like Fredson Bowers, Rosalie Colie, Frederick Crews, Leon Edel, E. D. Hirsch, Robert Spiller, James Thorpe, and Eugene Vinaver—not to mention Marx and Freud—all of whom find it highly appropriate to link literary works in one way or another with the specific contexts of their origins. This fact proves little. Perhaps these critics constitute a deviant idiolect within the linguistic community. But the burden of proof is on the proposer of the definition. If the definition rests on usage, one wants to know whose, and how the information was attained.

Is it the case (assuming that literary professionals don't count as speakers of the language) that the "ordinary reader" of poems or novels regards it as "inappropriate" to raise questions about the connections between them and the context of their origin? I have not done Ellis's lexicographical research either, but I believe it is not unusual for the man in the street to ask questions like: Who wrote it? What was he like? Was he mad? What do you suppose he meant by that? Why do you think he wrote it *that* way? Do you suppose he wanted us to admire that character? Or even: Do you think people in Dickens's day considered that sad or funny? Did the people of Shakespeare's time really talk like that? Did they really feel that way about kings then? Or (when someone points out a complicated metaphorical pattern): Did he really intend to make it all fit together that way? Such questions (I aver) do not raise eyebrows. Neither do they violate linguistic or social conventions. Indeed they seem intimately connected with the institution of literature, and I suspect it would seem perfectly natural and in no way ungrammatical, even if slightly metaphorical, if someone were to claim that he read literature for the express purpose of connecting himself to the past.

In this respect it is noteworthy that Ellis himself, when his guard is down, frequently talks as if he were referring texts to their originators. We find him saying, for example, that "authors do not always write about the same thematic issues" (p. 225), and that "poets are men who have a gift for using language to produce structures of words that will say what they want to say, have implications that they wish to imply, and leave carefully open what they want to leave open" (p. 124).

As one might expect, Ellis's definition has some very peculiar consequences. If, for example, one reads Swift's "A Modest Proposal" as referring to the Irish problem of the 1720s, one is not reading it as literature. To read it that way is "to trivialize the meaning of the satire, to prevent ourselves from thinking about its relation to life in the deepest sense" (p. 139). Why a recognition of the situation Swift was referring to should prevent us from thinking of the general and timeless significance of the satire Ellis does not say. What one would like to know is how a reader could possibly think anything at all about "the depth of Swift's meaning," or recognize its universality, *without* knowing what Swift was referring to.

Similarly, one cannot read contemporary literature as literature, for one is then too close to the context of its origin. For Ellis the contemporary work has not yet become a work of literature: "The contemporary audience's response to the contemporary text is not only a local one, but a fundamentally untypical one too; that is, untypical of what is to be the text's most normal and most literary situation, in which it is distinctively not a document in ordinary contemporary language" (p. 148). What has happened to Ellis's deference to "the speakers of the language" and to the community's use of literary works? Is there a social convention to the effect that one can either read literature or a current bestseller but not both at once?

If we return to the preliminaries that led up to Ellis's definition, we find at least three other propositions regarding what we do not do when we "treat a piece of language as literature." Let us examine each of them briefly:

1. *We do not "accept any information offered as something to act upon."* This may sometimes be true, in a sense, though the notion of acting upon information is very vague. If we accept as acting upon information such things as forming expectations and making decisions and judgments about what is going on in the work, the proposition is clearly untrue. If it refers only to physical actions like voting for Willkie or going to the store to buy a quart of milk, then it is sometimes true, but also true of most ordinary speech and most writing. We received a letter

from our son this morning reporting on his first two days at camp. Fortunately it called for no overt action; but it was literature only from a doting parent's point of view.

2. *"We do not generally concern ourselves with whether what it says is true or false."* This, as I have stressed before, is false. Novels contain statements about the world of the novel and the world outside it, and we frequently have to decide as to their truth. If Frost's poem "Nothing Gold Can Stay" had begun "everything precious endures," and continued in that direction, the reader would be concerned about more than the rhythm.

3. *We do not "regard it as relevant to any specific practical purpose."* This is sometimes true, but it is also often true of the way we treat historical, philosophical, and scientific texts, as well as cocktail party chatter. If, with Arnold, we regard "learning how to live" as a specific practical purpose, it may well be false.

Since all of Ellis's prescriptions about how one ought to study, interpret, and evaluate literature are derived from these propositions about what we do not do when we read something as literature, we need not pursue them. The propositions themselves are wrong. First, they are wrong because they are based on a misunderstanding of the reading process, a reductive and exaggerated contrast between literary and ordinary uses of language. Second, they are based on a thoroughly distorted notion of what uses of the word "literature" speakers of the language would regard as "appropriate and inappropriate." If Ellis were correct, references to the history, sociology, or psychology of literature would seldom occur, and when they did, they would be regarded, if not as self-contradictory, at least as deviant expressions.

Jonathan Culler, in *Structuralist Poetics*, has presented an institutional theory of literature that has several advantages over Ellis's.[28] Like Ellis he is promulgating "the study of literature itself as an institution" (p. 118). He wants to investigate, for example, "the conventions of reading which comprise the institution of poetry" (p. 115). But instead of starting with what we do *not* do when we read, he explores what we do. And instead of working from a single convention of literature reading, he recognizes that there are many and that they may vary from genre to genre. Culler's book is the clearest and most judicious

explanation in English of the ideas of the so-called structuralists—
writers like Roland Barthes, A. J. Greimas, Roman Jakobson,
Julia Kristeva, Claude Lévi-Strauss, and Tzvetan Todorov. His
goal is much like mine: "to specify how we go about making
sense of texts" (viii). He has made what I regard as an unusually
valuable contribution to the study of criticism. For these reasons,
I want to explore Culler's notion of poetics in some detail.

Culler's model for the study of literature as an institution or
set of conventions is the linguist's analysis of linguistic competence as that concept has been defined by Chomsky. A
speaker's competence—his knowledge of a language—is that
system of rules and conventions which he must be presumed to
know how to follow if he is able to form new sentences in the
language and to understand new and unfamiliar sentences in the
language when he hears them. It is "the implicit knowledge
possessed by those who successfully operate within the system":

> Though the rules of *la langue* may be unconscious they
> have empirical correlates: in the case of language they
> are manifested in the speaker's ability to understand
> utterances, to recognize grammatically well-formed or
> deviant sentences, to detect ambiguity, to perceive
> meaning relations among sentences, etc. The linguist
> attempts to construct a system of rules that would
> account for this knowledge by formally reproducing
> it. [P. 9]

What Culler seeks to describe is not linguistic but literary
competence. As he points out:

> To read a text as literature is not to make one's mind a
> *tabula rasa* and approach it without preconceptions;
> one must bring to it an implicit understanding of the
> operations of literary discourse which tells one what to
> look for.
>
> Anyone lacking this knowledge, anyone wholly un-
> acquainted with literature and unfamiliar with the
> conventions by which fictions are read, would, for
> example, be quite baffled if presented with a poem.
> His knowledge of the language would enable him
> to understand phrases and sentences, but he would
> not know, quite literally, what to *make* of this strange
> concatenation of phrases. He would be unable to

read it *as* literature ... because he lacks the complex
'literary competence' which enables others to proceed. He has not internalized the 'grammar' of literature which would permit him to convert linguistic
sequences into literary structures and meanings. [Pp.
113–14]

Among the facts that a description of *linguistic* competence
seeks to explain are the following: that a speaker who knows a
language can both utter and understand sentences that have
never been uttered before, that he can distinguish between
grammatical sentences ("The boy climbed the tree") and ungrammatical sentences ("The boy climb a trees"), that he can
relate sentences to other sentences in certain ways ("Are you
hungry?" is like "Are you happy?" in one respect, and like "I am
hungry" in another), and so on. The facts that a theory of
literary competence should explain, according to Culler,

can be of many kinds: that a given prose sentence has
different meanings if set down as a poem, that readers
are able to recognize the plot of a novel, that some
symbolic interpretations of a poem are more plausible
than others, that two characters in a novel contrast
with one another, that *The Waste Land* or *Ulysses* once
seemed strange and now seems intelligible. [P. 123]

What, then, are the conventions that constitute literary discourse? What is it that a reader must have internalized if he is to
make sense of a poem and know how to take it? Let us consider
"the expectations with which one approaches lyric poetry, the
conventions which govern its possible modes of signification":

The primary convention is what might be called the
rule of significance: read the poem as expressing a
significant attitude to some problem concerning man
and/or his relation to the universe. [P. 115]

To write a poem is to claim significance of some sort
for the verbal construct one produces, and the reader
approaches a poem with the assumption that however
brief it may appear it must contain, at least implicitly,
potential riches which make it worthy of his attention.
Reading a poem thus becomes a process of finding
ways to grant it significance and importance, and in

that process we call upon a variety of operations which have come to form part of the institution of poetry. [P. 175]

For example, "attempt to read any brief descriptive lyric as a moment of epiphany. If an object or situation is the focus of a poem, that implies, by convention, that it is especially important" (p. 175). Or again, "another convention of a different kind, especially useful in the case of obscure or minimal poems where the fact that they are presented as poems is the one thing we can be certain of, is the rule that poems are significant if they can be read as reflections on or explorations of the problems of poetry itself" (p. 177). Or yet again, "typographic arrangements can be given spatial or temporal interpretations" (p. 162).

The second major convention is that we read poems as atemporal and impersonal. That is, we do not regard the "I" and the "you" of a poem as referring to "empirical individuals," and when a poem begins with the word "yesterday," we do not relate that reference to the day before the poem was written or to the day before our reading of it. Though such "spatial, temporal and personal deictics" may force us to construct a fictional situation within which the poem makes sense, "we are aware that our interest in the poem depends on the fact that it is something other than the record of an empirical speech act" (p. 165).

Another "fundamental convention of the lyric is what we might call the expectation of totality or coherence":

> Ordinary speech-acts need not be autonomous wholes because they are but parts of complex situations to which they contribute and from which they derive meaning.... Even if we deny the need for a poem to be a harmonious totality we make use of the notion in reading. Understanding is necessarily a teleological process and a sense of totality is the end which governs its progress. Ideally, one should be able to account for everything in a poem and among comprehensive explanations we should prefer those which best succeed in relating items to one another rather than offer separate and unrelated explanations. [Pp. 170–71]

Closely related to this convention is the convention according to which we expect "metaphorical coherence" and "thematic unity" (p. 115). Culler includes an account of metaphor, synecdoche, and metonymy, which, along with other figures, "serve as a set of instructions which readers can apply when they encounter a problem in the text." "One identifies phrases which require semantic transformation and considers what kind of move seems justified in each case.... Our conventions lead us to expect and to value metaphorical coherence and thus to preserve the vehicles of rhetorical figures and to structure them while we are investigating possible meanings" (pp. 181–82).

Now Culler's discussion of these expectations and conventions, particularly when fleshed out with his well-chosen examples, is unquestionably instructive. It is instructive in much the same way that a good, sophisticated poetry text "with apparatus" is instructive: it offers a set of tips, of things to be on the lookout for, of good questions to ask about the poem at hand. Culler does not and could not, after all, tell us what we are sure to find in a poem; we may search for significance or coherence and not find it because it is not there. He points rather to things worth seeking in an effort to make sense of the poem. I do not mean this comparison to be in any sense disparaging. A treatise on poetry does not have to be of theoretic or definitional value to be very valuable indeed. The point is to understand its value correctly.

By this time the reader will have anticipated my reservations about Culler's structuralist poetics; they are reservations, however, that do not deny, but merely redescribe its value. He has enumerated conventions and expectations relevant not to the reading of poetry alone but to the careful, attentive, and sensitive reading of most writing. That is, he has not distinguished the institution of poetry from the institution of writing.

I do not intend to deal with each convention in detail, since many of them have already received attention in other guises elsewhere in this study. The "expectation of totality or coherence," for example, is closely related to the "coherence criterion" which we employ to sort out correct from incorrect interpretations. (See chap. 4.) I believe that it applies, however, to our reading or hearing of any sentence, paragraph, speech, essay, or scientific explanation or theory. Grasping a principle according to which the parts of something may be seen to cohere is so closely related to the general notion of understanding something that it hardly seems possible to claim this as a peculiarly poetic expectation. We *do* read "teleologically" because we assume that speakers and writers order their words to some purpose. It is true that in many poems the principle of coherence will be much harder to discover than that of an everyday sentence, that the poem may be complicated and difficult. This in itself is sufficient to justify admonitions of patience and care and other interpretive procedures that would not usually be necessary for reading newspapers and dime novels. It is as if Culler's poetics, here and elsewhere, were a way of saying "read closely" and a demonstration of how to do it.

Since Culler does not claim that figures of speech are peculiar to poetry, it is clear that the explanations he gives of them are as relevant to our understanding of figures of speech whether they occur in speech, prose, or poetry. One may expect, perhaps, more, and more subtle, figurative speech in poetry, but as Culler points out, there is no essential difference between the "properties of the language of poems" and the properties of "language of any kind" (pp. 162–63).

Consider next the "primary convention . . . the rule of significance." "Read the poem as expressing a significant attitude to some problem concerning man and/or his relation to the universe."

It is certainly true that by offering something to the world as a poem the poet is claiming, as Culler says, that there is something here worth attending to. The special typography, the rhyme and rhythm, the divisions between stanzas, and so on, are, apart from whatever special effects they may have in individual occurrences, ways of saying, in effect, "read me with care." These framing devices are part of what identify poems as poems. But philosophical treatises, sermons, and newspaper editorials have their own framing devices, each of them making the same claim. Indeed there is something oddly nebulous about Culler's discussion of this convention. Does not the very act of speaking to someone presume by convention that the act will be "worthy of attention," whether or not it turns out to be so? How significant an attitude do we expect? If our expectations are too high, we will often be disappointed or take a light poem too seriously. Or is the emphasis on the word "attitude"? Do we expect poetry to express attitudes in some way that other utterances do not? If so, Culler does not specify how. Certainly many kinds of nonpoetic utterances and even nonlinguistic behavior express attitudes.

Does one attribute a different sort of significance to a group of sentences when one reads them as a poem than when one reads them as something else? One of the "facts" that a theory of literary competence is called upon to explain is the fact "that a given prose sentence has different meanings if set down as a poem." But it is not obvious that this is a fact at all; or if it is one it is not clear in what sense it is true. Consider Culler's remarks on William Carlos Williams's poem "This Is Just to Say":

> THIS IS JUST TO SAY
>
> I have eaten
> the plums
> that were in
> the icebox
>
> and which
> you were probably
> saving
> for breakfast
>
> Forgive me
> they were delicious
> so sweet
> and so cold[29]

A note left on a kitchen table which read 'This is just to say I have eaten the plums which were in the icebox and which you were probably saving for breakfast. Forgive me, they were delicious: so sweet and so cold' would be a nice gesture; but when it is set down on the page as a poem the convention of significance comes into play. We deprive the poem of the pragmatic and circumstantial functions of the note (retaining simply this reference to a context as an implicit assertion that this sort of experience is important), and we must therefore supply a new function to justify the poem. Given the opposition between the eating of plums and the social rules which this violates, we may say that the poem as note becomes a mediating force, recognizing the priority of rules by asking forgiveness but also affirming, by the thrust of the last few words, that immediate sensuous experience also has its claims and that the order of personal relations (the relationship

between the 'I' and the 'you') must make a place for
such experience. We can even go on from there and say
that the world of notes and breakfast is also the world
of language, which cannot assimilate or stand up to
these moments when, as Valery says, 'le fruit se fonde
en jouissance.' The value affirmed by the eating of
plums is something that transcends language and cannot be captured by the poem except negatively (as
apparent insignificance), which is why the poem must
be so sparse and superficially banal. [Pp. 175–76]

Culler says that an actual note comprised of these words
would be a "nice gesture." I would add that the actual poem is a
nice poem. But I am not sure that the meaning Culler finds in the
poem is not to be found in the note. The note itself *is* a
"mediating force, recognizing the priority of rules by asking
forgiveness. . . ." This is a good interpretation of the note as
note: of what the note writer was doing (asking forgiveness), of
why he felt obliged to do it (the priority of rules), and of how he
justified his deed (the claims of sensuous experience). This is just
what a reader would make of the note if he understood it, and it
is a requisite beginning, at least, for understanding the poem.

I am not sure that the last part of Culler's explication is right,
whether we are thinking of the poem or the note. Is the poem
sparse and superficially banal because Williams is saying indirectly that "the value affirmed by the eating of plums is
something that transcends language," or because Williams is
imitating the simple language one would find in a note, and
could not do that successfully if he ran on too long? Is it even the
case that language fails to stand up to this moment? Isn't "they
were delicious / so sweet / and so cold" precisely adequate to the
purpose of the occasion? (They were *so* delicious that I think you
will forgive me.)

Culler says later that "the convention that poems may be read
as statements about poetry is extremely powerful. If a poem
seems utterly banal it is possible to take banality of statement as
a statement about banality. . . . The ability of this convention to
assimilate anything and endow it with significance may give it a
dubious status. . . ." (p. 177). That is correct. If it is legitimate to
take this poem as being about the limitations of language, I see
no reason why we could not take this note as being about the

same thing. Not everything that a sentence or poem entails, implies, or presupposes can be regarded as its topic or as what it is about. "I have eaten the plums" entails "I have eaten at least one plum," implies that the speaker believes he ate some plums, and presupposes that there were some plums to be eaten. The sentence is nevertheless not an assertion about any of those facts. But if we allow any of them as relevant to the significance of the poem, we could just as well allow them to be relevant to the significance of the note.

It seems to me very questionable, then, that "a given prose sentence has different meanings [in Culler's sense] if set down as a poem." But this does not deny that a poem calls special attention to the meaning (and implications, presuppositions, and entailments) of the sentence, just as one might call attention to the meaning (and beauty) of the note by saying, "look at this note Joan left. Isn't it lovely?" And the typography serves to slow the reading down, order it, emphasize certain words, and so on. It is not that the poem gives the sentence more significance, or a different meaning, but that it invites us to explore and appreciate the meaning and significance it has. Perhaps such invitations, whether in poetry or in life, ask us also to generalize the significance somewhat, to see the sentences as fine examples of something, as representing certain characteristics of human relationships, say.

There are, of course, many sentences which we would not be surprised to find in literature but which would amaze us on the street ("The invisible worm that flies in the night . . ."; "Season of mists and mellow fruitfulness . . ."). But they would mean the same thing if they were said outside of literature. Insofar as the context helps to determine the significance of an utterance, it might have a different significance depending on its occurrence in this poem rather than that, this life situation rather than that, and so on. If Joan had written the note we were considering for Jack, its significance would have been different in the sense that its nouns and pronouns would have had real rather than fictional referents. But that is not a nonpoetry-poetry distinction. The note as we have been considering it hypothetically in the preceding paragraphs also has fictional referents (Joan and Jack, for example).

The convention according to which we treat poems as atemporal and impersonal is one we have discussed before. It is certainly true that we do read poems, as we read most other kinds of writing, as "something other than *the record of* an empirical speech act," if by that we mean a written transcription of a prior oral speech act. True, too, that we often devise "fictional constructs" which we employ as interpretive devices. On the other hand, we surely read a poem as the trace of "a specific and individual act"—namely the poet's act of writing the poem. What one wants to avoid is overstating the case for poetry as fiction. When we read "I placed a jar in Tennessee," we don't care whether Stevens ever did that, but we read it (or ought to) as a poem Stevens wrote about the effects of introducing a foreign object in a scene on the way we perceive the scene. More to the point, however, we certainly read "The Convergence of the Twain" as a poem Hardy wrote about the loss of the Titanic. And "Elegy for Jane" is a poem Roethke wrote about a student of his who was thrown by a horse. The poem opens "I remember the neckcurls ... and her quick look."[30] Surely the "I" is Roethke and the quick look Jane's. Different conventions are appropriate for different poems, and we find out which are appropriate by reading them.

I do not propose to consider Culler's "poetics of the novel," since doing so would be by and large repetitious. I will refer to it obliquely, however, by returning to the list of exemplary facts that a "model of literary competence" ought to explain:

1. *"That readers are able to recognize the plot of a novel."* What is it about this fact that requires explanation? Culler seems to find it surprising that "readers can tell that two texts are versions of the same story, that a novel and a film have the same plot.... A theory of plot structure ought to provide a representation of readers' abilities to identify plots, to compare them and to grasp their structure" (p. 205). Now in fact Culler does not deal with this question; he goes on to discuss instead various proposals, by Propp, Todorov, Greimas, and others, for *classifying* plots. This is understandable, since the reader's ability to recognize the plot of a novel calls for no explanation, is not remarkable or problematic. A reader who can follow the sequence of events reported in a newspaper story, a biography, a history, and recognize the way the events are related to each other has all the competence he needs to recognize the plot of a novel. Or if a reader's ability to recognize all of these calls for

explanation, it would be explained in terms of our capacities to recognize differences and similarities, to ascribe causes and reasons to events and actions, to imagine people doing things, and the like. These same capacities account also for our ability to recognize two very different sequences of actions, whether recounted in a novel or anywhere else, as similar on some abstract level—as instances, say, of a fall from greatness, a biter bitten, an equilibrium destroyed and restored, a successful quest, a progress through release to clarification, an expulsion of a scapegoat, and so on.

2. *"That some symbolic interpretations of a poem are more plausible than others."* The only explanation that Culler gives of this fact is that we prefer those interpretations "which best succeed in relating items to one another rather than offer separate and unrelated explanations." This is true as far as it goes, and it is equally true of why we find some interpretations of anything more plausible than others.

3. *"That two characters in a novel contrast with one another."* This seems no more in need of explanation than the fact that we can recognize the plot of a novel.

4. *"That* The Waste Land *or* Ulysses *once seemed strange and now seems intelligible."* I find nothing in Culler's book that would distinguish this problem from the problem of why any act, artifact, or utterance that initially seems strange may with time seem intelligible, from "Nude Descending a Staircase" to the mechanisms under the hood of a car, from the policies and pronouncements of statesmen like Bismark and Disraeli to any everyday action which puzzles us at first because we don't understand its reasons and causes. Aren't the poem and novel now intelligible (insofar as they are) because readers worked on them and discovered reasons that explain what Eliot and Joyce were doing and how the parts of the texts are related to each other?

In short, it is not at all certain that these facts require a special *literary* theory to explain them, or that a model of *literary* competence is needed.

We can get some perspective on Culler's attempt at a poetics if we reflect upon what a model of *linguistic* competence can and cannot do. Knowledge of a language is necessary for understanding sentences in the language, but it is never sufficient for understanding an actual sentence fully. Similarly, linguistics describes the rules we must know in order to create and understand sentences, but it doesn't fully explain how we create and understand them. Chomsky, in a recent lecture, pointed to one of the "mysteries" which linguistics has yet to solve—the mystery of why a given person utters the sentence he utters.[31] That mystery could never be explained by a reference to a system of conventions alone, but it can be explained easily by reference to what the speaker wants to say or do and why he wants to say or do it.

Laertes' linguistic competence was necessary for him to understand Claudius's "the Queen his mother lives almost by his looks," but it does not account for his ability to know what queen Claudius was referring to, nor could it have told him why Claudius said what he said. For that, a knowledge of the full nonlinguistic situation is necessary.

It is easy to exaggerate or misconstrue the significance of linguistic competence as an explanatory model, and it is not always clear what sort of explanation is required by certain facts of language behavior. For example, Chomsky once pointed out that the two sentences "I persuaded John to leave" and "I expected John to leave" are not parallel in structure, though on the surface they appear to be. In some sense (though these are not quite Chomsky's terms) "John" in the first sentence is the object of "persuaded" and the subject of "to leave," while in the second "John" is the subject of "to leave" but it is the whole phrase "John to leave" that is the object of "expected." Chomsky explained our different ways of understanding the two sentences by postulating an "internalized grammar" which "assigns very different syntactic descriptions to these sentences." The sentences are "very different in the deep structure that underlies them and determines their semantic interpretations." This internalized grammar "may very well not be immediately available to the user of the language."[32] If our question, however, is simply what a speaker needs to know to understand the difference between the meaning and structure of the two sentences, we could answer it by saying that he needs to know what persuading is and what expecting is. If he knows that, he knows that one can expect events, but that one cannot persuade them; one can only persuade people. In fact this knowledge has a certain priority over the ability to "assign syntactic descriptions," since

if "persuading" denoted an act you could perform on events—
that is, if it meant something other than what it means—no one
(not even a linguist) could assign a different syntactic description
to the two sentences. One advantage of the semantic over the
syntactic explanation is that it invokes no knowledge of which
the speaker is not fully aware.

Of course knowing the meaning of the words one uses is part
of one's linguistic competence. Knowing what sort of activities
"persuading" and "expecting" regularly denote is knowing two
of the "rules" that constitute English. The point is simply that
even in linguistics there can be questions about what sort of
knowledge needs to be presumed in order to explain some fact of
linguistic behavior. Before a particular theory is developed to
explain something, it is important to be clear about what it is
that stands in need of explanation.

There is an additional sort of murkiness in discussions of
linguistic competence. Chomsky was talking about the competence involved in knowing a language, period. He was not
talking about competence in a sense that admits of degree, a
sense that would distinguish among more or less competent,
skillful, lucid, or cogent speakers of the language. Nor was he
talking about the full competence needed to understand actual
utterances. Culler, it seems to me, was trying to follow Chomsky
in this regard, determining what it is that makes it possible to
read literature, period. Ideally (and Culler admits that this ideal
may be unattainable) a theory of literary competence in this
sense would distinguish reading literature from reading nonliterature just as a theory of linguistic competence would distinguish knowing a language from not knowing a language, or
knowing English from knowing French. I am not sure whether
Chomsky's abstract Competence is a postulate linguists need or
not. I have tried to show that in literature not only is the ideal
unattainable; there is no need for such a theory, for anyone who
can read can read literature.

This is not to say, however, that some readers of literature are
not more competent than others, or that everybody who knows
English is equally competent at reading English poetry. Knowledge of literary traditions, of many individual works, and of life
can contribute to one's ability to read literature competently,
sensitively, intelligently. And sometimes knowledge of some

special set of facts is necessary for understanding a particular work. One could speak in a vague but useful way of something called literary competence just as one could speak of rhetorical, culinary or diplomatic competence, or competence at diagnosing symptoms or predicting the weather. But it is not a competence that could be spelled out in such a way as to explain anyone's ability to understand this or that particular work. Nor could it be acquired in a way that would guarantee understanding, any more than rhetorical competence can guarantee an orator's ability to persuade the next hostile audience he faces.

There may be some danger of confusing the knowledge that is needed to describe a piece of language and the knowledge that is needed to understand what is being said in it. Consider, for example, some of those terms that denote literary works and nothing else, like "sonnet," "picaresque novel," "morality play," *Bildungsroman*, or (in their literary senses) "interlude," "plot," or "invocation." Obviously a knowledge of these terms is essential if we are to identify a sonnet as such, call it by its name, and converse with literary critics. But it is not always the case that one has to know what a sonnet is in order to understand a particular sonnet (Keats's sonnet "On the Sonnet" is a notable exception) any more than it is necessary to know what a noun phrase is in order to use or understand a noun phrase in a sentence. On the other hand, knowing that there is a sonnet tradition may help us understand a particular sonnet more easily: we may be on our toes for certain arrangements of ideas and spot them more quickly. One builds up a sort of expertise through wide reading and through making the sorts of discrimination that our list of terms is designed to achieve.

The general and not very surprising rule, for literature as for other kinds of understanding, would seem to be "The more you know the better," with the proviso not to let your knowledge mislead you. One can understand Anthony Hecht's poem "The Dover Bitch" to some extent without knowing "Dover Beach," but one won't know what Hecht was parodying. To understand Ishmael Reed's "I am a Cowboy In The Boat of Ra," you have to know something about the Egyptian pantheon, the Old West, the heroes of modern jazz, and a good deal of jive talk. Sometimes you have to know about other literature and sometimes not. It depends, in literature as in life, on what the speaker or author is referring to, mimicking, parodying, or working with.

CONCLUSION

If we step back a short distance from the several kinds of literary or poetic theory we have been examining, we should be able to see why there is no reason to expect a theory of literature as an institution to succeed where attempts to define the essential nature or function of literature had failed. For if there were a single and definable set of special activities that one engaged in when reading something "as literature," it would presumably be related to a special set of qualities that those things we read as literature possess and to the special function that literature performs. Peckham himself tried to establish such a triangular relationship among the institution, the function, and the qualities of literary works. The three concepts—what it is, what it is used for, how we use it—are closely related. If I am using something as a shovel, it must be because it has certain properties that enable me so to use it, properties that allow it to perform certain jobs. The specificity with which we can define any one of the three members will determine in large measure the specificity with which we can define the others.

One might ask why it is that, if one can specify neither the function of literature, nor its essential attributes, nor what special things readers of literature do or need to know, one can still use the word, know what it means, and even understand someone who speaks of reading a nonliterary text *as literature*. The answer is that there are many qualities that we do tend to associate loosely with literary works: fictiveness; special care taken with form or with language; the use of concrete and sensuous detail; a stress on unity and "self-containedness"; emotiveness, perhaps, and entertainment value; or perhaps high seriousness and a special blending of the particular and the universal; and so on and on. None of these attributes is possessed by all literary works, and all of them can be found outside of literature. Some we associate more with some genres than with others. But they permit us to carry on perfectly well. A statement to the effect that I am reading something as literature may suggest any one or more of these qualities, depending on the context. It suggests one thing if I say it with reference to the sign along the highway ("Conviction means loss of license"), something else if I am referring to Boswell's *London Journal*, and something still different if I am referring to an Eskimo legend.

I said that we know what the word "literature" means, and indeed we do. It means "novels, poems, plays, and things like that." Dictionaries tell us what the word means, usually ostensively, by pointing out some exemplary kinds. (Sometimes the definitions are theory laden too, however.) W. E. Kennick has pointed out that if you sent someone into a very large and variously stocked warehouse and asked him to bring out all the works of art he would be able to do so. But ask him to get all the objects possessing "significant form" and he will be at a loss.[33] Knowing the meaning of a term, knowing how to use it and to recognize members of the class it denotes do not depend on having a theory about it.

We seem to have a classic case, then, of a concept defined by a rather open-ended series of what Wittgenstein called "family resemblances" rather than by a set of necessary and sufficient characteristics. And this should not surprise us when we consider the enormous range of works that "literature" denotes, from lyric poems to dramatic monologues to epics, from imagistic haikus to political satires to allegories like *Everyman* and *The Faerie Queene*, from science fiction to Arthurian romance to the nonfiction novel. Why indeed should we expect a single function or set of qualities to cover such variety and such plenty? And why would one wish to write off as "unliterary" any way of understanding a good poem that tells us something true and useful about it?

I want to reiterate at this point the nature of the objections I have raised to theorizing about literature. They are objections to two things: first, to claims that such and such is *the* essential, fundamental, or privileged way to talk about or read literature; second, to a tendency to exaggerate the distinction between the literary and the nonliterary. The two are connected. The search for distinguishing features leads to a dwelling on differences and a brushing aside of similarities. But these objections do not entail the dismissal of the theorist's terms and concepts as irrelevant to the study of literature. There is a simple but crucial distinction between saying that literature is whatever we read without regard to its origins and saying that one can often find a great deal of value in a literary work without inquiring deeply into its origins; or between saying that it is the function of literature to provide the experience of cognitive tension and saying that some literature does provide that experience and that it may be worth exploring in those terms. The first formulations lead toward prescriptiveness and a narrowing of vision, the second toward exploration and new insight.

M. H. Abrams, with his customary intelligence and lucidity, has come to the defense of "theorizing" about literature in a similar fashion.[34] Abrams invites us to see definitions of literature as they have been employed by the great theorists, not as "legislative" but as "working" definitions, serving to block out an area of inquiry, and to introduce some categories useful in organizing that inquiry. Speaking of Aristotle's *Poetics* he writes:

> The body of the theory does not consist of an attempt— whether vain or successful—to support and "prove" the definition. It consists instead of putting to work the terms, distinctions, and categories proposed in the initial definition (which are supplemented, in a way consistent with this definition, as the need arises) in the analysis of the distinctive elements, organization, and characteristic powers of various kinds of poetic art.

Such a theory "provides ... knowledge how to experience and enjoy works of art ... by providing terms and analytic devices which enable us to experience them in a discriminating rather than a crude way." "This is the primary service of a good critical theory, for in bringing us, with new insights and powers of discrimination, to individual works of art in their immediacy, it enhances our appreciation of the only places where artistic values are in fact realized" (pp. 21–22).

A theory for Abrams is a "speculative instrument." As such "it has its particular angle and focus of vision, and what for one speculative instrument is an indistinct or blank area requires an alternative speculative instrument if it is to be brought into sharper focus for inspection" (p. 25).

Abrams is very close in spirit to Kennick, who, though he has insisted upon the futility of attempting to discover "some distinctive set of characteristics which serves to separate art from everything else," nevertheless recognizes the value of definitions as "instruments of instruction or reform." What Clive Bell had discovered in his development of the concept of "significant form" was not the essence of art but *a new way of looking at pictures.*" "Read Aristotle's Poetics," Kennick urges, "not as a philosophical exercise in definition, but as instruction in one way to read tragic poetry." It all comes down, then, to the question of what one expects a theory to do.

We have seen in this chapter how natural it is to construe literature in terms that reflect whatever the critic finds valuable in it. Some works will prove more suited than others for fulfilling a given function, just as some will display more abundantly than others the attributes designated by a particular definition of literature. It might appear that in the absence of a tidy theory of literature there would be no way to evaluate literary works. But the reverse is true. Not only would a theory of literature be of no use to the critic who wishes to say what is good about a work; he can get along nicely without one, as the following chapter is designed to show.

6

Evaluation

There was a time when most critics and aestheticians presumed that evaluating literary works was an important activity for the critic, if not, indeed, his primary goal. But that time is no more. The most insistently judgmental critics of the mid-century, Yvor Winters and F. R. Leavis, were regarded even in their heyday as moralizing mavericks, and now they are treated with only condescending respect. Stanley Fish was no doubt speaking for a multitude when he wrote: "I regard evaluation not as a theoretical issue but as a subject in the history of taste."[1] And so was Northrop Frye, asserting that when value judgments "are fashionable or generally accepted, they look objective, but that is all. The demonstrable value-judgment is the donkey's carrot of literary criticism, and every new critical fashion ... has been accompanied by a belief that criticism has finally devised a definitive technique for separating the excellent from the less excellent. But this always turns out to be an allusion of the history of taste." A value judgment, Frye goes on to say, "is not a statement of fact."[2]

To talk this way is to yield, of course, to the divorce between fact and value urged by the logical positivists, and to their relegation of ethical judgments to the realm of the emotive, the expressive, or (what is even more discouraging!) the meaningless. It is not easy to maintain in this climate of opinion that the critic who tries to demonstrate that the poem under consideration is a good one may be adding importantly to our sum of knowledge about it. But one would no more wish to fall victim to fashionable skepticism about the making of value judgments than to fashionable value judgments themselves.

Philosophers have been less inclined than critics simply to dismiss value judgments in the arts. Instead they have tried to attribute a peculiar logic (or illogic) to them, as special, non-assertive speech acts, or as claims supported by unique kinds of justification, as anything, indeed, but assertions that might be either true or false. I want to consider several such reinterpretations of critical evaluation to show why they won't do, and then I will try to show that when we say that a work is good in some respect, and provide the right sort of reasons for our judgment, we are describing the work, and our description may be true or false. Hence whatever other purposes evaluation may serve, one of them is to increase our understanding of the work in question. We will find, however, no "five easy steps to correct evaluation." We will discover neither that evaluating is easy, nor that it is easy to determine whether a particular assessment of a work is accurate. With critical judgment, as with descriptions in any field, it is always possible that relevant facts will be brought to light which would necessitate revising the assessment. All that we will see is that, though some critics may make monstrous judgments, evaluative statements are not logically monstrous simply by virtue of being evaluative. They are ways of describing literary works from an evaluative, and sometimes moral, point of view.

Perhaps the most naive yet persistent reinterpretation of value judgments is that they are expressions of preference, of likes and dislikes. "It's a good play" means "I liked it." And this emotivist view is often supplemented with the idea that value judgments are ways of commending. "It's a good play" means "I liked it and you will too; try it." The view is naive not because there is *no* connection between thinking something good and liking it. That something is good may be a reason for liking it, and liking it (the favorable first impression) may lead us to suspect that it's good. But the two locutions simply aren't interchangeable. As Isabel Hungerland has pointed out, if someone claimed to like Yeats's "Sailing to Byzantium," it would be odd to disagree with him or tell him that he's mistaken (though one might, of course, accuse him of lying). On the other hand, it would not be odd at all to disagree with someone who said it was a very good or a very bad poem.[3] Our ordinary uses of the term presuppose that the goodness of something is arguable in a way in which reports of liking or preference are not. We wouldn't find it contradictory to hear someone say "I *know* it's a terrible novel, but I like it anyway," or "I loved the play, but I haven't decided whether I think it's really good," or "That's a good detective story, but detective stories always bore me." Commendation is subject to the same objection: though we ought to commend a poem to someone only if we think it's good in some respect, saying that it's a good poem is not necessarily commending it. If someone says that *Portrait of the Artist* is a bad novel and I reply that it's a good novel, I'm not commending it to him (he's already read it); I'm disagreeing with him.

Now someone might say that our ordinary uses of words like "good" are fallacious, founded upon the *illusion* that we are predicating a quality of something when we call it good, the *illusion* that the goodness, value, or merit of a literary work is arguable. Such a person might maintain that "I like it" is all that "It's good" *can* (reasonably) mean, the best that can be said for it. But such a claim is difficult to substantiate, resting as it does on the presumption that no other satisfactory explication of its meaning has been or could be found.

But the desire to segregate evaluation from ordinary description runs deep. Morris Weitz, in *Hamlet and the Philosophy of Literary Criticism*, divides critical activity into four categories: description, explanation, evaluation, and poetics. And as that division indicates, he holds that *evaluating* is different from *describing*. The latter may be true or false, but the former is not. For Weitz, evaluation is tantamount to praising and condemning. To call *Hamlet* a great play is to praise it, but not to describe it truly or falsely.[4]

For the aesthetician Margaret Macdonald, too, value judgments are distinguished sharply from descriptions. They are, instead, like "the impersonal verdict 'He is guilty.'" And a verdict, she says, "does not describe the accused." Verdicts "are not true or false." The critic, when he evaluates, "affirms merit or demerit. By calling a work 'good' he places the hall mark on an artistic performance. But he does not describe it."[5]

Now it is certainly true that when we call something good we may be praising it, just as it is also true that we often evaluate highly what we like, and often commend something to somebody because it is good. But it by no means follows from these facts that we are not describing the thing, or not saying something that may be true or false. Indeed it is hard to see how we would be justified in commending or praising or affirming the merit of something if it were not really good in the way we claim it to be good. In the words of Milton, "all praising is but courtship and flattery" unless "that only is prais'd which is solidly worth praise."[6]

As for verdict giving, it seems to me that Macdonald is confused. To say "He is guilty," no matter how impersonally, is surely to describe the accused, and the statement is either true or false depending on whether the accused did or did not do whatever he was accused of doing. It is true that the judge's "I *pronounce* the defendant guilty," said in a context of legal authority and convention, has consequences that the layman's verdict lacks. But critics (at least those who survive) don't say "I pronounce, dub, christen, and declare this poem good." They say that it is a good poem, and then go on to justify their description.

Even if we allow that critics often like, praise, and commend the works they judge to be good, we want to resist the notion that that is all evaluation consists of. Not just because the notion is wrong (and we have just seen it to be), but because it is demeaning to good criticism and has authoritarian implications in which we ought not to acquiesce. Macdonald concludes her essay, for example, by asking:

> Does it follow from this that all judgments about art are of equal value, which I began by denying? I do not think so.... Instead, they are generally appraised in relation to qualities of the critic. The judgments of a skilful, sympathetic, widely experienced critic are better than those of one without these, and other appropriate qualities. But "better" and "worse" judgments are probably all that can be achieved in this field. No critic, even the best, is infallible and sometimes we may be well advised to trust our own judgment rather than that of any expert. [P. 604]

Now if judgments can't be true or false, how can we know whether a particular critic is skillful at making them? Or whether his wide experience has paid off in a particular case? How can we know whether a judgment is better or worse? But we may take some solace in Macdonald's avowal that "no critic is infallible," for we may then conjecture that one of the ways in which a critic may fail is by offering an evaluation that is incorrect.

These attempts to make evaluative statements out to be nonassertive speech acts of a special kind are doomed to fail because they confuse the meaning of the terms employed in evaluation with the possible uses of some of the sentences in which they appear. "You're a good boy!" may be used to bestow praise, but none of the following sentences is:

Is he a good boy?
Be a good boy!
I had a good time, but Joan didn't.
I use this battered old portable because I can't afford a good new one.
I hope we'll have good weather tomorrow.

Furthermore, the act of praising something is not nondescriptive. To call the boy in question well-behaved, intelligent, and friendly would be to describe him *as well as* to praise him. The relationship between liking, commending, and praising on the one hand, and evaluating on the other, is not semantic. It consists only in the fact that what is good is often commendable, praiseworthy, and likeable.

Another approach to evaluative statements is through an analysis of the kinds of reasons that can be offered in their support. One common view, for example, is that all one can do to justify the claim that a work is good is to go on describing the work, pointing out its various features. This notion goes back to an influential article by Helen Knight, called "The Use of 'Good' in Aesthetic Judgments," published in 1935:

> Suppose I say that Cézanne's "Green Jar" is a good picture and someone asks me "why?" or "what do you mean?" I should answer by describing it. I should point out a number of facts about its organization, for example: that apple is placed so that it exactly balances the main mass on the right; the lines of tablecloth, knife, and shadows repeat each other; the diagonal of the knife counteracts the diagonals of the shadows. All these objects, I might continue, are exceedingly solid and the shadows exceedingly deep—each thing "is infallibly in its place." I might point out a number of

important problems that Cézanne has solved; for example, that he combines a geometrical scheme with the variety we get in natural appearances. And finally I might allude to the profundity and gravity of the picture. In this description I have pointed out criterion-characters; the "Green Jar" is good because it possesses them.[7]

This, Knight maintained, is all we can do by way of explaining why "Green Jar" is a good picture. But do such pointings back to the picture constitute an explanation or justification at all? Of course to the viewer who has his own reasons for thinking that the features pointed to are good, the description may be helpful; and any full argument about its goodness would have to point to features. But why place the burden on the viewer? Has the critic no recourse, if someone asked him what's so good about counteracting diagonals, but to point to them again? What would he say to someone who said, "Oh, no, those diagonals *ruin* the painting," or to someone who pointed to altogether different features to justify a favorable judgment? Mrs. Knight's implied answer to these questions is a retreat to cultural determinism, her version of Fish's and Frye's history of taste: "What is the guarantee of a criterion? What determines the truth of 'so-and-so is a criterion for goodness in pictures'? The guarantee, I would answer, lies in its being used as a criterion. Organization of groups, space, composition, profundity, etc., are criteria of goodness because they are used as such" (p. 595).

A recent version of Mrs. Knight's position appears in John Casey's *The Language of Criticism*.[8] Casey pairs off two views of critical judgments. The first of these, which he rejects, is that they are "deduced" from "*a priori* standards" (p. 57), "general principles" (p. 138), or "an absolute and unquestioned standard" (p. 135). He exemplifies this view with the writings of Yvor Winters. The second view, which he attributes to F. R. Leavis, is that specific judgments are supported not by "proceeding from the particular to the general" (p. 154), but by citing other "facts on the same level" (p. 166). Speaking of Winters, Casey writes: "The idea that particular judgments, if they are to be objective, have to be deduced from general principles, or entailed by general descriptions, is the fundamental fallacy. To defend a judgment of a poem one has to go on describing it, relating it to other poems and so on, until the person one is trying to convince is satisfied." But this is a misleading opposition. It does not follow that, in the absence of general principles or "absolute standards," the only recourse is to wallow in the details of the work. His position is as disappointing as Knight's. Having quoted a comment by Leavis to the effect that a passage from *The Cenci* is "voluminously emotional," he says that to substantiate the attendant value judgment we "cite facts on the same level," as follows:

> 'Voluminous emotionalism is usually bad because it is a form of insincerity.' Then, 'Why is insincerity bad?' 'Well, look at this speech by N' (a notably insincere politician). Our opponent can, of course, reply 'Well, what is wrong with it?' He can go on doing so whatever examples of insincerity we bring forward. We may then show more fully what we mean by insincerity— may show it how it is connected with, and made up of many qualities—let us call them $a \ldots n$. If, by the time we have reached n, he is still unwilling to concede any sense in which insincerity might be bad, we may well be at a loss what to say; for nothing we have shown entails the judgment of value that we wish to elicit. [Pp. 166–67]

This is an improvement on Mrs. Knight's version in one respect. Casey is at least willing to allow the critic to show his opponent what he means by the quality he attributes to the work, and if the other qualities he shows it to be "connected to" turn out to be qualities that the opponent already has reasons for considering bad, the critic's rhetoric has been effective. What he will *not* allow the critic to do, however, is to be explicit about any "sense in which insincerity might be bad." And since he seems willing to concede that there is such a sense, why not let the critic say what it is?

The reason for this stubbornness, I suspect, is that fundamentally Casey holds to the view that evaluative claims are tantamount to mere expressions of liking or preference, so that an evaluative argument is no more, finally, than an attempt to get the opponent to like what the critic likes. For Casey, "the measure of the success of a critical argument is that we come to 'see' a picture or poem in a certain way" (p. 22). This measure taken alone naturally invites rhetoric to dominate reason. What would one say, in the absence of a nonrhetorical measure, if the critic brought one reader to "see" the poem as good but not another? Casey forcefully rejects the identification of value judgments with the expression of feeling, but the identification comes in the back door in several passages. He says with apparent approval that "for Leavis valuing is a complex of activities (or a family of activities), 'finding that this wears well,' 'coming back to that' and so on. All this adds up to evaluating; there is no gap to be bridged between it and evaluating" (p. 168). He makes no distinction, as this passage shows, between evaluating highly and what he calls "valuing highly" (p. 57). But surely there is an important distinction, for we may come back to something again and again, and value it greatly, then be persuaded (by a doctor, say, or a critic) that what we valued highly *ought not* to have been valued highly because it is not good, and wasn't good even when we valued it highly. My valuing something highly may lead (or mislead) me to think that something is good, but it is not a reason for its being good. We would not say "This is a good poem because I value it highly," though we might say "This poem ought to be valued highly because it is a good poem."

THE MEANING OF "GOOD"

All the accounts of critical judgments we have glanced at are alike in regarding them as essentially irrational and as distinct in kind from nonaesthetic judgments. One would not, after all, if faced with a challenge to a claim that a certain man or posthole digger or backhand volley was good, merely *point* to the person, object, or shot. Nor would we need to rest content with describing it or enumerating its characteristics. I believe that aesthetic judgments are not distinct from practical and moral judgments in the ways implied by these accounts, and that it may be clarifying to explore briefly a simple, everyday example of evaluation to see how it can shed light on the evaluation of literature.

Let us suppose, in true philosophical fashion, that Jones is planning to fix *Suprêmes de Volaille* for Smith, and while discussing the preparations, Smith says, "I have a good poultry knife you can use," and shows it to him. Jones (who hasn't had much experience with this sort of thing) asks him why it's a good poultry knife. And Smith points out that its blade is long, narrow, sharply pointed, fairly unbending, its handle hefty and comfortable. Jones persists: Why do those qualities make it a good poultry knife? And Smith answers: "It's those qualities that make the knife suitable for separating the breast meat from the bone. A good poultry knife is one that's suitable for doing that."

In this exchange "good" seems to mean "suitable for fulfilling some function." Even Jones probably knew that, so that Smith's last sentence was clarifying but redundant. The reason-giving part of the argument consists of saying what the function is, and pointing out the characteristics of the thing that make it suitable. (Note that "good" doesn't mean "suitable for boning chicken," nor does it mean "long, sharp, and possessed of a hefty handle." These notions help convey the entire concept of a good poultry knife, but not the single concept of goodness, which remains constant from poultry knives to pianos to cars to human deeds.)

I have rendered the meaning of "good" as "suitable for fulfilling some function." This roughly Aristotelian definition has been formulated in slightly different ways by two contemporary philosophers, F. E. Sparshott and Paul Ziff. For Sparshott, to say that something is good is to say that it is "such as to satisfy the wants of the person or persons concerned."[9] For Ziff it means "answering to certain interests."[10] Though Ziff makes some fine and useful distinctions among these and similar renderings, I am content with the fact that all three share the connotation of instrumentality. All three suggest that something that is good must be good *for* something, and that the goodness of something must be relative to something else—fulfilling a function, satisfying a want, answering an interest.

There is a traditional philosophical distinction between "instrumental" and "intrinsic" goodness. When an object is evaluated in terms of its capacity to perform a specified function (e.g., a good augur is one that drills holes well) we are said to be attributing instrumental goodness to it. An object is said to be intrinsically good if it is good apart from any purpose or use. In such cases we follow "it is good" with such tags as "per se," "in itself," or, more mysterious still, "in and of itself." Thus R. M. Hare writes: "A good bath is good both instrumentally (in that it is conducive to cleanliness) and intrinsically (for we should not have nearly so many baths if our only purpose in having them were to become clean)."[11]

I regard this as a false distinction and suggest that whenever we evaluate something as good there is a tacit reference to some function, purpose, want, need, or interest. The fact that we take more baths than our want of cleanliness would call for indicates not that baths are intrinsically good, but that there are other reasons for bathing, such as relaxing tired muscles. My children frequently bathe not to get *clean*, but to get *away from the family*.

When Smith calls his a good poultry knife, is he describing it? Though his statement may appear elliptical to someone unfamiliar with preparing poultry, it seems clear that he is describing his knife, and that his claim is true if the knife has the features he says it has and those features do suit it for the task. As for the elliptical quality of the description, if Jones had wanted to, he could have asked Smith for further analysis: for example, why are the length and narrowness and stiffness of the blade important? And if those are qualities that truly aid in boning chicken, an answer could be given to the question. How far such analysis has to be carried out depends on how much it takes to get someone to see the connection between the qualities and the function.

Note that Smith is only claiming that the knife is good in one respect—namely, as a poultry knife. It is good as that, but not as a breadknife or an outboard motor. If we find an object on the beach and don't know what it is, we could wonder what it might be good for, and think of some use it could serve, some need it might fill. But what would it mean to call it a good object? Or good "in general"? Or "good—period!"? In the collection of Roman artifacts in the London Museum there is an object labelled "Dodecahedron: use unknown." It's hard to say whether it survived the ravages of time because, being a good one, it received careful treatment, or because, being a bad one, it avoided the wear and tear of daily use. It appears to be a good example of a dodecahedron, however.

At this point we should acknowledge at least one crucial difference between poultry knives and literary works. For if the function of poultry knives is clear and indeed implicit in the meaning of the term, the function of a literary work is not. As we saw in the previous chapter, "literature" is not a functional term, nor are all literary works designed for the performance of some single task, the satisfaction of a single want or interest. It is possible to specify what are sometimes called the "criteria" of a good poultry knife or other functionally defined object. They are those characteristics (length and firmness of blade, for example) that render it suitable for performing its function. Hence a degree of definiteness about what makes a good poultry knife is possible: one may even try to derive the criteria from the function and the available materials, much as Aristotle derived the criteria for a good tragedy from the end he assigned to it. Of course one cannot be *too* definite, even with things like poultry knives and mousetraps, since someone may discover a better way to bone chicken or catch mice.

It might be thought that some objects are functional, and that for them rational evaluation is possible, but that for other objects it is impossible. But that is not the case. First, there are degrees of functional specificity associated with terms. There is a progression from specific-function terms like "barometer" and "spade" to terms like "weapon" and "writing implement" to terms like "utensil" and "tool," a progression from "trotter" to "brood mare" to "horse," from "comedian" to "entertainer" to "man." One can see a similar range in critical terms, since some generic names connote a fairly specific function while others do not. Note, say, the progression from a good joke, piece of slapstick, detective story, to a good comedy, satire, or romance, to a good poem, novel, or work of literature. If someone describes a joke as good, you can be pretty sure that he means it will strike a listener as funny. If something is presented as a good satire, you expect that it ridicules something effectively, and perhaps that what it ridicules merits abuse. But a high summary evaluation of a poem or novel is highly elliptical and needs filling out. The question "Good for what?" comes quickly to mind.

Furthermore, in the case of an object whose function is not specified by its name, rational evaluation is still possible, and that in at least two ways, both of them calling for elaboration and analysis on the part of the appraiser. First, one may designate a function prior to examining the object and then analyze the object to see whether it is designed in a way that makes it effective for serving that function. For literary works the function designated might range from creating suspense or diversion, to arousing pity and fear, to exposing human folly or inculcating Christian doctrine, to providing an opportunity for the rehearsal of cognitive tension—whatever function or want or interest the critic is curious about. If he finds that the work *is* so designed, he has found one thing that the work is good for, something which it offers, a respect in which it is a good literary work. This is the *procedure* followed by a critic like Yvor Winters, who characteristically assessed literary works with a single, though general, function in mind. There is nothing wrong with such a procedure, and Winters was a skilled practitioner of it. But its results must be correctly understood. They may show a respect in which the work is good or not good, but they cannot establish that the work is good, period, or a better work of literature than any other except with regard to the designated function. And since literature is not a functional concept, no function can claim precedence as literary or aesthetic. As E. D. Hirsch demonstrated from another angle, there are no "privileged criteria" in literary criticism.[12]

The second, more inductive procedure is to examine the work and discover what it has to offer, what readerly interests it might satisfy, what sort of an experience it will provide. To recuperate the terms of chapter 3, the inductive critic tries to find out what the author is *doing* to the reader. One approaches a work in this way not with a specific function in mind, but with whatever range of possible values, hopefully plural and diverse, one has learned to look for in different kinds of literature. What such a critic may discover will be the specific value or values of the text in question. And if he has read it with understanding he will then know what to praise it for and what not to praise it for, what sort of a person to commend it to, and so on.

The need to specify the function we have in mind when we are evaluating a literary work is closely related to the fact that even a functionally designed object, like an augur or a poultry knife, is good as a fulfiller of that function, not good in general. It is easy to run aground if we think of critics as always asking questions like "Is *Waiting for Godot* a good play or not?" "Which is the better novel, *Clarissa* or *Tom Jones*?" "Which is better, lyric poetry or the dramatic monologue?" Questions such as these assume the existence of some single standard or set of qualities (other than goodness itself) which a work must possess in order to be good. Since it is possible for a work to be good in some respects but not in others (and it is difficult to imagine a work good in every respect in which a literary work may be good) such questions are misleading. One might decide, after deliberation, that the virtues of one work are more weighty, significant, indeed better, than those of another, and hence conclude that it is, all in all, the better work. But this would amount to a summary of findings, useful perhaps, but less informative than the findings themselves.

There is a curious corollary of the position I am advocating, and it should be acknowledged. Since words like "novel," "poem," and "literature" do not connote a specific function, want, or interest, a statement like "this is a good novel," though highly uninformative and vague in the extreme, is descriptive and always true (when said of a novel). The novel may be good for producing tedium or for illustrating the shortcomings of an author or genre or for illustrating by contrast the virtues of some other book. Or, less frivolously, it may be a good indicator of its author's state of mind when he wrote it or a good reflector of the social values of the culture in which he worked. In other words, an evaluation becomes usefully and informatively descriptive only when we have some idea of what the novel is good *for*. And its truth becomes demonstrated only when the characteristics that make it good for that end are pointed out and their connection to the end explained. One wishes to preserve Knight's and Casey's emphasis on pointing back to the shape and content and details of the work itself; but in an evaluative argument they need to be related to some end beyond their mere existence.

The Shape of an Evaluative Argument

What sorts of functions are actually referred to in assessing a literary work? We may decide that some aspect of a work is good (or effective) in relation to something else in the work. We might, for example, say that the Gloucester subplot in *Lear* is good because it both intensifies and qualifies the meaning of the main plot. We might show how the rhythm or syntax of a passage of poetry contributes to the characterization of the speaker or the feeling expressed in the poem. In such cases we are designating what we may think of as an internal function, and if the value of performing that function is accepted or assumed, the evaluation may stop there.

Such arguments, crucial as they are in analyzing the form of the work itself, are nevertheless oddly incomplete, like demonstrations of how a machine works that fail to discuss the job that the machine is designed to do. One of the peculiar features of goodness is that, once it has been established, one can raise the further question, "Well, what's so good about that?" Once we have shown how the Gloucester subplot qualifies the meaning of the central action, someone may always query: "But what's good about that? *Should* the meaning of the main plot be intensified and qualified that way?" That is, we may ask why the purpose served is a good one to serve. And that question will lead (depending on the perseverance of the questioner) outside the text to the goodness of the work with respect to the reader. Indeed this move toward persons seems implicit even when the functions are "internal," since qualifying meaning and characterizing speakers are not intrinsic goods but good for satisfying the wants or interests of someone concerned with the play or poem.

At this point, with the move from internal relations to the work's capacity to affect the reader, satisfying certain wants or interests, let us say that the evaluative argument takes on a moral dimension. The argument enters the realm of human wants and interests, which may be, after all, in competition with each other, and which may be different in different situations. They nevertheless remain subject to rational debate and justification. Since it is always possible to ask of something, including the answering of some human interest, why it is good, there is no limit implied by the meaning of "good" on the reaches of evaluation. The definition in no way suggests, for example, that some popular writer's novels, because they apparently satisfy a widespread need, are therefore as good as any other novels, or good in any other sense than as a fulfiller of that need. It is not contradictory to say that something is good for doing something which it is not good to do; in fact, a definition that did *not* allow for that sort of distinction would not accurately represent many of our ordinary uses of the term. A good "Saturday night special" may be a bad thing to produce and make accessible, and a vegetarian bystander might have initiated a quarrel with Jones and Smith over the value of preparing poultry. That is why no definition of the essential nature or function of literature, even if there were such a thing, could clinch an evaluative argument; for one may always ask of such a function or set of properties, "What's good about *that*?"

Analyses of internal functions—of the way certain features of a work reinforce others—are like demonstrations of an author's skill as it is manifested in a work. One can speak of a well-made poem or of a difficult problem effectively solved or of a writer's capacity to achieve certain effects, and yet we realize that such descriptions fall short of demonstrating that the work in question is a good one and that skill, as Socrates was at pains to show the rhetorician Gorgias, may be used in a good or bad cause. I have in mind criticism like F. R. Leavis's characterization of Henry James as "an incomparable master at differentiating national tones and qualities,"[13] or Erich Auerbach's celebration of Dante's language:

> If we start from his predecessors, Dante's language is a well-nigh incomprehensible miracle. There were great poets among them. But compared with theirs, his style is so immeasurably richer in directness, vigor, and subtlety, he knows and uses such an immeasurably greater stock of forms, he expresses the most varied phenomena and subjects with such immeasurably superior assurance and firmness, that we come to the conclusion that this man used his language to discover the world anew.[14]

We stand in awe of great artistry, and of course I don't want to suggest that either James or Dante turned their skills to ignoble uses. The point is simply that not every skillfully made poem is a good poem, and that the latter judgment can be reached only by discovering and assessing the effects which the poem is well made to achieve.

In my view, then, a full critical evaluation will consist of an analysis of the effect of the work on the reader—of precisely what sort of cognitive and emotional experience it is designed to afford—coupled, if the need arises, with justification of the value of that experience. The whole will be a string of connected functional statements: "*A* is good for intensifying *B*; together they evoke *C* and make it clear that *D*; these in turn help to achieve *E*"; and so on. Each step in the argument is a clarification of the context in which the function previously specified may be regarded as good. In such an argument the value of the work is not "deduced" from some absolute standard of excellence or from some general proposition about art or literature. Instead it relates the very specific nature of the individual work to human experiences, concerns, and choices.

It might appear that the view I am advocating would, if put into practice, transform every critical essay into a treatise on morality and social ethics. On the one hand, of course, no critic will carry his evaluative argument beyond the point where he assumes that his readers will accept the terms of his assessment, the value of doing whatever he has shown the work to be capable of doing. But on the other hand it is essential to recognize the direction such an expansion would have to take in order to be well and fully reasoned, or to counter the challenge of someone who refuses to accept the critic's moral assumptions. The practical problem that besets criticism is that critical terms harden with respect to their evaluative connotations, and as they do so, the rationale on which they may once have rested may disappear from view, however sound it may originally have been. I am thinking of terms like "unified," "moving," "hackneyed," "superficial," "vivid," "intense," "sentimental," and so on, that sometimes indicate, even as they describe, whether the critic is judging the work favorably or not. Critics often write for readers who share their moral vocabulary. This is good insofar as it saves time, but like any intellectual shortcut it is bad insofar as it discourages a reassessment of the reasons that underlay that vocabulary and the discoveries such a reassessment can produce.

If we look again at Casey's remarks about insincerity, we can again see why the mere enumeration of qualities won't do. Even if we waive the difficulties involved in determining whether a particular expression is or is not sincere, there remains the incontrovertible fact that one can imagine instances of insincerity which contribute to the value of a work, or works which, though insincere, are so good in other respects as to render the charge of insincerity virtually silly and beside the point. The same can be said of sentimentality. It may be wrong always to feel emotions in excess of the facts, but it is certainly not always wrong to feel emotions in excess of the facts. And if one might fault a writer for being incapable of skeptical, reasonable responses, one could also fault a writer for being incapable of sentimental responses.

Leavis, though his criticism is permeated with certain recurrent notions that may have undergone a degree of hardening, is more reasonable on this score than Casey's picture of him suggests. In an essay cited by Casey, Leavis writes of Tennyson's "Tears, Idle Tears": "It moves simply forward with a sweetly plangent flow, without check, cross-tension or any qualifying element. To give it the reading it asks for is to flow with it, acquiescing in a complete and simple immersion."[15] Surely any reader unfamiliar with Leavis's predilections would be hard put to say whether this description will be used for or against the poem. One can easily imagine the argument turning toward praise. But Leavis is interested in the sense in which these qualities have negative implications:

> There is no attitude toward the experience except one of complaisance; we are to be wholly in it and of it. . . .
> It is plain that habitual indulgence of the kind represented by *Tears, idle tears*—indulgence not accompanied and virtually disowned by a critical placing—would be, on grounds of emotional and spiritual hygiene, something to deplore.

The connections between the form of this assessment and the view of evaluation we have been exploring should be obvious. Leavis by no means treats the quality of sentimentality as self-evidently deplorable wherever it occurs. In fact it is not sentimentality that he deplores at all, but rather the habitual indulgence of it, by either reader or writer. He is not even asserting that the poem is bad rather than good; he is merely pointing to a respect in which the attitudes it embodies bear watching or are potentially detrimental. And if he were asked to elaborate the notion of emotional and spiritual hygiene, the natural tack for him to take would be to detail the possible consequences—the human needs fulfilled and needs thwarted—of the sort of indulgence he portrays.

Before turning to some further examples of evaluative criticism, we should note an apparent paradox implicit in the view of evaluation presented here, taking as our text Socrates' confidential remarks to Glaucon at the beginning of book 10 of the *Republic*:

> Speaking in confidence, for I should not like to have my words repeated to the tragedians and the rest of the imitative tribe—but I do not mind saying to you, that all poetical imitations are ruinous to the understanding of the hearers, and that the knowledge of their true nature is the only antidote to them.[16]

Let me hasten to dissociate myself from the master's generalization about "all poetical imitations" and dwell simply on the notion that a knowledge of the true nature of a work of art or literature *is* the proper antidote to any potentially ruinous effects it might have. For if Socrates is right on that score, a full understanding of a poem (including an understanding of the effects it is designed to produce) is tantmount to a correct assessment of it. A correct assessment not only depends on a correct interpretation but becomes superfluous to the extent that the interpretation succeeds in relating the text to the reader and to the domain of human values. The sort of linked argument I have described could, after all, be presented without the words "good" or "bad" or any of their near synonyms putting in an appearance. Just so, Smith might have said of his poultry knife: "This knife will make it easy to bone chicken because it has a long firm blade suitable for . . . ." He need never have troubled to introduce an explicitly evaluative vocabulary. Suppose a critic demonstrates that a novel is designed, through its blandishments, to make the reader admire a sort of behavior that is essentially selfish and destructive or that the hidden political assumptions on which the techniques of a particular satire rest are totalitarian, or anarchic, or fallacious. To do so *is* to evaluate the work by accurately describing it, thus unfolding what it has to offer. And such a demonstration will serve, harking back to Socrates, to keep a reader from being taken in. Or, to hark back to chapter 3, where our paradox was also present, it will show the reader how he *ought* to respond to the work (i.e., warily, and with a recognition of the true nature of the behavior he is asked to admire, the assumptions he would be accepting by joining in the spirit of the satire). Of course the critic I've imagined here might be called on to go further: *Ought* that sort of behavior to be rejected? What's wrong with accepting those assumptions? But these questions, too, can be answered, the linked argument extended, without the help of "good" and "bad."

If all the information contained in an extended evaluative argument can be conveyed without those terms that we associate with evaluation, does it follow that those terms are dispensable? By no means. But to see why, we must speculate a bit on what they are doing in our language, what *their* function is, what *they* are good for. They are in our language, I would argue, because we are interested in the consequences of things and acts, interested in the connections things have with our lives as individuals and as social, political animals. Questions about the respect in which something is good are like the always impudent question "So what?" We want to know whether something ought to be sought after or avoided, whether it is worthy of time and attention, whether it is of some conceivable use or interest. Fancy a critic saying truly of a poem that it contains an unusually large number of fricatives. He is, of course, telling us something the poem has to offer, an element of the experience of reading the poem aloud or of hearing it read. But if he goes no further we are likely to ask, "So what?" "Who cares?" Or "What's good about that?" We often use "good" as a way of saying that something is suitable when the question of suitable for what is apparent. (Good weather is weather suitable for doing what we plan to do.) But we also use it for pressing each other, asking for further reasons, insisting on more detailed accounts of consequences, relevance, and importance. The need to know these things is surely the same need that initiates criticism, justifies it, and sustains it. "Knowledge for its own sake" is an empty slogan, after all, like "poetry for poetry's sake." It is by means of the evaluative lexicon that we raise pointed questions: Good in what ways and for *whose* sake?

Coda

I have a suspicion that the best evaluative criticism takes place not in print at all but in conversations, classrooms, and colloquia. I mean the sort of criticism that is tempered by persistent questioning, that leads back to a reexamination of the text itself, and also to an exploration and expansion of the reasons offered in support of the judgment. Not every private muse is persistent with the question "What's good about that?" Other persons help. But there is an analogue to the virtues of discussion in the ongoing debate in print over the merits of a classic work. Take, for example, the criticism of *Huckleberry Finn*, the consideration of a small segment of which may serve as our conclusion.

Our part of the story begins with Lionel Trilling's essay "The Greatness of *Huckleberry Finn*," which served as an introduction to the Rinehart edition of the novel published in 1948.[17] "Wherein," Trilling asks, "does its greatness lie?" First, he tells us, the novel's greatness lies "in its power of telling the truth." And the sort of truth it tells is truth about "the virtue and depravity of man's heart." That is, the novel shows us things about human nature, its characters serving as instances of actual human traits and tendencies. Second, it affords us, in the character of Huck himself, a model hero, an essentially good person faced with moral "crises" and responding to them well. (Trilling says of Huck, for example, that "responsibility is the very essence of his character," that "his sympathy is quick and immediate" in spite of his "profound and bitter knowledge of human depravity.") The result, Trilling avers in eloquent if hyperbolic language, is that

> No one who reads thoughtfully the dialectic of Huck's great moral crisis will ever again be wholly able to accept without some question and some irony the assumptions of the respectable morality by which he lives, nor will ever again be certain that what he considers the clear dictates of moral reason are not merely the engrained customary beliefs of his time and place.

At the risk of stating the obvious, let me offer a few comments by way of relating Trilling's observations to the themes of the present study.

First, how would one challenge Trilling's claim that the novel is great because it tells the truth? The first challenge, pointing back to the novel, would be on the order of "Does it say what Trilling claims it says?" The second, pointing toward consequences and the reader, would be "Why is it good to tell those truths?" Are they important, trivial, worth knowing? Is it good to be made skeptical about the grounds of the dictates of what we take to be moral reason? Either challenge would be appropriate in principle. Several others would not be. It would be illogical to argue, say, that truth telling is a moral and not a literary virtue. If *Huck Finn* is a novel, a work of literature, and if it tells a truth that merits telling, then it is a good work of literature in that respect. It would be likewise inappropriate to argue that fiction *can't* tell the truth. Trilling is obviously using truth telling loosely to mean something like presenting characters whose behavior is typical of human behavior in some specifiably important ways, or, in Dr. Johnson's finer speech, characters who "act and speak by the influence of those general passions and principles by which all minds are agitated and the whole system of life is continued in motion."[18]

As for Huck's honesty, his sense of responsibility, and his humane sympathies, I take it that Trilling's argument is remediably incomplete: the presence of a good character doesn't make a novel good. But it is implicit in the very tone and energy of Trilling's description of Huck that he sees the novel as perfectly calculated to make us admire the boy and the qualities he possesses. (As Sidney said of another character, "Who readeth *Aeneas* carrying olde *Anchises* on his back, that wisheth not it were his fortune to perfourm so excellent an acte?"[19]) Again, the retorts available are: *Does* Huck possess the qualities in question? *Is* the book designed to make us admire them? *Ought* we admire them?

To get on with the story, in which we will see Trilling's claims both challenged and defended, let us turn to what has proven to be a hotly debated section of the novel, the concluding eleven chapters, which recount Tom Sawyer's elaborate scheme for freeing Jim from the hut where he is imprisoned at the Phelps's farm. Tom, recall, already knows that Jim has been freed by Miss Watson, his former owner, in her will. But Tom doesn't tell; it's the "adventure" of the escape that he's after. Huck, though baffled by the unnecessary intricacies of Tom's plans, plays his part, as does Jim.

This concluding episode had fallen under heavy, though terse, attack before Trilling wrote his essay. Hemingway warned that "if you read [the novel] you must stop where the nigger Jim is stolen by the boys. This is the real end. The rest is cheating."[20] And Bernard DeVoto had said that "in the whole reach of the English novel there is no more abrupt or more chilling descent."[21] Trilling, though he acknowledged that the ending constitutes "a falling off," attributes to it "a certain formal aptness":

> It is a rather mechanical development of an idea, and yet some device is needed to permit Huck to return to his anonymity, to give up the role of hero, to fall into the background which he prefers, for he is modest in all things and could not well endure the attention and glamour which attend a hero at a book's end. For this purpose nothing could serve better than the mind of Tom Sawyer with its literary furnishings, its conscious romantic desire for experience and the hero's part, and its ingenious schematization of life to achieve that aim.

And T. S. Eliot, two years later, argued in a similar vein:

> It is right that the mood of the end of the book should bring us back to that of the beginning. Or, if this was not the right ending for the book, what ending would have been right? ...
>
> For Huckleberry Finn, neither a tragic nor a happy ending would be suitable. No worldly success or social satisfaction, no domestic consummation would be worthy of him; a tragic end also would reduce him to the level of those whom we pity. Huck Finn must come from nowhere and be bound for nowhere.... He has no beginning and no end. Hence, he can only disappear; and his disappearance can only be accomplished by bringing forward another performer to obscure the disappearance in a cloud of whimsicalities.[22]

Concerning Trilling's qualified defense of the ending, we may note that it is based on some notion of internal necessity. The ending is a good one, a "comfortable" one, perhaps, *for Huck*, satisfying his preference for anonymity. If we try to extend the argument to the reader, we can do so only, it seems, by saying that this ending would answer the reader's interest in Huck's comfort. We like Huck, and we wish him to be happy; to fulfill this wish, "nothing could serve better" than the ending as it stands. Eliot's argument is similar, and even less satisfactory. Why must an ending be "worthy" of a protagonist? (And what does "worthy" mean in this context?) Why would it be wrong to have an ending that led us to pity Huck? In what sense does Huck have no beginning and no end, and why, if that is true, can he *only* disappear? And why can the disappearance *only* be accomplished . . . ?

There is a suggestion running through the argument that an episode is good if it unifies the novel or is consistent with something else in it. Thus it is right that the novel end in the "mood" with which it began and good that Huck metaphorically "disappears" behind a cloud because disappearance is consistent with metaphorically having "no beginning and no end" (whatever that means). But surely the demonstration that something is unified, or contributes to unity, establishes for it only the most minimal sort of goodness. The ending may be good for returning us to the mood of the beginning, but why is it good to do that? It is not just that the sort of unity in question is superficial, but that unity, no matter how "profound" and no matter how diffuse and complex the elements unified, is a neutral quality, like skill, or complexity, simplicity, or confusion itself. The most that can be said for unity is that in a vague way a work must be unified if it is to be understood. To demonstrate that something is unified is to show that there is some principle according to which its parts are related. Now if one cannot discover such a principle, that is tantamount to being unable to understand the "something" as a whole. And if one cannot understand something, it is hard to say whether or in what respects it is good or bad. But unity, like any other quality a literary work may possess, cannot alone establish the value of a work. If a novel is unified, one needs to ask: Unified in the service of what end, and is the end a good one? The answer, "in order to provide a unified, coherent reading experience" is a beginning, but a beginning of the vaguest sort.

Trilling's and Eliot's attempts to defend the ending of Twain's novel against charges like those of Hemingway and DeVoto at least served to initiate a critical conversation; the next participant in it was Leo Marx, with an essay entitled "Mr. Eliot, Mr. Trilling, and *Huckleberry Finn*." What Marx offers us, as we shall see, is a new interpretation of the novel which is also a new assessment of it. His general thesis is that the major portion of the novel presents a truth which the ending obscures and betrays and that "the return, in the end, to the mood of the beginning . . . means defeat—Huck's defeat; to return to that mood *joyously* is to portray defeat in the guise of victory."²³ To understand Marx's point we must see what that truth is and how the ending signals a defeat for Huck.

Huck and Jim, according to Marx, are engaged in "a quest for freedom":

> From the electrifying moment when Huck comes back to Jackson's Island and rouses Jim with the news that a search party is on the way, we are meant to believe that Huck is enlisted in the cause of freedom. "Git up and hump yourself, Jim!" he cries. "There ain't a minute to lose. They're after us!"

Huck's "unpremeditated identification with Jim's flight from slavery" places the two of them in sharp opposition to "the polite lies of civilization," the greed and complacency, represented by the society they reject. But by its very nature, the quest cannot succeed, for the freedom and friendship that Huck and Jim find on the raft cannot be realized in the culture. The latter is "an image of solid reality," the former "an ecstatic dream."

Since the novel "affirms" the code by which Huck and Jim live on the raft and "aims a devastating criticism at the existent social order," yet also recognizes the impotence of the code, and since this vision of society is true, "a satisfactory ending would inevitably cause the reader some frustration." The conclusion for which he *rightly* wishes cannot be. In Marx's view the ending consistent with all that is best in the novel would affirm the quest but make it clear that it cannot be realized.

Instead, Twain "yielded to [the] essential complacency" of the existing order. Jim is in fact set free through the deathbed conversion of Miss Watson: Huck "makes himself a party to sport which aggravates Jim's misery"; Jim, "who bleeds ink and feels no pain," is "made over in the image of a flat stereotype: the submissive stage-Negro"; yet the novel ends, in spite of these degradations, on a note of "jubilation," in "a scene fairly bursting with approbation of the entire family." The ending thus vindicates the very "persons and attitudes Huck and Jim had symbolically repudiated when they set forth downstream." Hence:

> During the final extravaganza we are forced to put aside many of the mature emotions evoked earlier by

the vivid rendering of Jim's fear of capture, the tender-
ness of Huck's and Jim's regard for each other, and
Huck's excruciating moments of wavering between
honesty and respectability.... Moreover, the most
serious motive in the novel, Jim's yearning for freedom, is made the object of nonsense.

Marx's critique, then, radically reinterprets the novel. For
Eliot and Trilling, Huck and Jim were passive (though observant
and compassionate) characters, swept along by the river through
a picaresque series of adventures; for Marx their journey has a
positive, conscious motive, the quest for freedom. Recalling the
terms of our first chapter, "picaresque" and "quest" are narrative
models not both of which, as these critics employ them, could be
correct. Aligning his narrative model with the values symbolized
by Huck, Jim, and the culture they flee, Marx finds a meaning in
the journey which neither Trilling nor Eliot had seen. But more
than that: Marx simply introduces into the discussion issues and
episodes which his predecessors had overlooked, such as the fact
that Huck does *not* manifest at the end that moral sensitivity
which Trilling admired; the fact that Miss Watson ("the enemy")
is the agent of Jim's release from slavery; the fact of Jim's
humiliation and physical suffering. It is in this sense that
criticism, like science, can be progressive. Whether Marx was
right, or only partly right, or all wrong, subsequent attempts to
understand and evaluate the novel must deal with these facts,
either by demonstrating their irrelevance, or by showing their
significance to be other than Marx claimed.

Marx's argument reminds us of how value judgments push us
not only back to the text, but also outward toward the reader.
The ending forces us "to put aside many of the mature emotions
evoked earlier...." A demonstrated inconsistency between the
body of the novel and the ending would no more be proof of
failure than demonstrated unity would be proof of success. It is
implicit in Marx's argument, I think, that for the reader to share
uncritically in the affirmative feelings of the ending would be for
him, too, to yield to complacency. The ending, à la Marx,
allows the reader to escape a recognition of the consequences of
those moral yearnings he had experienced earlier. We are
allowed to have our abolitionist cake, and eat it too.

But Marx's criticism did not go unanswered. James Cox, for

one, reinterpreted the novel in a way that virtually stands Marx's thesis on its head. For him, the fact that Huck is involved in freeing a slave from a tyrannical society is not the *point* of the novel, but a conventional device for assuring "moral approval from the reader." Twain is not *saying* that Huck's behavior is admirable, but *assuming* it.

> What, after all, was courageous about writing in Hart-ford twenty years after the Civil War—or what is courageous about reading in a post–Civil War world—a book about a boy who was helping a slave to freedom? Such an act would be roughly equivalent to writing a novel in our time about a boy in Hitler's Germany helping a Jew to the border.[24]

The point of the novel, for Cox, lies elsewhere. For him, the chief complacency is located not in the society that Huck flees but in the reader's self-indulgent and sentimental approval of Huck, the wish that he be granted "recognition for his achievement." The ending not only frustrates that wish; it punishes the reader for having entertained it:

> If the reader sees in Tom's performance a rather shabby and safe bit of play, he is seeing no more than the exposure of the approval with which he watched Huck operate. For if Tom is rather contemptibly setting a free slave free, what after all is the reader doing, who be-gins the book after the *fact* of the Civil War? This is the "joke" of the book—the moment when, in out-rageous burlesque, it attacks the sentiment which its style has at once evoked and exploited. To see that Tom is doing at the ending what we have been doing throughout the book is essential to understanding what the book has meant to us. For when Tom proclaims to the assembled throng who have witnessed his per-formance that Jim "is as free as any cretur that walks this earth," he is an exposed embodiment of the complacent moral sentiment on which the reader has relied throughout the book.

If freedom from social and political oppression is not a central theme in the novel, what is? For Cox, the true rebellion of *Huckleberry Finn* is an "attack upon the conscience," and not just the "Southern" conscience represented by Miss Watson, the

Widow Douglas, Tom, and Sunday School, but any conscience whatever, including those feelings that impel Huck to save Jim from the slave hunters and to tear up the letter he writes to Miss Watson offering to turn Jim in. The reader hopes that Huck will discover and abide with this "Northern conscience" (so Cox calls it), but Huck successfully evades it, governed as he is by the "pleasure principle." "Comfort and satisfaction are the value terms in *Huckleberry Finn*," and conscience of any sort is uncomfortable. When Huck decides at the very end, "I reckon I got to light out for the Territory ahead of the rest, because Aunt Sally she's going to adopt me and sivilize me and I can't stand it," it is conscience which he flees, comfort which he seeks.

Twain, then, used the "moral sentiment" evoked by the novel—the approbation of Huck's most humane motives and actions—only as a device to win the reader's assent. But the narrative itself not only puts the reader down for having assented; it proposes an alternative to the sentiment in the form of the pleasure principle. Whether Cox regards Twain as advocating or endorsing the "comfort" ethic by which, he says, Huck seeks to live is not altogether clear. He goes so far as to say, however, that Twain's humor depends on Huck's steady adherence to it, which is tantamount to endorsement, even if only through default.

If Cox's reinterpretation of the novel is right, then he has refuted Marx's judgment of it, for he proposes a very different notion of what Twain was doing, of his stance toward Huck's various actions, and of the effect the novel is designed to have on the reader. And though Cox refrains from taking much of a stand on the value of the novel, we can see what direction evaluative questions would have to take: *Is* our approval of Huck's humane instincts reprehensible? *Ought* it to be attacked? If the novel endorses pleasure and comfort as the grounds on which decisions ought to be made, *should* it? (Cox writes about critics "retreating from the pleasure principle toward the relative safety of 'moral issues,' " as if Huck's lapses into and evasions of conscience were somehow beyond morality. But under our broad definition of moral issues as those that pertain to the adverse or beneficial effects of actions on people, such a distinction makes no sense. A decision to seek pleasure on a raft rather than to engage in a political action falls into the domain of morality, as does a writer's manipulation of a reader's responses to such a decision.)

Prior to these reader-directed questions, of course, are questions about the correctness of Cox's interpretation. Before worrying about the value of the reading experience Cox sees the novel as affording, one wants to know such things as: How strong are the similarities between Tom's pretending to free a freed slave and the reader's approval of Huck's genuine efforts? What has Twain done to make those similarities apparent? How relevant is the fact that the Civil War is over? (Are the emotions aroused in *King Lear* by the blinding of Gloucester complacent and shabby because everyone takes it for granted now that pressing out the eyes of helpless old men is wrong?) Does the ending invite a stern judgment of Tom? Or is he presented ambiguously, as Marx claimed? Is it accurate to characterize the source of Huck's efforts to help Jim as his "Northern conscience," or does Twain suggest a distinction between that source, whatever it is, and other, culturally transmitted guides for conduct. Is Huck losing his identity when he makes a moral choice, such as his decision to "go to hell" rather than reveal Jim's whereabouts, or is he re-establishing an identity he had before, only to lose it once again when he arrives at the Phelps's farm pretending to be Tom?

If Cox interprets the novel in a way that is thoroughly incompatible with Marx's view, Richard Poirier, the participant in this conversation with whom we shall conclude, offers not so much a refutation as a refinement and extension of it. Poirier builds constructively on Marx's position, but does not seriously contradict it. Marx, he argues, has defined the subject of the novel too narrowly. And as we might expect, Poirier brings to the foreground episodes that Marx neglected:

> During these episodes, from Chapter XVIII to XXIX, the freeing of Jim is obviously not the subject of the novel. These chapters are indicative of the fact that the book is concerned with Negro slavery only as one aspect of a more general enslavement—of feeling and intelligence within inadequate and restrictively artificial modes of expression.[25]

Poirier argues that all of society, as Twain conceives of it in the novel, is artificial, incapable of accommodating individual

freedom or the expression of genuine inner feelings. The opening
chapters establish Tom Sawyer's world as the childhood version
of the adult world of Widow Douglas and Miss Watson. In both
of these worlds—societies built on "games, tricks, and illu-
sions"—people act according to roles assigned to them by
scriptural authority: the Bible itself, in the case of the adults; in
Tom's case, the romances he endlessly cites to justify the rules of
the game being played. Huck himself is torn between his
eagerness to establish a relationship with this society ("I did wish
I had some company") and his "impulsive need" for "freedom."
From the start there is a discrepancy between Twain's implied
criticism of the society and Huck's more affectionate feeling for
it. And the problem inherent in the novel—Poirier's more
general version of Marx's belief that the quest cannot succeed—
is that

> society, as the author conceives it, provides no op-
> portunity, no language, for the transformation of
> individual consciousness into social drama. The pro-
> vision is lacking because Mark Twain cannot imagine
> a society that offers alternatives to artificiality or that
> has in it, like Joyce's Dublin, evidences of an official
> culture that has historical dignity and value.

Marx had suggested that at the end of chapter 3 "Huck parts
company with Tom," allies himself with Jim and his cause,
troubled only now and then by his vestigial "conscience." But
Poirier points out that

> Huck is cultivating an imaginative association with
> Tom (and therefore society) all the way from Chapter
> III to Chapter XV. He consistently imitates him, and to
> that extent is, like the rest of this society, imitating
> "books" and "authorities." He repeatedly cites Tom as
> his own authority for tricks and adventures that are
> conspicuously at odds with both his feelings and self-
> interest.

This identification with Tom's ways continues through chapter
15, where Huck tricks Jim into believing that he had only dreamt
of being separated from Huck in the fog. But Jim's devastating
response ("Dat truck dah is *trash*; en trash is what people is dat
puts dirt on de head er dey fren's en makes 'em ashamed.")
moves Huck to shame and deep regret. This, and the following

chapter where Huck plays trickster *against* society by deceiving two slave hunters into believing that the raft houses his smallpox-stricken family, constitute the novel's crisis and the high point in Huck's moral growth and self-expressiveness. But from this point on the novel "goes to pieces." Huck takes the names of George Jackson and Tom Sawyer, and "the Huck Finn shown to us at what is obviously the dramatic crisis of the book is disguised thereafter even from the reader."

> *Huckleberry Finn* so insistently educates us to feelings of exasperation about tricks, games, and theatricality that we cannot have learned our lessons and want when we reach the last chapters still to be entertained by Tom's prolonged antics. The uncertainty that one feels, nevertheless, about the intended effect of the concluding scenes results from the fact that the weight of prejudice urged upon us by what precedes so brutally outbalances Tom's innocuous behavior.... The reaction of the reader ... is strangely muffled by Huck's presentation. It is apparent that he does not respond in the way the book has prepared the reader to respond, and that he is here glaringly unlike the character we have loved and respected earlier in the book.

It seems clear that Marx and Poirier offer slightly divergent models of "what happens" in the book, and hence slightly divergent versions of its meaning; clear, too, that Poirier has defended his interpretation on grounds of its greater completeness; clear, finally, that both critics (and Cox as well) are working to clarify Twain's intentions—what he was *saying* and *doing* to the reader. (For example, Poirier's argument is, in part, that Marx has provided no *reason* for Twain's having portrayed Huck's continuing reliance on Tom as authority.) What is not so clear, or at least so explicit, is the evaluative force of Poirier's argument. For though he acknowledges that the novel "goes to pieces," his primary interest is in the ways it exemplifies problems characteristic of a phase of nineteenth-century American fiction. Besides, he says, "I cannot imagine how *Huckleberry Finn* could have succeeded in resolving the issues that it creates." Nevertheless, like any penetrating reading of a literary work, it tells us, insofar as it is correct, what the novel importantly has to offer, what its effects are, and hence constitutes an assessment of it. If we wish to highlight the negatively evaluative aspects of the argument, we might note two implications of the way, according to Poirier, it goes to pieces.

First, since Twain sees no way for Huck to develop dramatically in his relationships with other characters, since he can only reiterate his portraits of an artificial society, the narrative becomes at times (the terms are Poirier's) repetitious, flat, feeble, lacking in vitality, cloying, uncertain in its intended effect, in contrast with earlier passages that are immediate, entertaining, compact, dramatic, exciting, amusing, heartbreaking. These are affective terms. Like the more general "boring" and "uninteresting," which have also been applied to the writing of the last chapters, they describe the experience the novel affords.

Second, if it is true that "we cannot have learned our lessons and want when we reach the last chapters still to be entertained by Tom's prolonged antics," then the reader who lets himself so be entertained, as the ending partly invites him to do, will be, as Marx also maintained, yielding to the enemy. We cannot share Huck's sentimental approbation of the family reunion without repudiating the qualities for which we had rightly respected him.

If this coda were aimed at settling the matter of *Huckleberry Finn*, we would have more work, and work of a different kind, to do. But our purpose has been, rather, to explore the connection between judging and interpreting, evaluating a novel and making sense of it. What impels and gives point to criticism's pursuit of ever more refined and true ways of making sense of a novel like *Huckleberry Finn* if not a desire to get its value rightly placed and understood? I will be content if I have shown that the questions raised by these critics matter. But an analysis of criticism should stop short of trying to provide answers, and should merely point, where the reader ought by now to want to go, back to the books.

Notes

Preface

1. Allan Rodway, *The Truths of Fiction* (London: Chatto & Windus, 1970), pp. 83, 95.

2. *Critics and Criticism, Ancient and Modern*, ed. R. S. Crane (Chicago: University of Chicago Press, 1952), pp. 8–9.

3. From the preface to the paperback edition of *Critics and Criticism* (Chicago: University of Chicago Press, 1957), p. v.

Chapter One

1. *Validity in Interpretation* (New Haven: Yale University Press, 1967).

2. "What Is Criticism?" in *Literary Criticism: An Introductory Reader*, ed. Lionel Trilling (New York: Holt, Rinehart & Winston, 1970), pp. 12–15.

3. The approach to criticism taken in this chapter owes much to conversations many years ago with Walter Clark, of the University of Michigan, and to his essay " 'Seeing As' and 'Knowing That' in Aesthetic Education," in Ralph A. Smith, ed., *Aesthetic Concepts and Education* (Urbana: University of Illinois Press, 1970), pp. 182–203. For an excellent treatment of myth criticism from a similar standpoint, see William Righter, "Myth and Interpretation," *New Literary History* 3 (1972): 319–44.

4. *The Language of Art and Art Criticism: Analytic Questions in Aesthetics* (Detroit: Wayne State University Press, 1965), p. 67.

5. See, for example, Norwood Russell Hanson, *Patterns of Discovery* (Cambridge: Cambridge University Press, 1958), chaps. 1 and 2, and F. E. Sparshott, *The Concept of Criticism* (Oxford: Clarendon Press, 1967), pp. 131–32.

6. *Selected Poems* (New York: Alfred Knopf, 1927).

7. *The Wheel of Fire* (Cleveland: World Publishing Co., 1957), pp. 3, 11.

8. *Shakespeare's Festive Comedy* (Princeton: Princeton University Press, 1959), pp. 4–6.

9. From *The Poems of Emily Dickinson*, ed. Thomas H. Johnson (Cambridge, Mass.: Harvard University Press, 1955), 1:225.

10. "The Heresy of Paraphrase," in *The Well-Wrought Urn* (New York: Harcourt, Brace, & World, 1947), p. 199.

11. R. S. Crane, *The Languages of Criticism and the Structure of Poetry* (Toronto: University of Toronto Press, 1953), p. 172.

12. J. Hillis Miller, *Charles Dickens: The World of His Novels* (Cambridge, Mass.: Harvard University Press, 1958), p. 21.

13. Georges Poulet, "The Circle and the Center: Reality and Madame Bovary," *Western Review* 19 (1955): 253.

14. "Falstaff," *South Atlantic Quarterly* 50 (1951): 86–95.

15. "The Pride of Lemuel Gulliver," *Sewanee Review* 63 (1955): 48–71; reprinted in the Norton Critical Edition of *Gulliver's Travels*, ed. Robert A. Greenberg, rev. ed. (New York: W. W. Norton & Co., 1970), pp. 326–28.

16. From *Personae* (New York: Boni & Liveright, 1926), p. 109.

17. "Five Types of Lycidas," in C. A. Patrides, ed., *Milton's "Lycidas": The Tradition and the Poem* (New York: Holt, Rinehart & Winston, 1961), pp. 223–24.

18. John Milton, *Complete Poems and Major Prose*, ed. Merritt Y. Hughes (New York: Odyssey Press, 1957), p. 124.

19. *Milton's "Lycidas,"* p. 229.

20. "Flowerets and Sounding Seas: A Study in the Affective Structure of *Lycidas*," ibid., pp. 133–34.

21. See Noam Chomsky, *Aspects of the Theory of Syntax* (Cambridge, Mass.: M.I.T. Press, 1965), pp. 21–25.

22. " 'Eager Thought': Dialectic in *Lycidas*," *PMLA* 77 (1926): 27.

23. "Literature as Context: Milton's *Lycidas*," in *Milton's "Lycidas,"* p. 209.

24. *The Poems and Letters of Andrew Marvell*, ed. H. M. Margoliouth (Oxford: Clarendon Press, 1927), 1:26–27.

25. "The Rationale of the Fourth Voyage," in the Norton Critical Edition of *Gulliver's Travels*, pp. 331–38.

26. *The Writing on the Wall and Other Literary Essays* (New York: Harcourt, Brace & World, 1970), p. 80.

27. For an analysis of this view of history see William H. Dray, *Philosophy of History* (Englewood Cliffs: Prentice-Hall, 1964), pp. 4–20.

CHAPTER TWO

1. I am greatly indebted in this chapter to several authors who have illuminated the dark domain of meaning: H. P. Grice, "Utterer's Meaning, Sentence-Meaning, and Word-Meaning," *Foundations of*

Language 4 (1968): 1–18; J. L. Austin, *How to Do Things with Words* (New York: Oxford University Press, 1965), and "The Meaning of a Word," in his *Philosophical Papers*, ed. J. O. Urmson and G. J. Warnock (Oxford: Clarendon Press, 1961), pp. 23–43; William Alston, *Philosophy of Language* (Englewood Cliffs: Prentice-Hall, 1964); John Searle, *Speech Acts: An Essay in the Philosophy of Language* (Cambridge: Cambridge University Press, 1969); and Dennis W. Stampe, "Toward a Grammar of Meaning," *Philosophical Review* 77 (1968): 137–74. Stampe's essay has been reprinted in *On Noam Chomsky: Critical Essays*, ed. Gilbert Harman (Garden City: Anchor Press, 1974), pp. 267–302, and it is to the reprint that I shall refer.

2. As Barbara Herrnstein Smith, to whom I owe this example, says, "pointing to Bill and offering an analysis of the 'concept' of folly will probably not answer [the] question." See her "Poetry as Fiction," *New Literary History* 2 (1971): 266.

3. The phrase comes from S. I. Hayakawa's influential *Language in Thought and Action* (1939), 3d ed. (New York: Harcourt Brace Jovanovich, 1972), p. 55. Hayakawa mistakenly identified the meaning of a word with what someone uses it to refer to on a specific occasion and with memories evoked by words in the minds of individuals who read or hear them.

4. "Toward a Grammar of Meaning," p. 275.

5. *Meaning and Truth* (Oxford: Clarendon Press, 1970), p. 4.

6. On this point, see *Philosophy of Language*, pp. 44–47.

7. See, for example, Noam Chomsky, *Aspects of the Theory of Syntax* (Cambridge, Mass.: M.I.T. Press, 1965), pp. 113–20, and Jerrold J. Katz, *Semantic Theory* (New York: Harper & Row, 1972), pp. 43–47, 89–97.

8. The term "category mistake" comes from Gilbert Ryle, *The Concept of Mind* (New York: Barnes & Noble, 1949), p. 16. The term "sort-crossing" is Colin M. Turbayne's phrase for a category mistake. See his *The Myth of Metaphor* (New Haven: Yale University Press, 1962). It was Turbayne who developed Ryle's notion into a definition of metaphor.

9. *Philosophy of Language*, pp. 98–100.

10. *Syntactic Structures* (The Hague: Mouton, 1972), p. 15.

11. Quoted from *On Noam Chomsky: Critical Essays*, ed. Gilbert Harman (Garden City: Doubleday & Co., 1974), p. 1.

12. *The Myth of Metaphor*, p. 18.

13. *Philosophy of Language*, pp. 39–44; *Speech Acts*, pp. 54–71.

14. A subtle and richly illustrated treatment of irony, and one that happens to concur that a claim about irony is a claim about intentions, is Wayne C. Booth's *The Rhetoric of Irony* (Chicago: University of Chicago Press, 1974). See the index entry "intentions."

15. Samuel Langhorn Clemens, *Adventures of Huckleberry Finn*, ed.

Sculley Bradley, Richmond Croom Beatty, and E. Hudson Long (New York: W. W. Norton & Co., 1961), p. 7.

16. *Ada or Ardor: A Family Chronicle* (New York: McGraw-Hill Book Co., 1969), p. 3. Strictly speaking, statements like Huck's that entail the existence of nonexistent referents are false, but may be thought of as fictionally or make-believedly true. Works of fiction contain fictional assertions from each of four categories: the really true (about the real world), the make-believedly true, the really false, and the make-believedly false. For an intriguing development of these ideas see two essays by Kendall L. Walton, "Pictures and Make-Believe," *Philosophical Review* 82 (1973): 283–319, and "Points of View in Narrative and Depictive Representation," *Noûs* 10 (1976): 49–61.

17. *Lost in the Funhouse* (New York: Bantam Books, 1969), p. 86.

18. *The Good Soldier* (New York: Alfred A. Knopf, 1951), p. 3.

19. The famous opening sentence of Jane Austen's *Pride and Prejudice*, ed. Donald J. Gray (New York: W. W. Norton & Co., 1966).

20. *Great Expectations* (San Francisco: Rinehart Press, 1948), p. 1.

21. *New Literary History* 6 (1974): 319–32.

22. *The Portrait of a Lady* (Baltimore: Penguin Books, 1963), p. 5.

23. Searle's general criterion for fiction is authorial pretense. At one point in the essay, however, he seems to admit the nonreality of referents as a criterion: "Normally not all of the references in a work of fiction will be pretended acts of referring; some will be real references as in the passage from Miss Murdoch where she refers to Dublin, or in Sherlock Holmes when Conan Doyle refers to London" (p. 330). This criterion seems untenable, for reasons already suggested. Suppose we have a sentence that refers both to a fictional person and a real place, or vice versa. If Dr. Watson refers to Paddington Station, it certainly looks like a fictional reference to a real place. A sentence from Iris Murdoch's novel *The Red and the Green* cited by Searle goes: "So thought Second Lieutenant Andrew Chase-White [a fictional character] . . . as he pottered contentedly in a garden on the outskirts of Dublin." Are we to call the sentence part fictional, part nonfictional? Or are we to call the whole sentence a fictional one that happens to contain a reference to a real place? The latter solution seems true to how we read fiction. We regard the sentences in a novel as of a piece, thoroughly fictional, unless the evidence for the pretense having been dropped becomes persistent and strong.

Similarly, Searle regards a sentence like "Happy families are all happy in the same way, unhappy families unhappy in their separate, different ways," from the beginning of *Anna Karenina*, as "not a fictional but a serious utterance. It is a genuine assertion." Why it should be regarded as such, Searle doesn't say. But its inclusion in a novel rather than in a treatise on the sociology of the family places the burden of proof on Searle. I think it ought to be regarded, like the teatime passage from *The Portrait of a Lady*, as a proposition the author *puts before* the reader without asserting it.

24. Haim G. Ginott, *Between Parent and Teenager* (New York: Macmillan Co., 1969), p. 88.

25. *Ragtime* (New York: Random House, 1974). The passages referred to appear on pages 29–33.

26. *Freud: Master and Friend* (Cambridge, Mass.: Harvard University Press, 1944), p. 85.

27. *The Life and Work of Sigmund Freud* (New York: Basic Books, 1955), 2:55–60.

CHAPTER THREE

1. The ideas in this chapter are deeply indebted to G. E. M. Anscombe's *Intention*, 2d ed. (Ithaca, N.Y.: Cornell University Press, 1963) and A. R. Louch's *Explanation and Human Action* (Berkeley: University of California Press, 1966). Though neither writer is concerned with literature or literary criticism, each has altered my understanding of how we can talk about people and their actions, and hence of how we can talk about writers and readers and the books they make and read.

2. *Dante* (New York: Macmillan Co., 1966), p. 106.

3. *The Comic Sense of Henry James: A Study of the Early Novels* (New York: Oxford University Press, 1960), p. 224.

4. *Mimesis* (New York: Anchor Books, 1957, originally published 1953), pp. 10, 12.

5. Reprinted in W. K. Wimsatt's *The Verbal Icon: Studies in the Meaning of Poetry* (New York: Noonday Press, 1958), p. 5.

6. See Anscombe, *Intention*, pp. 9–12 and passim. For a view of interpretation similar to my own, see Quentin Skinner, "Motives, Intentions, and the Interpretations of Texts," *New Literary History* 3 (1972): 393–408.

7. *The Verbal Icon*, pp. 3, 4.

8. F. R. and Q. D. Leavis, *Dickens the Novelist* (London: Chatto & Windus; New York: Random House, 1970), pp. 65 and 68. Mrs. Leavis's appraisal of the ending is shared by other critics who approach the novel from different angles. See Mark Spilka, *Dickens and Kafka: A Mutual Interpretation* (Bloomington: Indiana University Press, 1963), pp. 172 and 194; and Barbara Hardy, *The Moral Art of Dickens* (New York: Oxford University Press, 1970), p. 126.

9. *Structuralist Poetics: Structuralism, Linguistics and the Study of Literature* (Ithaca, N.Y.: Cornell University Press, 1975), pp. 27, 29–30.

10. *The Poetry of Robert Frost*, ed. Edward Connery Lathem (New York: Holt, Rinehart & Winston, 1969), pp. 257–60.

11. *The Poetry of Robert Frost: Constellations of Intention* (New York: Oxford University Press, 1963), pp. 193–94.

12. See Anscombe, *Intention*, p. 24.

13. See, for example, Theodore Mischel, "Concerning Rational Behavior and Psychoanalytic Explanation," in *Freud: A Collection of Critical Essays*, ed. Richard Wollheim (Garden City: Doubleday & Co., 1974), pp. 322–31; and D. W. Hamlyn, "Unconscious Intentions," *Philosophy* 46 (1971): 12–22; A. C. MacIntyre, *The Unconscious: A Conceptual Analysis* (London: Routledge & Kegan Paul, 1958), pp. 55–79.

14. Among the best studies of the reader as an element in criticism are Wayne C. Booth, *The Rhetoric of Fiction* (Chicago: University of Chicago Press, 1961); Walter J. Slatoff, *With Respect to Readers* (Ithaca, N.Y.: Cornell University Press, 1970); Stanley Fish, "Literature in the Reader: Affective Stylistics," *New Literary History* 2 (1970): 123–62; Wolfgang Iser, *The Implied Reader: Patterns of Communication in Prose Fiction from Bunyan to Beckett* (Baltimore: Johns Hopkins Unviersity Press, 1974). Essays on the subject by French critics include Roland Barthes's *Le plaisir du texte* (Paris: Editions du Seuil, 1973) and Georges Poulet's "Criticism and the Experience of Interiority," in *The Languages of Criticism and the Sciences of Man: The Structuralist Controversy*, ed. Richard Macksey and Eugenio Donato (Baltimore: Johns Hopkins University Press, 1970). Three good examples of practical rhetorical criticism more recent than those of the Chicago critics are Stephen Booth's "On the Value of *Hamlet*," in *Reinterpretations of Elizabethan Drama: Selected Papers from the English Institute*, ed. Norman Rabkin (New York: Columbia University Press, 1969), pp. 137–76, and Fish's studies of Milton and seventeenth-century poetry, *Surprised by Sin: The Reader in "Paradise Lost"* (New York: St. Martin's Press, 1967), and *Self-consuming Artifacts: The Experience of Seventeenth Century Literature* (Berkeley: University of California Press, 1972). Norman N. Holland's *The Dynamics of Literary Response* (New York: Oxford University Press, 1968) is a psychoanalytic study of responses to literature.

15. *The Poetics of Reverie: Childhood, Language, and the Cosmos*, trans. Daniel Russell (Boston: Beacon Press, 1971), p. 9.

16. "Literature in the Reader: Affective Stylistics," pp. 123–25. Ralph Rader has objected to Fish's analysis on somewhat different grounds in "The Concept of Genre and Eighteenth-Century Studies," *New Approaches to Eighteenth-Century Literature*, ed. Phillip Harth (New York: Columbia University Press, 1974), pp. 87–89. Earlier in the essay Rader states with admirable concision a view of interpretation very similar to my own.

17. For a more detailed account of these matters, see Anthony Kenny, *Action, Emotion and Will* (London: Routledge & Kegan Paul,

1963), pp. 60–75; and G. Pitcher, "Emotion," in *Mind* 74 (1965): 326–46. It is sometimes asserted that there are objectless emotions: vague feelings of apprehension, fear, depression, and the like. Such emotions are not, however, lacking in an object; rather their objects are vague, general, or ill-defined. The person who is afraid but says "I'm not sure what I'm afraid of" is nevertheless afraid that something threatening has occurred or will occur. These cases need not concern us, however, since we are dealing with emotions and attitudes whose objects are very specific, namely, the characters and events in individual literary texts.

18. *The Languages of Criticism and the Structure of Poetry* (Toronto: University of Toronto Press, 1953), pp. 170–72.

19. For a brilliant and sustained analysis of the reader's developing responses to *Tom Jones* see Crane's "The Concept of Plot and the Plot of *Tom Jones*" in *Critics and Criticism: Ancient and Modern*, ed. R. S. Crane (Chicago: University of Chicago Press, 1952), pp. 616–48.

20. "The Affective Fallacy," in *The Verbal Icon*, p. 34.

21. "Psychological Processes in the Reading of Fiction," *British Journal of Aesthetics* 2 (1962): 133–47.

22. *With Respect to Readers*, p. 42.

23. Richard Wollheim makes this point cogently in "Identification and Imagination: The Inner Structure of a Psychic Mechanism," in Wollheim, ed., *Freud: A Collection of Critical Essays* (New York: Anchor Press, 1974), p. 186.

24. *Fiction and the Unconscious* (Boston: Beacon Press, 1967).

Chapter Four

1. This exchange took place at a symposium in 1966. It is reprinted, along with other papers and discussions, in *The Languages of Criticism and the Sciences of Man: The Structuralist Controversy*, ed. Richard Macksey and Eugenio Donato (Baltimore: Johns Hopkins University Press, 1970), pp. 72, 84, 85.

2. *Validity in Interpretation* (New Haven: Yale University Press, 1967), p. 164.

3. *Hamlet and Oedipus* (New York: W. W. Norton & Co., 1949), pp. 77–86.

4. "The Pride of Lemuel Gulliver," in *Sewanee Review* 63 (1955): 48–71; reprinted in the Norton Critical Edition of *Gulliver's Travels*, ed. Robert A. Greenberg, rev. ed. (New York: W. W. Norton & Co., 1970), pp. 314, 326.

5. *The Collected Poems of Wallace Stevens* (New York: Alfred A. Knopf, 1954), p. 76.

6. *Yvor Winters on Modern Poets* (New York: Meridian Books, 1959), pp. 15–16.

7. For an example of such an interpretation, see Frank Kermode,

Romantic Image (New York: Vintage Books, 1964), p. 48.

8. For an excellent discussion of these criteria from a slightly different vantage point, see Hirsch, *Validity in Interpretation*, chap. 5. Hirsch, as we shall see, does not regard these criteria as sufficient for settling critical disputes.

9. *The Verbal Icon* (New York: Noonday Press, 1958), pp. 12–14.

10. *Validity in Interpretation*, pp. 181, 227–44.

11. Beardsley himself has argued persuasively that the text of the poem supports the view that the speaker's tone is calm and "consoled." See *The Possibility of Criticism* (Detroit: Wayne State University Press, 1970), pp. 44–48.

12. "Shakespearean Persuasion: *Antony and Cleopatra*," in *Language as Symbolic Action: Essays on Life, Literature, and Method* (Berkeley: University of California Press, 1966), pp. 105–6.

13. *The English Novel: Form and Function* (New York: Harper & Brothers, 1961), pp. 125–38.

14. *"Hamlet" and the Philosophy of Literary Criticism* (Chicago: University of Chicago Press, 1964); *The Language of Art and Art Criticism: Analytic Questions in Aesthetics* (Detroit: Wayne State University Press, 1965).

15. *Hamlet and Oedipus*, p. 80.

16. I owe this and the following observation to Elder Olson's *"Hamlet* and the Hermeneutics of Drama," *Modern Philology* 61 (1964): 225–37.

17. Theodore Spencer, *Shakespeare and the Nature of Man*, 2d ed. (New York: Macmillan Co., 1961), pp. 94–103.

18. Elmer Edgar Stoll, *Art and Artifice in Shakespeare: A Study in Dramatic Illusion and Contrast* (Cambridge: Cambridge University Press, 1933), p. 119.

19. "What Is Criticism?" in Barthes's *Critical Essays*, trans. Richard Howard (Evanston: Northwestern University Press, 1972), p. 257.

20. "Wanted: A New Contextualism," *Critical Inquiry* 1 (1975): 635.

21. *The Classic: Literary Images of Permanence and Change* (New York: Viking Press, 1975), p. 124.

22. My point has been made forcefully by E. D. Hirsch, first in *Validity in Interpretation*, pp. 40–44, 133–39, and more recently in *The Aims of Interpretation* (Chicago: University of Chicago Press, 1976), especially chaps. 2 and 3.

Chapter Five

1. *Theory of Literature*, 2d ed. (New York: Harcourt, Brace & World, 1956), p. 8.

2. *The Possibility of Criticism* (Detroit: Wayne State University Press, 1970).

3. *The Poetry of Robert Frost,* ed. Edward Connery Lathem (New York: Holt, Rinehart & Winston, 1969), pp. 222–23.

4. *The Well-Wrought Urn* (New York: Harcourt, Brace & World, 1947).

5. *The Languages of Criticism and the Structure of Poetry* (Toronto: University of Toronto Press, 1953), p. 176.

6. *The Function of Criticism* (Denver: Swallow Press, 1957), p. 21.

7. *The Mirror and the Lamp: Romantic Theory and the Critical Tradition* (New York: W. W. Norton & Co., 1958), chap. 1.

8. See *The Languages of Criticism and the Structure of Poetry*, pp. 80–139.

9. See, for example, Morris Weitz, "The Role of Theory in Aesthetics," *Journal of Aesthetics and Art Criticism* 15 (1956): 27–35; William E. Kennick, "Does Traditional Aesthetics Rest on a Mistake?" *Mind* 67 (1958): 317–34; Mortimer R. Kadish, *Reason and Controversy in the Arts* (Cleveland: Case Western Reserve University Press, 1958); E. D. Hirsch, Jr., " 'Intrinsic' Criticism," *College English* 36 (1974): 446–57.

10. *Oxford Lectures on Poetry* (London: MacMillan & Co.; 1911), p. 4.

11. *Anatomy of Criticism* (Princeton: Princeton University Press, 1957), pp. 6–7.

12. *PMLA* 85 (1970): pp. 423–28; 86 (1971): 128–30.

13. *Aesthetics: Problems in the Philosophy of Criticism* (New York: Harcourt, Brace & World, 1958), p. 527.

14. *The Language of Art and Art Criticism: Analytic Questions in Aesthetics* (Detroit: Wayne State University Press, 1965), pp. 43–44.

15. *The Artistic Transaction and Essays on the Theory of Literature* (Columbus: Ohio State University Press, 1963), pp. 166–67.

16. *Creation and Discovery* (New York: Noonday Press, 1955), p. 73.

17. *Feeling and Form* (New York: Charles Scribner's Sons, 1953), p. 26.

18. *Essays of John Dryden,* ed. W. P. Ker (New York: Russell & Russell, 1961), 1:36.

19. Page references in the text are to *Man's Rage for Chaos* (Philadelphia: Chilton Books, 1965), preceded by *MRC,* and to *The Triumph of Romanticism* (Columbia: University of South Carolina Press, 1970), preceded by *TR.*

20. Among the questions that might be raised about Peckham's theory as it applies to literature are the following: (1) Peckham stresses the idea that the reader must be *trained* in the poetry reader's role. Is it not the case that part of that training involves learning *not* to expect metrical regularity and learning to deal with unusual syntax? Won't the

trained reader experience less cognitive tension than the novice? (2) For Peckham the artist's function is to offer a problem, but *"not* a problem to be solved."* The point is to keep the reader disoriented. But isn't the problem afforded by difficult syntax very much a problem to be solved? (3) Why do most plots not only postpone solutions but (eventually) offer solutions? (4) What reason or evidence is there for thinking that "important" characters are unpredictable, their personalities "discontinuous"? No character's exact behavior can ever be predicted with certainty, and if it is totally inconsistent with earlier behavior, the characterization is likely to be regarded as flawed. Furthermore, there are a host of important, flat, stereotyped, and fairly predictable characters in literature, especially in such genres as comedy, romance, and folktale, where predictability may serve any of several important functions.

21. For these references, see Sidney's *Defence of Poesy*, ed. Dorothy M. Macardle (New York: St. Martin's Press, 1962), p. 7; book 2, chap. 8 of *The Advancement of Learning*, in James Spedding, Robert Leslie Ellis, and Douglas Denon Heath, eds., *The Works of Francis Bacon* (London: Longmans & Co., 1883), 4:315–16; Robert Frost, "The Figure a Poem Makes," in *Robert Frost on Writing*, ed. Elaine Barry (New Brunswick, N.J.: Rutgers University Press, 1973), p. 126; and T. S. Eliot, "Poetry and Drama," in *On Poetry and Poets* (New York: Noonday Press, 1961), p. 94.

22. *The Sense of an Ending: Studies in the Theory of Fiction* (Oxford: Oxford University Press, 1966).

23. Michael Ruse, *The Philosophy of Biology* (London: Hutchinson & Co., 1973), p. 183.

24. *Explanation and Human Action* (Berkeley: University of California Press, 1966), pp. 165–71.

25. For these references, see John Dennis, *The Grounds of Criticism in Poetry* (1704), chap. 2, in *The Critical Works of John Dennis*, ed. Edward Niles Hooker (Baltimore: Johns Hopkins Press, 1939), 1:335; Leo Tolstoy, "What Is Art?" in *Tolstoy on Art*, ed. and trans. Aylmer Maude (Boston: Small, Maynard & Co., 1924), p. 173; Victor Shklovsky, "Art as Technique" (1917), trans. Lee T. Lemon and Marion J. Reis in their *Russian Formalist Criticism: Four Essays* (Lincoln: University of Nebraska Press, 1965), p. 12; and Frederick Crews, "Anaesthetic Criticism" in Crews, ed., *Psychoanalysis and Literary Process* (Cambridge, Mass.: Winthrop Publishers, 1970), p. 13.

26. *The Theory of Literary Criticism: A Logical Analysis* (Berkeley: University of California Press, 1974).

27. See, for example, ibid., pp. 71, 84, 112, 133, 134.

28. *Structuralist Poetics* (Ithaca, N.Y.: Cornell University Press, 1975).

29. *The Complete Collected Poems of William Carlos Williams 1906-1938* (Norfolk, Conn.: New Directions, 1938), p. 179.

30. *The Waking: Poems 1933-1953* (New York: Doubleday & Co., 1953), p. 112.

31. Delivered at Williams College, April 28, 1975.

32. *Aspects of the Theory of Syntax* (Cambridge, Mass.: M.I.T. Press, 1965), pp. 21-27.

33. "Does Traditional Aesthetics Rest on a Mistake?"

34. "What's the Use of Theorizing about the Arts?" in *In Search of Literary Theory*, ed. Morton W. Bloomfield (Ithaca, N.Y.: Cornell University Press, 1972), pp. 1-54.

CHAPTER SIX

1. "Facts and Fictions: A Reply to Ralph Rader," *Critical Inquiry* 1 (1975): 891, n. 7.

2. *Anatomy of Criticism* (Princeton: Princeton University Press, 1957), p. 20.

3. *Poetic Discourse*, University of California Publications in Philosophy, vol. 33 (Berkeley: University of California Press, 1958), p. 92.

4. *"Hamlet" and the Philosophy of Literary Criticism* (Chicago: University of Chicago Press, 1964), pp. 274-76.

5. "Some Distinctive Features of Arguments Used in Criticism of the Arts," reprinted in W. E. Kennick, ed., *Art and Philosophy: Readings in Aesthetics* (New York: St. Martin's Press, 1964), pp. 597-604.

6. *Areopagitica*, in Milton's *Complete Poems and Major Prose*, ed. Merrit Y. Hughes (New York: Odyssey Press, 1957), p. 718.

7. Reprinted in Kennick, *Art and Philosophy*, p. 590.

8. *The Language of Criticism* (London: Methuen & Co., 1966).

9. *An Enquiry into Goodness and Related Concepts; with Some Remarks on the Nature and Scope of Such Enquiries* (Toronto: University of Toronto Press, 1958), p. 122.

10. *Semantic Analysis* (Ithaca, N.Y.: Cornell University Press, 1960), chap. 6.

11. *The Language of Morals* (New York: Oxford University Press, 1952), p. 138.

12. "Privileged Criteria in Literary Evaluation," in *Problems of Literary Evaluation*, ed. Joseph Strelka (University Park: Pennsylvania State University Press, 1969), pp. 22-36.

13. *The Great Tradition* (London: Chatto & Windus, 1948), p. 146.

14. *Mimesis: The Representation of Reality in Western Literature* (New York: Doubleday & Co., 1957), p. 159.

15. " 'Thought' and Emotional Quality," *Scrutiny* 13 (1945): 59.

16. *The Dialogues of Plato*, trans. B. Jowett (New York: Random House, 1937), p. 852.

17. Trilling's essay has been reprinted in the Norton Critical Edition of the *Adventures of Huckleberry Finn*, ed. Sculley Bradley, Richmond Croom Beatty, and E. Hudson Long (New York: W. W. Norton & Co., 1961), pp. 310–20.

18. "Preface to Shakespeare," in *Johnson on Shakespeare*, ed. Arthur Sherbo, vol. 7 of *The Works of Samuel Johnson* (New Haven: Yale University Press, 1968), p. 62.

19. *Defence of Poesy*, ed. Dorothy A. Macardle (New York: St. Martin's Press, 1962), p. 22.

20. *The Green Hills of Africa* (New York: C. Scribner's Sons, 1935), p. 22.

21. *Mark Twain at Work* (Cambridge, Mass.: Harvard University Press, 1942), p. 92.

22. Eliot's essay, which appeared in 1950 as the introduction to the Cresset edition of the novel, also appears in the Norton Critical Edition, pp. 320–27.

23. *The American Scholar* 22 (1953): 423–40, reprinted in the Norton Critical Edition, pp. 328–41.

24. *Mark Twain: The Fate of Humor* (Princeton: Princeton University Press, 1966). My quotations are from pp. 169–84.

25. *A World Elsewhere: The Place of Style in American Literature* (New York: Oxford University Press, 1966), see pp. 175–207.

Index